Withdrawn

A LONG
STONE'S
THROW

A LONG
STONE'S
THROW

by Alphie McCourt

STERLING & ROSS PUBLISHERS

NEW YORK § TORONTO

Published by
Sterling & Ross Publishers
New York, NY 10001
www.SterlingandRoss.com

Library of Congress Cataloging-in-Publication Data

McCourt, Alphie.
  A long stone's throw / by Alphie McCourt.
    p. cm.
  ISBN 978-0-9814535-5-2 (hardcover : alk. paper)
  1. McCourt, Alphie. 2. Irish Americans--New York (State)--New York--Biography. 3. Immigrants--New York (State)--New York--Biography. 4. Drinking of alcoholic beverages--Social aspects--New York (State)--New York. 5. New York (N.Y.)--Biography. 6. Limerick (Ireland)--Biography. I. Title.
  F128.9.I6M36 2008
  304.8'7471041945092--dc22
  [B]
                                          2008032672

Cover design by Nicola Lengua.
Composition/typography by Rachel Trusheim.

The author has written these events, people and places as he remembers them. He has made minor changes, particularly in changing names, to protect privacy.

10 9 8 7 6 5 4 3 2 1

Printed in the United States of America.

To Lynn, my wife and my pulse

To Allison, my daughter, the music in my life

To my brothers, Frank, Malachy and Michael,
for blazing more than a few trails

· ACKNOWLEDGMENTS ·

Most of my life story is laid out in this book. In one way or another, I owe it all to my mother, Angela, who kept us safe and together, and to my father, Malachy.

In my life I have received many a kindness and, in the finishing of this book, I have received a ton of support and guidance. When it comes to the events described, and to the finishing of the book itself, I can make no distinction among those I would like to thank. Thank you to Katharine Myer, who cheered from the beginning. To Seamus O'Dwyer, good friend of my memory. And to Michael Ryan, old friend, for standing fast. To Sean and Mary Costelloe, for the songs. And to my teachers: Jack Noonan, "Midge" Malone and Tony Brommel, for the fostering. To Carol and Sam Gibbon for the Christmas and the house. And to Michael and Cathy Miro for the green sock. Thank you to Brendan Keany, for standing by and for so long. Thank you to Henry Allen for giving me a chance. To Brendan Halligan for his early praise. To the Rogers family for opening a door. To Elizabeth O'Brien for opening it wide. And to Lincoln Anderson for leaving it open. To Cecily O'Flaherty for setting us up. To Jim Salestrom for his enormous talent and energy in creating the "calling card." To Drew Nederpelt, at Sterling and Ross, for taking a chance on this book. And to Rachel Trusheim, Executive Editor, for her inspired skill and limitless patience in bringing order and a fresh approach.

An infinite thank you to my brothers, Mike, Malachy and Frank for leaving me a variety of coattails. And to Lynn who typed the first, and then endured, the forty-seven versions that followed.

1960

I OFTEN DON'T TALK much. There is a rhythm to talk, a definite beat. Sometimes my mind wanders and I lose the cadence of the conversation. Especially when I'm in a group of five or six or more. Once, during a lull in the conversation, I was thinking out loud. "Too much," I said, "I think I live too much in my own mind."

I have been in New York for two months, on a visitor's visa, and my future status is uncertain. Not yet a legitimate immigrant, I am a bit nervous about looking for work. Through an employment agency, I find a job with First Boston Corporation. Downtown in the Wall Street area, as one of a group of four, I spend my days feeding a giant gloppiter-gloppiter mainframe computer. At prescribed intervals, the monster must be fed. The frame in use must be removed and replaced.

"Why?" I ask. "Why do we have to replace it?"

"Don't worry about it. Just do it," I am told.

Comes Saint Patrick's Day, my first Saint Patrick's Day in New York City. It is my duty to celebrate and I do. "A little more than a little" proves to be "by much too much" and, on the morning after, I fail to go to work. On the following day I don't go either. When I do arrive at work I am instructed to report to personnel. "And bring your coat," I am told. The woman in personnel is greatly disappointed. She had great faith in me and in my potential. When she tells me that she doesn't understand my behavior, I feel bound to assure her that I don't understand it either, but joke as I may, I am sorry to have disappointed her. She had been decent to me.

Through another agency, I find a job with British and Irish Railways in New York. I issue rail and boat tickets to those poor souls setting out to tour Shakespeare's birthplace in England or to visit the ancestral cottage in the bogs of Ireland's County Leitrim. Tickets are important, but there are other, more important, matters to attend to. Every morning at ten o'clock comes the call:

"Joh-on, is the kettle on?"

"Yes, Ken," is the call in response.

Again, ten minutes later, "Ke-ehn, tea's ready."

Soon followed by, "Right-o, John." This ritual is repeated every morning and afternoon.

I respect their devotion to the custom. They have brought a little bit of England to New York. Still, sometimes, I have to laugh at the predictability of it all. But when I sing, "I like New York in June," they're the ones who laugh.

"Just you wait," they tell me. "Wait till it's ninety degrees. You'll sweat even when you're lying down. You won't be singing then." They are veterans of one New York summer.

In late spring I submit an application for an alien registration card. The card will allow me to become a permanent resident of the United States. I am given an appointment for mid-summer. My new permanent resident status, a mere formality, will be readily granted, but on the back of the letter from Immigration there is a caveat. I am instructed not to leave the country between now and the date of my appointment.

That's fine with me. I have no travel plans. June, as predicted by John and Ken, brings on the hot and humid. Then I hear about the trip to Montreal. I am invited to travel up to Montreal to play a rugby football game with Manhattan Rugby Club, the team I some-times play with in New York. I have been instructed not to leave the country, but I'm just twenty years old and I can't resist. There will be plenty of beer and—Montreal. Who knows? There might even be a French-speaking woman. Will *this* be the weekend?

Friday night, on the bus from New York to Montreal, we stay up all night drinking beer, singing the shut-eyed Irish songs and the bawdy English rugby songs. By game time on Saturday afternoon, we are not well. By a score of a thousand points to none we lose the game. The great Tom Reid once played for Ireland in a game against England. Ireland lost by thirty points to nil. "We were lucky to get nil," said Tom. And so were we.

"Losing doesn't matter," our English teammates assure us. "It's not the winning or the losing that counts; it's the game itself, the songs and the beeyah awfterwards." That may be all right for you to say, I want to tell them. You've already conquered Africa and India and half the world. Here I am, with sleeves rolled up, socks hanging down and shin guards long gone. That is if I ever had them. We despised shin guards when I played for Young Munster in Limerick. All I want is to win a game once in a while and all they can come up with is a shower of shite about "the game itself and the beeyah awfterwards."

On Saturday night after the game, there's more beer, much too much beer. Now it is late on Sunday afternoon and away goes the bus. Moving slowly, the bus gathers speed. And I am not on it. My team-mates, hanging out the windows, are cheering, laughing and waving. My brother Malachy is on the bus. He isn't laughing or cheering, but wave he does and I wave back.

On the way back to New York from Montreal, as I attempted to reenter the U.S., I had been ordered off the bus at the United States border post. As a result, I end up in no man's land, stuck between bor-ders, sandwiched between Canada and the U.S. I explain my situation.

"Sorry," the U.S. Immigration official tells me, "but your visitor's visa can no longer be honored. And your new status is not yet in place, so we can't let you in. Better you go back to the Canadians. They will have to let you in, since you came out of there."

I begin to walk away from my adopted country, away from the United States border post, and back toward Canada. "You can't come in," I am told by the Canadian Immigration official.

I head back to the U.S. side. Again I am refused entry. I return to the Canadians, with no success. Back to the American side I go again and back again to the Canadians.

Now it is twilight. Have I worn them down? Or is it the changing of the guard? I will never know, but in the end, the Canadians wave me in and I board a bus bound for the city.

In Montreal, Chesley Milliken, a friend of Malachy's, puts me in touch with Vincent O'Doherty. I move in with Vincent and his three roommates, in their huge four-bedroom apartment on Queen Mary Road at the junction of Cote de Neige. Martin Beausang, a friend of Vincent's, arranges a Canadian visa for me and I become a landed immigrant in Canada.

At the Dorchester Hotel, I find a job as a bellman. The guests are open and friendly. The other hotel workers, French-speaking for the most part, claim to have trouble communicating with me. I don't think it matters, as most of the hotel guests are American and they speak English. But it does matter. At the end of my first day I'm punished for my lack of culture, fired because I don't speak French.

At the Bank of Montreal in Westmount, after a short training period, I become a teller. Every morning, just before opening time, the assistant manager calls out, "Tellers!" and my stomach rises into my throat. I feel as if I'm back at school where mathematics was always the first subject of the day. I never seemed to have my homework done and I knew that I would be found out. "Tellers!" means pick up your trays of cash and count your money before you enter into battle. It is obvious, even to me, that I have no feel for the rhythms of check cashing and money counting. Soon I am transferred to a desk job. Is this a promotion?

After two days of training in "collections," I am so foolish as to ask, "Collections, what are collections?"

Natasha, my tutor, mentor and tormentor to be, my fuehrer in a dress, says only, "Don't worry about it, just do the job."

"But I'll do better if I know what I'm doing and why I'm doing it."

"I'm telling you not to worry about it. Just do it."

I sense that Natasha is unsure of herself in her new position. I sympathize, but I need to know, so I persist with my questions. Turning fierce, she hisses at me with no more than half an answer. "Why the tenth of the month? Why the fifteenth and why the twentieth?" I ask again.

"Because that's when they're due, why can't you understand that?" I can't and I don't. Throwing back her head she goes clunking, elephant-footed, away from me. With her heavy heels, she murders the bare wooden floor.

Even so, Natasha declares me qualified to do her job, before beating a hasty escape to the glories of her new position. Left by myself, I fake it. Every day I fumble through the accordion file, extract a number of notes at random and send them on their way through the system. For a few weeks I get away with it, until, one day, a small red-faced man arrives, pushes his way into the manager's office and slams the door. We can hear him shouting. Single words and short phrases, "Collection...idiots! Serious problems...embarrassments...and who the hell is the imbecile?" come gusting on the waves of his anger, even through the closed door of the manager's office. Ten minutes later he emerges, glares all round him, jams his little hat on his head and stomps out the door of the bank. But he is only a little man, I think to myself, hysterical, ridiculous in his anger.

Yes, indeed he is ridiculous. Until the following day, when I am called into the manager's office. Mr. England, the manager, always with a boutonniere, is a florid-faced and kindly man, awaiting only the day of his imminent retirement. He does his best to paint a positive picture of the career that will soon embrace me. Downtown, in the bowels of the bank's main office, my contact with the public will be minimized. My encounters with little men in little hats, in particular, will be at arm's length. As chief caretaker of safety deposit boxes, I will deal mostly with the dead.

Before I undertake my new job, I am told a cautionary tale about the bedraggled man who had asked admittance to the safety deposit box area. Turned away because of his appearance, he proved to be a substantial citizen and a valued customer of the bank. There is no transfer from the security of the safety deposit boxes, no place lower than the bowels of the bank. The custodian in charge had been fired. After my experience with "collections," I am forever wary of little men in little hats. Now I must keep a weather eye out for scruffy-looking millionaires.

Six months later, I leave the vault, answer an ad in the newspaper and become an encyclopedia salesman. Into the hinterland of outlying Montreal housing estates we journey, to bring the joys of learning to housewives and children. In their houses and apartments we perch on couches and chairs that, by the look of things, are being paid for on the "installment plan." Their furniture may well be repossessed the next day. I try to persuade them to buy, but my heart isn't in it. Only when the crew chief, Bill, from Northern Ireland, does the spade work, bringing to bear his great flair for selling, do I make one sale after a whole month of trying.

A year has passed and I've had enough. New York is where I want to be. At the U.S. border I am greeted by the same Immigration official who had put me off the bus the year before. I remember him. And he remembers me.

"You have some trouble coming through here about a year ago?" he asks.

"Yes, I did, but I am now a permanent resident of Canada, coming to the U.S. for a visit."

He's dubious as ever, but he lets me through.

· NEW YORK ·
1961

IN NEW YORK I CONTACT Immigration and they give me an appointment. On the appointed day we're only a few minutes into the interview when I gain the impression that the Immigration agent is playing with me. When he tells me that I will have to be deported, I can neither beg nor plead. Nerves, weariness and frustration take over. I start to laugh and when the official asks me to what country I would like to be deported, I choose Australia just for devilment. This will be complicated. Should they send me back to Canada or to Ireland or should they send me to Australia? What are the guidelines? The official doesn't seem to know. Or maybe it's all part of the game. "Wait here," he tells me and he leaves the room. He's consulting with his superiors, maybe, or having a good laugh at my predicament. Ten minutes later, he returns. He instructs me to come back to his office, in four weeks, to pick up my alien registration card. "Do not leave the country in the meantime. No matter what. Game or no game, do you hear me?" he bellows.

"I hear you, I hear you," I promise. "And thank you." One month later, I receive my alien registration card.

❧

Once again I inflict myself on brother Malachy and his family on the West Side of Manhattan until I find a furnished room on West 95th

Street and a job as a clerk at the Army and Air Force Exchange Service, down on 14th Street. I will hold onto this job for a year, in itself a miracle, given my habit of staying up half the night, reading, or going out drinking beer and being late in the morning, or not going to work at all.

Eventually I will work only night jobs to avoid the morning doldrums. Anyway, I am planning to go to college. Frank urges me to go to school. My brothers' friends all tell me to go to school. "Go to school, go to school, are you going to school?" is a familiar refrain. Everywhere I go I hear people chanting at me to "go to school, go to school."

But am I not destined for greatness? I spend all my time dreaming at the stars, although with my head up my arse, which is an odd vantage point for a visionary. And I am still hampered by my childhood habit of trying, every day, to remember which shoe I put on first the day before. Was it the right or the left, so that I will put the other one on first today and not favor either one?

So many quandaries for a young man in New York. Miserably unsure of myself and so lacking in confidence, despite my few accomplishments, that I can't climb the hill to any kind of motivation. In my early twenties I live in a tent of teenage angst, an angst that has not yet been invented. Had I suffered from it in my teen years I would have been a pioneer. Now I am only a fool for falling foul of it in my twenties.

Each of my brothers has a sphere of influence and a circle of friends in the Village and on the Upper East Side. I have been introduced to all, but I am unable to find any footing. Everyone I meet is friendly and convivial, but I sorely miss the contexts of my life in Limerick. I don't miss the predictability, but I miss having a place among the givens and the customs. I speak English. Why then, is it so difficult to find my place in New York? My brothers had not followed the path of the typical immigrant. Two of them had been born in New York. Assimilation came relatively easy, but beyond that, they had already achieved a certain prominence in Manhattan. By comparison, I can never imagine making a dent or any kind of a name for myself.

It doesn't occur to me to start working at whatever is at hand, to start to build something, a basic framework, and then to build something else on top of that. No, everything will fall into my lap. My work will always be noteworthy and exciting. Why shouldn't I be paid plenty of money? And why shouldn't I be treated with respect and admiration, me with my Honors Leaving Certificate from Limerick? Still, with all my illusions and my foolish expectations, when I do work, I do my best. I do as much as I can and I worry that I am not doing enough.

From my low-level white-collar jobs I earn barely enough to live on and I carry a load of guilt at leaving my mother floundering, at her age, in New York. In moving to New York, she has become disconnected from all that was familiar. Her life must revolve around her sons, all of them struggling to construct their own lives.

❦

In June of 1962, in my furnished room on West 95th Street, the temperature is rising. Tempers begin to flare among old-time Irish, Italians and African Americans and the more recently arrived Puerto Ricans. Something is brewing. Seamus Collins is a few years older than I am. He and I work together. Seamus and his roommate, both of them Irish immigrants, are looking for a third man to share their apartment in the Bronx. Am I interested? I most certainly am.

One week after I move, a newspaper account describes an incident on 95th Street. An African American woman scolded or hit a Puerto Rican child, or vice versa. In protest, a hail of plants and garbage erupts from the surrounding rooftops, provoking a general riot and summoning a host of squad cars.

Not many Irish immigrants get to live first in Manhattan before moving to the Bronx. It's lucky for me that I escaped the riot by moving, just in time, back among the Irish. Seamus Collins, Eddie Deary and I live at Apt 1C, 1917 Walton Avenue. Seamus writes to his father in Ireland. His father, in writing back, addresses his letter to "The Aptic, 1917 Walton Avenue." He has assumed, no doubt, that his son is doing well. Isn't he living in a building with a fancy name? The apartment is on the ground floor and to the rear. There's little daylight and only one bedroom. The living room is the second bedroom.

The building, I would guess, had seen better times, when it was younger and held a predominantly Jewish population. The synagogue next door abuts the bedroom window where I sleep. On Saturday mornings in the summer, long before air-conditioning, it is always ninety degrees and a full-bodied bluebottle fly buzzes the bedroom. Periodically he touches down on my forehead. Repeatedly I shoo him away. His antennae are dulled by the fumes of last night's beer. He himself is lulled, no doubt, and calmed into slow motion, as I am, by the stately Sabbath chant as it drifts upward from the synagogue, soothing my ravaged gentile spirit.

In this secure Irish and Italian neighborhood, life is simple and straightforward if you are not too ambitious and your sensibilities are not hanging out all over. Two bars and a Catholic Church are within shouting distance of "The Aptic." I can't afford the church, but I make an obeisance at Behan's Bar whenever funds will allow. Exile from exile, this is sanctuary. The family name is not known here, as it is in Manhattan, in the Village and in the saloons of the Upper East Side, where the brothers have made their mark.

Here am I, up from my brief apprenticeship in the world of Manhattan cocktail parties, where the tinkle of polite conversation matches the gentle rattle of the ice in the glasses. Manhattan, where elegant women of the Upper East Side, women in black dresses and pearls, will ask me with glittering, if brittle, interest, if I am going to school. And I tell them yes, I am. That seems to be what they want to hear. Yes I am, I tell them. Yes I can. Yes I will. Yes I would. Anything you want, anything, just say the word, I would tell them, if I were not so tongue-tied. I can only nod in agreement as the blood rises to my face and they shine at me and tell the brothers that I am very bright.

Especially on New Year's Eve when Malachy and his wife arranged a date for me. She was the daughter of a well-known literary personality. We were to attend a formal party. I had no tux, so Malachy lent me his old one.

In *The Cruel Sea*, Nicholas Monsarrat describes a woman whose clothing was equipped with a quick-release device. She was always ready.

Malachy's suit must have had some thousands of miles on it. Somewhere along the line, the seam, which usually holds together the crotch part where the scrotum hangs out or hangs in, as the case may be, had abandoned ship, leaving a vacancy and a very breezy point. A hole in your pants, especially in that area, is not reassuring, especially when you're headed out for an evening. But, at age twenty-two, chance was all. Putting my best foot forward, I tried, really, to put both feet forward, both at the same time. Cheeks and thighs had to be held together at all times. Bow from the waist? I would if I had to. Just don't ask me to dance.

Miss Kate and I were chatting as we strolled the party. We tasted the food, drank some and toasted the New Year. We left the party early, stepping into the winter air, the very brisk winter air, but, at twenty-two neither snow nor sleet would stay. I had no doubt that Miss Kate was puzzled at my antics. I had moved around so casually at the party. Now, in the street, in an attempt to shield the jewels from winter chill and from revelation, I was walking sideways. Most of all, I was in mortal fear of being exposed.

Back at her parents' apartment we got together mighty hot and mighty quick on the couch. We moved along. My partner was a woman of some experience while I was ready, too ready and too ignorant. So anxious was I in my fear of discovery and so worried that she would come across the ripped seam that, in a short time, tension lit the spark and consummation was reached all by myself. The pants were christened. Rigor mortification set in, only adding to her puzzlement and I retired from the field, dejected by my momentary failure but hoping for another day.

In the Bronx, there are no black dresses or strings of pearls. There may be willing women, but I never find them. I don't know where the women dwell in the Bronx for there are no women in the streets after five o'clock. I would see them coming out of the church on Sundays after Mass, but otherwise they must be under wraps.

Behan's bar is peopled by old-time Irish Americans and immigrant Irishmen like myself. There is not much of the ice tinkling in the glasses, not much ice at all. Shots and beers and conversation are very basic among plumbers, carpenters, subway mechanics and factory workers who hang out there. I belong only because, by now, I have risen to the rank of service elevator operator in a residential building in Manhattan.

Bernard Baruch, financier, philanthropist and adviser to presidents, lives in the building, as does the British Ambassador to the U.N., Sir Patrick Dean. Both are decent men and, like a truly beautiful woman, these two truly accomplished men are approachable.

By this time I am a student, at Lehmann College in the Bronx, during the day. Running the service elevator at night allows me plenty of time to study. On that once-a-week evening when I must do tedious duty at the front door, I keep, on the bench by my side, a copy of *Plato's Republic*. Plato marks my spot. Plato's presence by my side will let them know, especially the good-looking daughter of the real estate mogul, that I am not only what I seem to be.

Sir Patrick Dean invites me for a tour of the U.N. Bernard Baruch asks me if I am going to school and is mighty pleased that I am, and proud that they have named a college after him. But in my uniform, even with Plato by my side, I am invisible to the mogul's daughter as she passes in and out. If she ever does notice Plato and me, she sure doesn't show it. All I ever get from her is a toss of her hair as she sashays away through the lobby.

Seamus Collins had come to the U.S. in his middle to late twenties and his age made it very difficult for him to make the adjustment to life in New York. Ideally he should have been here by age twenty-one in order to fit in, especially since he had a bit of the old Irish middle class in his origins. Strictly a suit-and-tie man, he works in insurance in an office.

For any special occasion, Seamus wears a cravat. At Behan's bar there are murmurings of too much gentility and a fool could mistake him for a bit of a dandy. But Seamus had been an amateur boxer. He is well able to handle himself and, strong as he is, he's a great man to have in your corner in any situation.

More émigré than emigrant is Seamus, as I would realize later. Still steeped in the manners and mores of his own country, he is dipping his toe, now, in a different culture. Too old to be so junior in position, he doesn't quite fit in with his peers at his office. Nor does he fit in with his fellow Irish immigrants, because of his old-fashioned manners and his unfailing courtesy.

Never afraid to branch out, Seamus mixes with people from Jamaica and Hungary and Korea, people with theatrical and artistic leanings. That's lucky for me. At one of their parties I meet Sally, a social worker and graduate student at Columbia University. Diminutive and pretty she is and she laughs at my jokes. We don't linger long at the party.

At International House, a residence for women students, men are not allowed upstairs. Evading capture, Sally and I shoot upstairs in the elevator and straight into her single bed. Furtive and anxious I am and in mortal fear of the arrival of the chastity shock troops. It happens fast, but it does happen. At last. She welcomes it with no begrudgery and no false modesty or fear. Just open arms and a warm welcome to the United States of Enlightenment.

After an encore it is time for me to go. Down the stairs I fly, running straight into the dawn, almost knocking over a sleepy, startled security guard who makes no attempt to stop me as I run out the door into the rising sun.

At Behan's she is a source of amazement, a real live woman in the bar. At this time, women do not frequent bars. She is a far cry from the broken-down alcoholic woman, escaping from husband and children, who sometimes appears. Nor does she resemble the desperate once-a-week woman, always chasing her drunken husband in an attempt to salvage something of his paycheck, which by now will have been well spent.

Neither of these two will cause any surprise in Behan's. But a young and good-looking woman (a real American, a Californian, mind you) obviously intelligent and educated, and with a hyphen to her name and pedigree? This is unheard of.

Before Sally's arrival the only halfway attractive woman ever to cross the threshold of the bar was the sometime girlfriend of Tommy, a hard-bitten factory worker from Glasgow, Scotland. And, as far as we know, his lady is married. She comes only on Sunday afternoons, when the crowd, in the best tradition, has already been in for the after-Mass beers, their reward for a hard week's work and for an hour of even more demanding piety.

She makes her entrance after the post-pious crowd has gone home to the heavy Sunday dinner, when only we hardy souls, with no wives and no expectation of any Sunday dinner, are still extant. On the jukebox, Roger Miller sings "King of the Road," the words of the song in a loose rhythm with the *shoosh* of the brass weights speeding down the length of the polished shuffleboard table. When the speeding weight hits a stationery weight, the *kathunk* is followed by a dull *thud* as the defeated weight is knocked off the table and into the sawdust in the trough.

Yes, Tommy's lady shows up on Sundays. Always with a touch of red: a scarf, a blouse or a pair of red shoes to add flame to her dark and exotic looks, hailing from Argentina, they say. "To hell with the Celtic mists that do be after rising. Is it on, or off the bog? I can't remember which. "Just give us a touch of the Pampas, will yeh?" I can hardly keep myself from saying it, but none of us stands a chance with her. Tommy is hard-bitten, as I said. And he is fully aware of us, as we put aside our shuffleboard lassitude, to stand straight up and give her our full regard.

For one or two drinks they stay, she smoking fast and nervous while Tommy, with pretended indifference, nurses his drink. Diverted by an occasional joke or a verbal toss into the ring by one of his mates, he rarely looks in her direction. Any overt sign of attention paid to her by Tommy will be construed as submission and will land him in a hell of taunts and imitations later on. But his command is absolute. At a nod from him, they leave and walk to his apartment, next door and just upstairs. Like a Carmen she had come, to ruin our shuffleboard reverie and to set us adrift on a raft of fantasy. Now she's gone and our imaginings, all of them foolish and futile, have gone with her. We resume the rhythm of the shuffleboard; the shoosh, the *kathunk* and the *thud* are companionable, comfortable and soothing.

Sally comes often to that bar with me. God knows what this California girl must think of those bleak streets. The IRT train pounds and rattles above our heads, bringing a constant drilling among glasses and bottles behind the bar. She is closely scrutinized by bartender and customers, but when I introduce her around, the novelty fades.

Mickey is an exception, Mickey of the no neck, arms extending all the way to his knees. Careful and deliberate in movement and an excellent shuffleboard player, he works as an elevator operator. God knows he has the perfect physique for the job. When I introduce him to Sally he is wary.

In conversation, later he remarks, "I never shpoke to a Prottishtant."

"Mickey," I ask him, "how do you know?" Mightily disturbed is he and, probably, forever. From that point on, he will keep his distance from Sally for he has guessed, I think, and correctly, that she is not a Catholic. She is, indeed, a Protestant, God Help Us. But Mickey is not unkind, as I discover when I find myself in need of work and he arranges a part-time job for me.

Soon I will be retired from my elevator operator job because I fail to show up on a couple of Saturday mornings at my ridiculous starting time of seven in the morning. Had I gone to work I could not have lain in bed, lamenting the effects of Friday night's beer and swatting at the solitary fly, just to let him know that somebody was taking note of his existence. Worst of all, I would have missed my arm's-length participation in the Sabbath service in the synagogue next door. There was probably a constitutional issue in my being fired, only I didn't realize it.

In the meantime, I have received a draft notice ordering me to report to Whitehall Street in Lower Manhattan for induction. When I write and tell them that I am a full-time student, they postpone my induction and request that I return the subway token they had sent me for transportation. I keep the token.

At the end of November, I am introduced to someone who

knows someone. He, in turn, introduces me to someone who knows someone else. Following an exhaustive and rigorous physical examination, with much probing of the rectum, which to me seems strange and downright stupid, at age twenty-three, I am hired by the Pennsylvania Railroad. Every evening our small crew stands out on a freezing railroad platform in Long Island City from four o'clock to midnight.

In sorting mailbags full of Christmas mail, we create a Christmas miracle of our own. Destination names are abbreviated and barely legible. Half of us can barely read and don't much care where the mail goes. The other half of us can read and we care even less. If any of that mail ever reaches its destination it is because of Divine Intervention, but, at ninety-six dollars a week, the pay is good. In the end, at four o'clock on the afternoon of Christmas Eve, when we report for work, the foreman hands us our pay. "Go on home, fellas," he tells us, "and have a Merry Christmas. You're all done." It is a mighty sweet ending.

⸎

Very early in the spring of 1964, Sally invites me to a party given by one of her friends and attended, mostly, by her fellow graduate student social workers. Pleasant manners they have, but there's little in the way of passionate argument or utterance and a slight hesitancy in their speech makes them seem overly conscious of their own breeding and their superiority. Or is it my imagination? For once, I am inside the room and actually at the party, but I still find myself peering in and puzzling at them. I wonder at their lack of fire and at the absence of zeal.

I could find more excited debate in a ten-minute conversation at Behan's Bar than I do in three whole hours at this party. I may be mistaken in my belief that there can be no dedication without passion, but I don't give up so easily. I have grown up with the idea of Christian charity. I haven't seen much of it, but the idea was always there. Social work is a whole new idea. Social work, in all its variations, will be their tool. It will lead them far away from traditional religious charity, for better or for worse. No longer will it be necessary to convert, in order to receive help. This is a new world. Food will become aid. Money will become funding. The rough hard edges of right and wrong will be rounded and smoothed into the merely appropriate and inappropriate.

Sally introduces me to one particular friend. Later she will tell me that she finds him to be effete, that he may even be of the other persuasion, but they are friends anyway. She admires his dedication to his work. Most appropriate, say I.

Sally has become my Manhattan connection for a few months of movies and the occasional cheap dinner at Tad's Steak House. When I am not holed up in the apartment, that is, and shouldering the burdens of Thomas Hardy and his *Jude the Obscure*, in the daytime, with all of Jude's misfortunes and lack of connection a mirror of my own life, I believe. *Tess of the d'Urbervilles*, tribulations and all, demands my attention at night. Between the two of them, Jude and Tess, I don't have a moment's peace. The Bronx is a perfect stepping aside from anything that might be expected of me. In the bar and in the beer I manage to step aside even from the stepping aside, but, in the end, I must always go home to face Jude and Tess, God bless 'em, and to face myself.

In February of 1964, I don the green uniform and cap of the Burns Detective Agency. Assigned to patrolling the grounds and outbuildings of a factory in the East Bronx, from four in the afternoon until midnight, every hour on the hour I punch a clock, brooding through my dark and solitary rounds.

The guard I relieve at four is a young black man a couple of years younger than I am. Packaged in a broad grin and a humorous if slightly mocking manner, he is tall and lithe. Cool and easy in his movements, of me he is the very opposite.

His shoes are still spit-shined, gleaming always to perfection for he is just recently out of the Army, with horror stories to tell of the fate that awaits me when my turn comes to be drafted.

And it does come, the Draft notice, in April. No longer a college student, I must report for induction on April 15th and now "The Leaving of Liverpool" takes on new meaning. I play it often on the jukebox as the Clancy Brothers and Tommy Maken sing:

> *I have shipped on a Yankee sailing ship*
> *Davy Crockett is her name*
> *And Burgess is the captain of her*
> *And they say that she's a floating hell*
> *So fair thee well my own true love*
> *And when I return united we will be*
> *'Tis not the leaving of Liverpool that grieves me*
> *But my darling when I think of thee*

I was born lonesome. We all are, some are more lonesome than others. Now I am lonesome again. Lonesome for what Sally might have been to me and for what I might have been to her. Lonesome for my Bronx cocoon and just plain lonesome, as the waves of the old Celtic melancholy roll in, constant as the sea.

Seamus Collins and company give a party for me. All the Behan's crowd shows up, to be welcomed by Seamus with his great wide smile, his thumb and forefinger held aloft about an inch and a half apart, as indication that shots of whiskey will be the order of the evening. Sally is a perfect hostess. She joins in fully and listens intently as we sing:

I belong to Glasgow, dear old Glasgow town
There's somethin' the matter with Glasgow
For it's goin' round and round
I'm only a common old working chap
As anyone here can see
But when I get a couple o' drinks on a Saturday
Glasgow belongs tae me

And "The Valley of Knockanure" and "Sean South of Garryowen" and "Annie Laurie":

Her brow is like the snowdrift
Her neck is like the swan
Her face it is the fairest
That ere the sun shone on
That ere the sun shone on
And dark blue is her e'e
And for Bonnie Annie Laurie
I would lay me doon and dee

Rich in songs we are, until the dawn comes up to remind us that Saturday night has passed; that the world has gone on without us and moved into Sunday morning, leaving all the friends to make their way, blinking, into the morning light. Replete with songs they are but humming, now, out of consideration for our neighbors.

A few days later, when I go to pick up my last paycheck from Burns Detective Agency, I am told that New York State has seized my check as payment for an old and forgotten tax bill of sixty dollars. There's no point in protesting. I wouldn't have it any other way. The timing is unfortunate, but the seizure is legitimate and, best of all, the irony is just priceless. "Render to Caesar the things that are Caesar's," I remind myself. And render to New York State the things that are New York State's. New York State has left me broke and I appreciate the new subway token, sent to me by the Draft Board, to ease the pain of traveling down to Whitehall Street.

1964

As a non-citizen I don't really have to go, I've been told. But then, if I ever leave the country, I might not be allowed back in. I'm told to drink a lot the night before and tell the doctors that I'm an alcoholic. I could have done that, but I figured that they would be wise to that tactic. Isn't it a well-known fact that being drunk is an Irishman's natural state of being? The doctors would just ignore my condition. And I am advised to claim homosexuality as my last line of defense.

On the appointed day of cheek spreading and general physical examination, I meet a fellow draftee named John F. Kennedy. Like myself, he is an immigrant Irishman. We lend each other moral support. Like an omen he seems, offering hope for us yet. President John F. Kennedy has been dead less than a year. But I'm held back and the president's namesake moves on. I will not see him again.

The doctors, in their puzzlement, scratch their heads and ears and noses. "Your ear drum, is it inside out, or outside in? Or is it back to front?" I don't know. "What happened to you? Was there some problem with your eye and your ear when you were a child?" I tell them that I had an ear infection as a baby and spent a few days in hospital. "What was the result?" the doctors want to know. Again I don't know and I apologize for my faulty eye and ear. Most of all, I apologize for not remembering what happened to me as an infant.

Three days later, after a visit to Elmhurst General Hospital in

Queens, for further tests, I am drafted. Vietnam is still not much more than a large twinkle in the eye of Uncle Sam, but he must know that something is coming. The Draft is accelerating.

Fort Dix, New Jersey is going through one of its episodic bouts of Asian Flu, Russian Measles or Spanish Fly. Such outbreaks are always foreign in origin. We are shipped off to Fort Jackson, South Carolina. On the overnight train trip I curse New York State for taking my last few bucks on the eve of my departure into the maw of Uncle Sam. And when I have to surrender my last few coins to the tip pool for the dining room steward, I curse even more.

At Fort Jackson, close by Columbia, South Carolina, we are herded in for orientation, information and the issuing of uniforms. On the third day one new "troop" stands in the doorway of the barracks, not moving. Holding a pair of boots in his left hand, he stares straight ahead. Still he stands, until they come to take him away for discharge. While I wish that God, or somebody, will help him if his state is genuine, if it is not, then his stillness, boots in hand, seems a much better ploy than alcoholism, flat feet or homosexuality.

Our heads are shaved, for sanitary reasons, and shower and toilet facilities are very much in common. There's not a shred of a partition for privacy, again for sanitary reasons. Or is it a further step in stripping away our individuality? I am a trainee, a "troop," now. I am three or four years older than the majority of the others who are mostly nineteen- or twenty-year-olds. Tough I am not. I'm approaching age twenty-four and I am no less fearful of the trials to come. By nature I am not assertive, worse, I have a great fear of falling short.

My nighttime schedule is turned upside down. Our day begins at four or five o'clock when we appear for formation, in a sea of sparkling white t-shirts, green fatigue pants and spit-shined boots. By some miracle, my boots are a perfect fit. I will go through all of Basic Training without even a blister.

Warming-up exercises are followed by the dreaded calisthenics. Then we set off on the morning run with the whole company of two hundred men running with rhythmic short steps, boots pounding in time, unstoppable in covering distance, and singing out, following our sergeant's lead:

I wanna be a Ranger, I wanna be a Ranger
A good old-fashioned Ranger, a good old-fashioned Ranger
Up the hill up the hill, Over the hill over the hill
Yaah, yaah, yaah, yaah

We are Charlie Company so we sing:

Everywhere we go-o, everywhere we go-o
People ask us, people ask us
Who we a-are, who we a-are
Where we come from, where we come from
So we tell them, so we tell them
We are Charlie, we are Charlie
Mighty mighty Charlie, mighty mighty Charlie
Mighty mighty Charlie, mighty mighty Charlie

The effect is terrific. I never could run worth a damn, but now I'm running. Caught up in the rhythm of it, I follow the man in front of me and keep ahead of the man behind, sweating along with the men on my right and left. During the first days, a few men will fall out and sit down, or walk, sick and exhausted but, before long, there will be no more falling out and no more sick men. Such is the hypnotic effect of the singing and the pounding of our rhythm boots, spurred on by the sergeant's lead and the insistent chanting, that the sun must come up, way up and fast, because we have done our incantations right and made offering of our plentiful sweat.

But the bars, a horizontal, ladder-like arrangement, are my terror.

We have to jump up to grasp a rung and swing our way along the ladder, rung by rung. It's simple, but I think I can't do it and so, defeated before I start, I never do get the hang of it. Painfully, one rung at a time I go through it. It is just a question of swinging the body and moving forward, hand over hand. We must go through the bars before entering the mess hall for meals. The alternative is ten push-ups, which I often gladly render.

Good and plentiful is the food. Some of my comrades complain of it and turn up their noses at grits and "shit on a shingle." They must have just come from the tender ministrations of their mammas and I sympathize with them, as I chow down on everything in sight. And I listen carefully to their complaints as I go through the line for seconds.

"War is hell," I often joke with my barracks mates. With bellies full and the sergeants, for a little while, at rest, we sit outside the barracks. Crickets chirp, cicadas cicada and our cigarettes glow in the near dark. Always, one of my comrades will reach for his wallet and show me a picture of "muh gurl." I, the wise one, elder by a few years, must nod, smile and intone, "she's beautiful." And I have to stop myself from saying to the misty-eyed kid beside me, "Hold on, ole buddy. We'll get through this, we'll get outta here soon, don't worry." Instead I sit back with the others as we smoke and spit-shine our boots and shoes.

In the daytime we run and climb and crawl under barbed wire. Once, and once only, do we crawl under live machine-gun fire. All of this I can more or less manage. It's the blasted ninety-degree heat I can't deal with. Now, on a particularly hot day, after going through my ordeal of the horizontal ladder, I am at a table in the mess hall. "Take all you want. Eat all you take." That's the rule in the mess hall. I have no appetite. Still remaining on my metal tray is a big slab of fish, very fried and very dead.

Poor fish. He died, not from being caught and cooked, I'm sure, but from the heat, as I am about to do. Fish and I understand each other. At this stage, I can no more eat him than he can eat me. I take my tray to the disposal area and try my best to evade the mess sergeant, but the mess sergeant will not be denied.

"What's that on your tray, troop?"

"Sorry, sir?"

"What's that on your tray?"

"Fish, sir."

"Gotta eat what you take."

"Can't, sir."

"You gotta eat what you take."

"Yes, sir."

I amble back to the table and force-feed myself with the poor fish. He gets the luxury of a round-trip ticket, because fish-going-down is meeting fish-coming-up. I will have to do something. I prevail on fish-going-down to shake hands with fish-coming-up, to make peace with him and to keep that peace long enough for me to get rid of my tray and to satisfy old eagle-eye sergeant. I run out of the mess hall and, just in time, I release both warring fish factions from captivity, by throwing up the whole lot at the sidewall of the mess hall.

<hr />

We are mountain men, farmers' sons and preachers' brothers. And there is a Puerto Rican contingent, all of us quartered at Fort Jackson. The Puerto Ricans, like the rest of us, are from the New York area. Their numbers in the Army seem out of all proportion to their numbers in the United States. It is a measure of the exclusiveness of Manhattan's East Side and of my own isolation in my Bronx ghetto that I have never come across any Puerto Ricans.

Basic Training they take in stride. Language presents no barrier.

Unlike me, they are lean and agile and they have no trouble with the cursed heat. Ever so smoothly do they swing through my nemeses, the accursed bars, their feet barely touching the ground on their way into the mess hall. And they register no complaints about the food.

So must Irishmen have seemed when, in great numbers, they joined the British Army and helped England to win all her wars, large and small. In the process they helped England to enslave and exploit millions across the world. The natives, after all, were only natives and, by definition, primitive. An Irishman in a uniform has already taken one step up from his own potato and poteen culture, from his shamrock syndrome of drinking, singing and fighting. Irishmen in the British Army won tons of awards for merit, valor and bravery with Victoria Crosses awarded out of all proportion to their numbers. Yes, they had to tip their caps, and to salute but they charged forward and they endured.

Our sergeants in dazzling white t-shirts and fatigues; their fatigues worn, aged and faded beyond their original green, beyond even a greenish blue, are transformed into a hazy gray. Mine is a fanciful and very private notion that while our sergeants may appear to serve at the will of the Federal Government, here, on the base, in Fort Jackson, South Carolina, there is more than a hint of the Confederacy.

Their accents, southern and western, are hard to pinpoint, especially for me, wide-eyed and gawking. I remember movies filled with wisecracking brave G.I.s and hard-bitten, kind-at-heart sergeants. In their faces, those faces burned from years spent in the outdoors, I look for some clue as to what we should expect.

Despite all my imaginings, their day's work is devoted to getting us in shape, nothing more and nothing less. At the end of the day of training they go home to their families. Like the British in India the sergeants are always right. Not only must they be right, they must be correct and always in command. In their demonstrated immunity to the heat, the British always stayed buttoned up, with their pith helmets firmly in place. Our sergeants dispense with the pith helmets. They indulge in no pretense and still manage to concentrate on getting us ready.

I become friends with Robinson. A hunter, well versed in the outdoors and in the care and handling of a shotgun, he is at home with our recently issued M14 rifle. He has a great West Virginia chuckle and no trouble grasping the refrain:

This is your rifle
This is your gun
This is for fighting
This is for fun

Medovar from Maryland is a farmer with an urban awareness and a bit of the Bible in his eye and in his jaw line. Tall and straight he stands. Robinson would be at home with a jug of moonshine and would do it justice. Medovar belongs more at the church social where maybe, just maybe, someone will spike the second bowl of punch while the men guffaw behind their hands and the ladies titter.

We all take a turn as kitchen police for a day. As part of our KP, it is our privilege to wash all pots, utensils, and metal trays as well as cutlery and to clean up the kitchen for the two hundred men in our company. We are happy enough when breakfast time passes without incident. Later, Medovar, my compadre, and I finish the lunchtime clean up. The mess sergeant casually runs his finger along the bottom of one of the two hundred metal trays. "Greasy," he barks. We must wash everything again. We are two ferocious fighting men in training. With two hundred metal trays we beat him down and take him apart. Most of him we shovel into the always simmering stock pot. Through the grease trap we render his fat. Only his uniform, his shoes and his belt buckle remain to be disposed of. We could have done all that. But we didn't.

Instead, we stand up straight and shout: "Yes, sir!" and "Yes, sir!" again and wash everything to his satisfaction.

In the evening, after our day's labors, we join the group for the nightly "spit-shining" session, that rare island of peace at the end of the day. With pleasure do we shine them up, our boots and our shoes. Some do a better job than others. There is one expert shiner who will do boots and "low cuts" for a fee. While most of us do our own, a few will pay him for this special shoeshine service.

One night "the expert" shines a pair of boots. The owner of the boots claims that he had already shined them. The expert demands payment on the spot, otherwise he will rub the boots in the sand and obliterate the splendid shine. A spit-shine war looms. The expert shiner is insistent, threatening and with language to boot. The owner of the boots refuses to pay.

The attendant night-owl smokers and spit-shiners hastily empanel a jury. The jury decides in favor of the owner of the boots. But it is decreed that he must pay half the normal fee, because the expert has greatly improved on the original shine, even though he had not been asked to do it. Payment is made and acknowledged. No trumpets are heard. Peace has arrived. And, indeed, with a great sigh of relief. Any argument, any noise or disturbance, will bring the sergeants down on our heads.

Showers, frequent and necessary, relieve the hot and sticky in the evenings. All will shower, except for the one who does not. When his bunkmates complain, the sergeant provides a rough brush and a cake of carbolic soap. "You guys take care of it yourselves," he advises. With little reluctance they advance on the smelly one. I'm not involved in the situation. But some fear is triggered in the back of my head, something I've seen or heard, or maybe something from my childhood. I can't place it but it nags at me.

I don't outrank any of the complainers and I never will be much of a soldier. I'm not much older than most of them, but I have been a few years away from home. Now, after some small persuasion on my part, the little mob gives up the brush and soap. I hand them to the smelly one with the suggestion that he should give himself a good wash. What I had seen bordered on bully rape, a kind of lynching, all just for being smelly. The smelly one heads toward the showers. The little mob, muttering its disappointment, is dispersed.

War is hell becomes the byword. After four weeks of it comes a letter from Sally. She has decided to marry her effete friend. In tandem, they will set off to bring the benefits of social work to the Native Americans of South Dakota. At the end of the letter she wishes me well. How kind of her to wish me well. I can't blame her. Her friend, effete or no, appears to be motivated. He, at least, has some prospects. My own ambition doesn't extend beyond the next two years in the Army. And, no doubt, like the girls of Limerick, she wants a man with steady employment and the probability of a house. There will be a pension at the end of it all, even if, unlike the women of Limerick, she must spend a portion of her life in the wilds of South Dakota.

The river of romance with Sally has dried up. Soon I find myself in the sandpits, where we are to learn hand-to-hand combat. Sand is up our noses and in our ears. Sand seeps sideways into our boots. Without apology, sand marches in and lodges in our pants. The little warrior is more gritty than usual that day. In burning sun and intense heat, each of us with a wooden peg in lieu of a bayonet, we are paired off in a one-on-one contest. "Subdue your opponent and you'll get a drink of water, a ten-minute break and a cigarette," we are told. In effect, kill and you will be free. We attack each other. Was I killed or did I kill? For the life of me, I can't remember.

And I'm in another kind of a sand pit, this one of my own making. I am bitter and I must cherish this bitterness. I know that it's bound to fall away, in time. Still, out of pure cussedness, I refuse the weekend pass. It's not all cussedness. I have another motive for my refusal. I know that most of the troops will accept the weekend pass. Those of us remaining in the barracks will have some peace and quiet.

Idling in the barracks during the day is never a good idea, not even on Sunday, our day off. Sergeants will often conduct a sweep through the barracks, rousting loungers and sleepers to be rounded up and sent to pick up garbage or to sweep the Company Street. And on top of that, whenever we walk from point A to point B, we are advised to carry a piece of paper. This will indicate that we are on an urgent mission and, therefore, not available to be press ganged into street sweeping or for any other detail.

Paper in hand, at noontime on a sleepy Sunday, in heavily starched Sunday khakis instead of weekday fatigues, to the library I go. I select a book, settle into a chair and soon fall asleep, prostrated by the heat and tired out by the rigors of the week.

Rigors of the week are not the only rigors. Physical fitness, deprivation and Sally's rejection soon give rise to more rigid rigors, to an erotic dream and to its conclusion. I wake up in a sweat, in the middle of the library. I start to sweat even more when I realize that I must be the focus of everyone's attention after such a monumental upheaval. I'm almost disappointed. It can't have been too monumental. No one is paying any attention to me but, when I look down, there is the evidence on my starched khaki pants.

How am I to leave the library and get back to barracks without being noticed and disgraced? How will I cover the stain? Could I cover it with my cap? Yes, I could. But we are required to wear our caps at all times and to salute all officers. I alternate. I hold my cap over the spot. When an officer approaches, I place cap on head with left hand, salute with right and offer an "Afternoon, sir." Then I quickly remove my cap with my left hand, cover the spot and so on. Fortunately, on this Sunday afternoon there aren't too many officers walking around the base, so I reach the empty barracks without being captured, take a shower and change clothes.

⌘

Well into the training I am selected to be interviewed as a possible candidate for Officers Candidate School. I have been selected, based on the tests I took when I was drafted. This comes as a surprise. One of the clerks at the Draft Board had looked at my test scores. In a snide aside, he remarked that I must have tried to fail the tests. It had been a peculiar situation. If I had set out to fail and was declared to be 4F, it would represent failure and would carry a stigma. On the other hand, being drafted is a pain in the neck and a total disruption. I didn't try to fail, but I didn't exert myself either.

Now I am being interviewed for O.C.S. Going to O.C.S. will mean signing up for an extra year. I'm no fierce warrior, so, when they ask, "You're surrounded and heavily outnumbered; you're alone, in fact. You have no food, no water and no ammunition. What do you do?" I just can't take this question too seriously. There are a million things I could do, a million answers I could give.

"Live to fight another day, I suppose," is the first answer that comes to mind. Not surprisingly, I am not encouraged to apply for O.C.S.

Our eight weeks of training come to an end with a great brassy passing-out parade, a reviewing stand, and speeches full of pride and congratulation. We are puffed up, if only for a moment, by the illusion that we have become soldiers. We don't throw our caps in the air. Officers and gentlemen do that. But we are happy, very happy, to get out of there and back into the world.

With Seamus, in the Bronx, I spend my ten-day leave. I'm proud of myself, proud that I survived at all. More than anything, I'm relieved that I didn't disgrace myself. I don't tell of my failures on the ladder or of my poor marksmanship. Unable to master the art of throwing from behind the ear, with a flick of the wrist, football style, I was still stuck on throwing from behind my back and over my head. "John Wayne-ing," they called it. I don't have to tell about that. But I joke about the day I almost beaned a training sergeant during practice with a dummy hand grenade. And I did joke that the training sergeants stayed home when they heard that it was my turn with a live grenade. On the day, I threw just fine, pretty much on target and didn't kill anyone.

We celebrate my return in Behan's Bar. Frank is a genuine veteran of World War II. During any lull in the conversation, with a great grin, he will declare himself an Irish Catholic, a Democrat and a Wounded War Veteran to boot. But with all his blather and buffoonery he retains a keen eye and a good heart. He offers me a handshake in congratulation and a warm welcome home.

I visit my mother and my brothers, but I am far away from them now. Lonely and lustful in Manhattan, I think of Sally. Unannounced, I go to visit her. Her roommate comes down to the front door, to head me off and to tell me that it will be better if Sally and I do not see each other. I rage at this rejection, but not too much. It's almost as if I expect myself to rage, as if the whole world and Hollywood all expect me to rage. Trouble is, Joan, the roommate, is even better looking than Sally and I have always had a bit of a yearning. This beautiful, intelligent, graceful girl is kind to me. She reasons with me, and with real sympathy. As she tries her best to talk sense into my thick shaven head, I begin to imagine possibilities.

When leave ends, I head off for Chicago, by plane, and at government expense. No more subway tokens for me. I am assigned now to the Veterinary Service of the U.S. Army. Wearing medical insignia, with a snake on each lapel, I have been sent to Chicago for two months, to learn to inspect food and to determine its fitness for human consumption.

I will witness the slaughter of cattle and the execution of sheep, by gas. I will smell the sausage up in the rafters of the smoke houses, taste butter and approve or reject it. A poor choice am I for such a task. As a result of growing up in Limerick, I am not inclined to reject any food. Especially the precious golden butter. The farmers' butter we grew up with, half salt and half butter, was basically self-curing. In a thousand years it wouldn't go bad. It could have been used to line the tomb of many a mummy, if the Irish had been into tombs and mummies. And, basically vegetarian by taste, though not by conviction, I don't take too easily to viewing the slaughter of animals, and especially at close range. But I will eat bacon and sausage, hamburgers and hot dogs, meatloaf and stew.

Most of our courses are written work with tons of charts and graphs that offer painfully precise methods for statistical sampling. A weekly practical and written test measures our progress. Housed in barrack-like quarters, in a converted warehouse on Pershing Boulevard, we have a cafeteria. There's no mess hall, but we receive a per diem allowance for food. Our food allowance is used sparingly. Most of it we spend on beer.

I had applied to attend the language school in Monterey, California. As a second choice, I wanted to work on an army newspaper, but Uncle Sam always knows better. Now I will help to protect the lives of all our boys and girls, in all services, worldwide. I will save them from bad food and drink. An unsung hero I will be. Highly unsung. And all without firing a shot. After the isolation and restriction of basic training, we are convicts on work release, our heads suitably shaven. Our classes finish at four in the afternoon and we are free until the following morning, with weekends off.

Written tests are multiple choice and the practical tests require only common sense, so we have plenty of time for our nightly explorations of Chicago. A congenial group it is, most of us just out of basic training, interested in getting through the school and moving on to a real assignment. Except for two. Of the perfect six-foot variety, blond-haired and blue-eyed, thick in the neck and broad in the shoulder, they are fresh from guarding the Tomb of the Unknown in Washington, D.C. The Tomb of the Unknown has been very much in the news since President John F. Kennedy's assassination. The metal taps on the heels of their shoes always announce their coming. Against all the rules, they go tap-tap-tapping around our barracks.

Parade ground soldiers and would-be Marines, they are looking to lord it over the rest of us. Or are they? As a minority of two, they may be just a little bit defensive. They are not too swift, as they say. Dumb as shite, in fact. But they single me out, this minority of two, because of my accent, maybe. They pick and pick and imitate and mock. I can do nothing. I would have little chance against either one, never mind both of them. And any fighting will bring heavy discipline, expulsion, even.

One day, after classes, I find one of them sitting down in the phone booth. The door is halfway open. With my left foot I jam the door in its half-open, half-closed position. Leaning in, I whisper into his right ear, "If the two of you don't stop fuckin' with me I'll get you. One by one, or both together, just as I have you jammed in now. There's no one around except you and me." The bullies back off. A coincidence? Very soon they are forced to leave the school because they can't keep up.

Again we graduate. After a short leave in New York, I report to Hampton Roads Army Terminal in Virginia. Assigned to Norfolk Naval Base I am to be a member of a team of army food inspectors living in barracks among about two million sailors. Responsible for all food used and served on the navy base and for all food loaded on ships for wider distribution worldwide, we must ensure that none of it is substandard or contaminated.

My working hours are spent in a warehouse. No. 10 cans must be checked, top and bottom, for swelling or popping, for dents or broken ridges. Sample bags of flour and rice are selected by rigid and precise application of statistical sampling procedures. They are opened and diligently searched for the presence of any foreign matter. Especially for bugs of any kind, weevils, in particular. The only weevil I know of is the boll weevil, the stuff of song and story. I'm greatly disappointed not to find any.

Trainloads of foodstuffs arrive at our warehouse and are passed through in good order except when I reject a shipment of some thousands of cans of tomato juice. The lids on the sample cans are poppers or springers, I can't remember which. And I reject a mislabeled shipment of canned fruit. Down comes the contractor from his plant in North Carolina. "And how much do you make in a month, soldier?" he demands. "Seventy-eight dollars a month, sir," Dopey Dan fires back. Is this the wrong answer? The contractor raises his eyes to heaven. He knows that I am hopeless. He takes back his whole shipment to be relabeled.

Was there more to his question than I knew? Have I gummed up the works of capitalism and cooperation?

There is another inspection area run by our unit and over there they check all the important stuff; all meat and fish and vegetables and it is staffed by enlistees, career soldiers and college graduates with degrees in agriculture or animal husbandry. These are serious men who will make a career in the food business, a business in which I have no interest, but as always I will do the job.

Our colonel, captain and lieutenant are all based in Hampton Roads Army Terminal a few miles away. Married sergeants live in married quarters. We seven or eight unmarried enlisted men live in a navy barracks. No cleaning and no KP for us. Strictly eight to four, we are, with weekends off, all nice and predictable. Our anthem could be:

The working class can kiss my ass
I got the foreman's job at last

Subject to no law outside of working hours except lights out and a reasonable standard of behavior determined by ourselves and our nearest navy neighbors in the barracks, we befriend our navy neighbors and our standard becomes theirs.

Across the street from our barracks is the mess hall and, further down the street, the WAVE barracks. In the evenings, from our windows, we watch the WAVEs as they saunter to the mess hall, accompanied by our whistles, growls and catcalls. "But your honor, we didn't do nuttin'. We wuz only havin' fun," we would have sworn if we were accused. Once in a while a WAVE will look in our direction and, just as quickly, turn away.

Especially do I watch the one young WAVE. Tall and slim, she steps long and slow, with care and dignity. This young black woman keeps her head high and her back straight. Of our whistles and yahoo catcalls she hears nothing or, if she does, she gives no sign. Is she just too proud, too much above it all or does she bear on her proud straight back the burden of all her people? Is it all nothing more than a romantic notion on my part? I will never know. Whatever the truth is, she doesn't flinch.

She needs only a touch of Spanish scarlet about her: a scarf, maybe, a handkerchief, even, or a red headband, to make her perfect.

To the sailors in the barracks we are and must be "the army guys." I'm partnered with Elvin B. J. "Buff" Roper. All-City in the 440 yards in Detroit, he is often scathing in his humor. Chronically laconic in demeanor, with laughter as his armor, Roper's flash of anger is as rare and as fleeting as lightning. And never will he be patronized, for his color or for anything else. Ever separate he will remain. And always more than equal.

In the warehouse by the railroad track, at the edge of civilization, our regular quota of work must be finished by the tenth day of the month. From then on we check shipments as they arrive. In between times there are crossword puzzles, epigrams and bananagrams, to be solved and completed. Impromptu comedy routines and two-man musical extravaganzas, brilliantly devised, will often burst upon the stage. All tap dancing is done on top of the one desk and we are careful not to put our heads through the dropped ceiling.

Roper introduces me to The Four Tops, to Ramsey Lewis and to the Boogaloo. I am working hard at perfecting my Boogaloo and Roper is wrestling with a crossword puzzle, when in come the officers: our seldom seen Colonel, our Captain and the Big Colonel down from Fort Meade on an inspection tour. We slam to attention. With a "carry on," our Captain puts us at ease. I go through the motions of tapping the tops and bottoms of the few No. 10 cans we keep on hand for use as step stools, when we have to climb onto the desk for tap dancing practice. Roper wrestles a bag of rice onto the desk. In doing so, he just happens to cover up his newspaper and the crossword puzzle. Our Captain checks the charts to see that we are up to date with our work and proclaims "good work," with a nod in the direction of the Big Colonel. Again we slam to attention and they move on to their next inspection.

The year 1965 brings rumblings and rumors from Vietnam along with tall tales of military advisers drawing hazardous-duty pay while living large in hotels in Saigon. Two of us offer to volunteer for this dangerous duty. To our great disappointment we are told that in our category, in our particular category of crossword-puzzle-maven-cum-Boogaloo-dancer, cum-food-inspection-specialist, they have five times as many volunteers as they need. By the time the situation changes I will be out of the Army forever.

In our disappointment, we find a disused tennis court on the base and start whacking tennis balls for diversion. Roper has played very little tennis. I have played none. Roper can lope and he covers the whole court in two strides. When I dare to approach the net he lobs the ball over my head. If by the base line I stay he will tap the ball just over the net and far from my reach. Rough treatment is this, almost as rough, I suspect, as fighting faceless guerillas in Vietnam, being booby-trapped and fired upon from the jungle, but somehow we survive.

Evenings after mess hall are bedlam. All radios in the barracks must be turned on. And all at the same time. As if by agreement, each radio is tuned to a different station. The result is a regional cultural cacophony. The volume is high enough to wake the dead and to make the insane crave asylum in the quiet grave. Not for me is the lying on the bunk, in the din and the dim, reading and rereading the letter from muh gurl. Besides, I don't have a muh gurl. Sally is probably married and residing among the Native Americans by now. And the slow shower shoe shuffle to the shower, toilet kit in hand, three times a night, just to pass the time, doesn't do much for me either.

I have never been much of an athlete. Now, desperate to escape the noise, I take up running. And I drag one or two of my barracks mates out to run with me, even against their will. We cover two or three miles each night. Geisinger is an athlete and he is in the U.S. Navy.

"Are you flat-footed?" he asks me, one evening.

"No, I'm not," I reply.

"Well, you run flat-footed," he tells me. "Don't you know you should run on the balls of your feet?"

"I know that," I tell him.

"Then why don't you do it?" I start to do it, there and then. As a result I am able to run faster and I weep to think that all these years a great athlete has been lost to the world. But it does not make me give up my daily pack of Pall Malls.

Dolbec runs with me on a Saturday afternoon. As we jog back to the barracks he is animated, as usual. And in his Vermont-French-Canadian way, he is, as always, puzzled as to why he is here to begin with. He is no more puzzled than I am; only he shows it more. Excitable, and prone to outrage as he sometimes is, he will often manifest indignation, magnificent in scale, and out of all proportion to his size.

Our two-mile run is done. We have played our two hours of tennis and we stop to watch two teams of sailors playing soccer, Columbian style. Their ship is docked in Norfolk for a few days. In need of a couple of players to fill out the two team rosters, they invite us to play. Dolbec is assigned to one team and I am assigned to the other. Dolbec has never played soccer before. My new team mates call out to each other to give me the ball. "Give it to thee gringo, give it to thee gringo," they urge each other. Should I be insulted at being called gringo or should I be more insulted at the idea that I can't get the ball for myself? It doesn't matter. Goodwill overrides all. They set me up with a can't-miss, right in front of the goal. I manage to score and they shake my hand and clap me on the back. This is generosity of spirit.

⁂

Word reaches us from the other world, our headquarters, at Hampton Roads Army Terminal, that the Army will pay our tuition if we take college-level courses. I sign up at Old Dominion College, founded in

1938, for a course in American history.

Mr. Savage is our teacher and the bulk of my classmates are in the military, mostly Navy and Marines. When, at a later date, I take driver's training at a local high school, my instructor is Mr. Slaughter. A logical historical progression, this, from Savage to Slaughter. Are the gods telling me something?

It turns out to be the best course I ever take in my life. It is a blessed relief to be dealing with American history, a chronology that makes sense, with principles and doctrines clearly laid out, instead of having to trudge through the tangled underbrush of European history as I had done before. No longer will I be tripping over knots of Hohenzollerns and Hapsburgs and tangles of Charles the First of Scotland, so easy to confuse with Charles the First of France, or whomever or whatever.

My sense of geography was never great and I really never gave much of a damn about the Seven Year War or Count Cavour and the Unification of Italy. I could only applaud Henry VIII for his accumulation of wives. "Good for you, Henry!" we cheered, in our boys-only, sex-starved Christian Brothers School. Our cheering had to be done very quietly. We were Catholics, after all. So, by comparison, American history makes more sense and is much more easily understood. The Puritans fled persecution. They came, they saw, they conquered. Along the way they devised principles, very sound principles, to buttress and to justify the seeing, the sawing and the conquering.

At Old Dominion I meet the Dinwiddies. A well-established Norfolk family, they have a bunch of children and they adopt me, wandering man that I am. I have a certain legitimacy because I am a foreigner and I am Army, not Navy. Being Army is a definite advantage. As soldiers, we are a very small minority. Sailors, on the other hand, descend on Norfolk in their thousands. Navy-enlisted men in Norfolk are held, not in low, but in no esteem, by the locals, just as residents of tourist towns despise the very tourists they depend on.

Yes, the Dinwiddies adopt me. On more than one occasion they feed me, but especially on Thanksgiving Day, when, in their Unitarian passion for enlightenment, they ask me to explain the origin and the nature of the conflict in Northern Ireland. And I do, so I do.

I reach back as far as I can into Irish history and mythology, detailing all that I can remember of every iota of injustice, every ripple of rebellion that had happened in Ireland, in nearly two thousand years: From the Fir Bolgs and the Tuatha De Danann to Cuchulainn and Fionn MacCumhaill. To Saint Patrick, the Shamrock and every snake of an informer in every rebellion that ever was. On to King Brian Boru who routed the Danes at Clontarf in 1014.

Not forgetting Cromwell, with his policy of "To Hell or to Connacht," to the Sieges of Limerick and Derry in the seventeenth century. To the rising of 1798, when Presbyterians and Catholics fought on the same side, and the infamous Act of Union in 1800. Followed, in 1803, by Robert Emmett's speech from the dock:

When my country takes her place among the nations of the earth, then and not till then, let my epitaph be written.

To Catholic Emancipation in 1829, when at that time, according to William Styron, the slaves of Virginia were well fed and well housed. The peasants of England and Ireland were not so well cared for, even though they were situated at the very elbow of the arm that rocked the cradle of democracy.

Nor did I spare them the rising of 1848 and the deportation of the leaders to Tasmania, all of whom escaped, dispersed and achieved distinction. So why should I not batter them with the Fenians of 1867, the founding of the Gaelic League and Sinn Fein? The Rising of 1916, the War of Independence, the first president a Protestant and women given the vote in 1919. I concluded with the Treaty, the Civil War and the declaring of a Republic in 1949 with the Northern Six Counties still gerrymandered and partitioned off.

Why in the name of God I did it and in such detail, I will never know. My only excuse might be that ever since I had arrived in New York, I'd been asked the same question a few times a year. In any bar, late at night, the question was bound to pop up. The questioner, after too many drinks, like a bee loaded with nectar was lulled into an expansive inquisitiveness. In what he thought of as a conciliatory way, "You guys are all white, right?" he would begin. "All Christians, right?" he would continue. And I would know what was coming next. "So why can't you get along with each other?"

Sometimes the man with the question was of first- or second-generation immigrant stock. Usually the common thread was there's us. And there's them. The us is all of us white Christians. The them is everybody else: Jews, Muslims, Hindus and Buddhists. And anyone who is not white.

There was an implied solidarity here. A solidarity that I did not feel. This was a race with too many horses in it. I could, maybe, ride one of them. I could discuss the differences between Nationalists and Unionists, Catholics and Protestants, respectively, in Northern Ireland. I could take a stab at talking about the exclusion of blacks and Jews. I can't do both. More importantly, I don't want to talk about any of it, so I avoid the question.

"Do you have a few hours, or a few days?" I ask. "It's very complicated and it's a very long story. Why don't we just have another drink?"

The Dinwiddies, unlike my friend at the bar, are kind and compassionate people. They would exclude no one.

Having finished both my dinner and my recitation, I look around the table. I am greeted by silence, amazement, shock and disbelief. Faint strangled sounds begin to emanate from my hostess. Is she giggling, I wonder? No, she's not giggling, you fool. She's too well bred to giggle. She seems to be half giggling and half sobbing. Is she sobbing at my tragic tale of Irish woe, betrayal and failure? What a great-hearted woman!

When she clenches her fists and shifts violently in her seat it begins to dawn on me that desperation is at work here.

"Thank you for a wonderful dinner," I say to the Dinwiddies as I leave their house. Would it not have been better, kinder and more merciful had I sung them one of my shut-eyed songs of rebellion and betrayal? A song, at least, would be finished in eighteen verses, or eighteen minutes, whichever comes first. And there would, at least, have been a touch of music in it for relief. But it is too late now. Had I a digression, I would have moved into it and covered my head for seven days and seven nights.

I don't hear from the Dinwiddies for some time. When I do eventually get in touch with them, they again invite me for dinner, brave and kindly souls that they are. Careful now, I confine my remarks to no more than one sentence. The Dinwiddies, as token of their forgiveness, introduce me to Margaret. In her mid-twenties, Margaret is tall, willowy, dark haired and has recently moved to Norfolk. Among her assets are an apartment and a car. Nice looking as she is, there is a touch of lingering melancholy about her. Who or what was he to have left her with such a melancholy? I never ask. A half-dozen times we go out together, ending, always, with passionate embraces and no resolution, up against the wall of her Confederate reserve.

God never closes one door, but he opens another. That's what they say. When the local Norfolk paper reports that a rugby club is starting up, I go and try out for it. Since I have actually played before, I am readily accepted by the founders, Bubba and Woody, and I get to play, along with the Whitley brothers. They could be twins, these two shortish blonde-haired, blue-eyed tanks. More accustomed to playing football, they play as if they're wearing helmets and padding. Rugby players don't wear helmet and pads. I can only thank God that I am on the same team with them, ferocious as they are. Like Young Munster front-row forwards they don't just play against the opposing players, they eat them up alive.

Our team includes locals, who have never played before and a couple of navy officers, one of them a hot-shot fighter pilot. On the short side, and dark haired, he has a tan and a great way with women. Hard as he tries, intense and athletic as he is, he should have stuck to racket ball. His intensity and lack of any sense of the ridiculous preclude any pleasure in playing rugby or any game. To him it is all competition and challenge, which is probably why women are attracted to him and why I can't stand him. I envy this wintry man with the perennial tan.

Woody and Bubba are friendly men just out for a good time. They are quick to tell me that in playing rugby with them, I am rubbing shoulders with some of Norfolk's oldest families. At the country club Bubba introduces me to his sister. We go on a few dates with plenty of alcohol on hand, but no clotheshorse am I and I don't fit in, with my old green leftover suit jacket and Farrah pants.

We have yet to win a game when, up in William & Mary College, we play our best game yet. Dominating from the beginning, we lead by three points at fulltime. The referee, by accident or design, fails to blow the final whistle until the other team is allowed to score a try and converts. We lose by two points.

⁂

An easy mark at home, we're always worse in away games. Still we travel, to the University of Virginia and to Duke at Chapel Hill, among others. One of our games is played in ninety-degree heat, on ground from which the grass is long gone. This is a very poor surface indeed for rugby football. We play into injury time. The game goes on so long that I get sunburned. After the game I drink my share of beer. Someone offers moonshine as a remedy for sunburn. I have some of that and I conclude my day by taking a nap on the one toilet in the house.

Awakened by haranguings, bangings and urgent shouts, I emerge to face a crowd of the dispossessed and the delayed. My sunburn is mistaken for chronic alcoholic flush and my nap on the toilet is looked upon as total disregard for the well-being of society at large. Hanging is mentioned, for holding up the line. In my defense, Bubba and Woody volunteer, "He's Irish, don't you know. You do know, don't you, about the Irish and their drinking. Besides, he is in no fit condition to be hanged." When I protest as to the reputation of the Irish and our capacity for drink, and when I look to defend the state of my condition, they tell me to shut up, bundle me into the car and, abruptly, we leave. Foiled, for once, is the hand of summary justice.

Walter Olsted comes along with me and plays once or twice. He is the senior man in our little group of "army guys." When his girlfriend comes to Norfolk to visit along with a couple of her girlfriends, Bergonzi and I are paired off with them. I have no car and no place to invite her back to. There are no expectations. All is done by gentleman's agreement. All proprieties are observed, red blooded and hot to trot though we are, beautiful and enticing as they are.

※

Bergonzi can find anything or fix anything. It is Bergonzi who discovers the beach at Nags Head in North Carolina. On weekends, having loaded up with camping gear borrowed from Special Services in addition to the hamburgers, hot dogs and steaks for which we bartered twenty-pound cans of coffee and having purchased enough beer for a year, we head off for a time of blessed peace on this deserted beach. There are no sailors and no radios; no sound but the cry of the birds in the wild and the rhythmic resonance of the ocean. Surf-casting is our main diversion. The only fish I ever catch is a giant jellyfish and I say, "Bye, bye, jellyfish," before returning him to the ocean.

Never afraid to try, Bergonzi prevails on two WAVEs to go with us to the beach and to spend the weekend with us in our two humble tents. These two ladies from the North are not burdened by any Confederate reserve. Mars and Venus settle their differences and enter into a state of conjunction. The soughing of the waves signals a new chapter and an end to a dreadful drought.

My first real taste of Americana is a scene right out of the movies. The beach is endless and deserted. A plentiful supply of driftwood allows us to keep a fire going all the time. Food is abundant and there's more beer than we can drink. For the whole weekend I wear nothing but an old pair of shorts: no hat, no shirt and no shoes. On Sunday evening, we set out on the trip back to Norfolk in Bergonzi's TR-whatever with the top down, while Bergonzi revs and roars with a *wheeeee*, as he always does, on a curve.

When I begin to shiver, I know then that I have a touch of sunstroke and a heavy dose of sunburn. Back to barracks I go, to shiver my way into bed until morning. Both feet are swollen and I am unable to jump down from my top bunk, as I usually do. With my back to the mattress, I slide down. All the burned skin leaves my back. Down to my warehouse work I hobble, wearing one combat boot in deference to authority and one shower shoe in defense of the more heavily blistered foot.

A sergeant comes by to verify the rumor of my death. In his disappointment that I am still alive, he threatens me with a court martial for bodily harm inflicted on myself. All morning the charge hangs in the air until, in the afternoon, I locate a friendly navy doctor. He covers my doleful arse by prescribing medicine for a severe burn. And, with a straight face, he makes a notation that the aforesaid burn was suffered in the line of duty.

Our Sergeant Carson is well beyond the point of sunburn, seasoned as he is and so tough and lean that even his lower jaw is sinewy. From underneath his crew cut, in his good ole boy manner, he chomps on his words as he speaks. He has bought a speedboat and invites us all to go waterskiing because he wants to learn.

We all take turns on the skis and manage to get up and stand on the skis, if only for a few seconds. Sergeant Carson tries once, and again and a third time but he fails to get up on the skis. Still he persists, with his body and his head underwater. Only the tip of his crew cut is visible, but still he will not let go of the towrope. He is skiing underwater. The driver, speeding heedless and headlong into murder, does not slacken speed. We shout at the driver, roar at him in unison, until, at last, he frees the towrope. Carson is forced to let go. His head appears and he coughs, once or twice, on a deep breath. He comes ashore bearing a wide grin. With a rueful shake of the head he tosses it all away and we know, now, why Carson has a Silver Star from Korea.

Korea is long gone. Vietnam, not much more than a loud rumor, as yet, is rapidly becoming a reality. I am conscious that something is definitely lacking in this dissolute, so-called military life. We all feel it.

And I am convinced, that were it not for my fearful appetite for food and beer, my one-pack-a-day cigarette habit and a constant preoccupation with sex, I could be a terrific ascetic. I lack the gaunt and haunted, or is it the haunt and gaunted, look. My unlined face does not lend itself to the part, still I crave a worn, more desperate look, with a bit of dissipation in it. It would be more attractive to women, I think. And had it not been for my sense of futility, after the zealotry of my Sinn Fein years, I might have pursued something. Or was it all just laziness.

Even so, weekday warehouse work and weekend warfare conducted on beaches, tennis courts and water skis, will take their toll on even the most battle-hardened warrior. Sometimes I accept an invitation to go north to visit the family of one of my comrades. One such weekend takes me to Dover, Pennsylvania and the "Hunting and Fishing Club" with Larry Coble. Inside the door of "The Club," we are greeted by a sign exhorting us to "License Communists, not firearms" and I know exactly where I am.

And once, in the company of Nelson Perry, I travel up to Washington, D.C. for a weekend. I will not see a white face for three days. There's a party for me on Saturday night. Friends and cousins alike embrace me, this white boy in the army uniform, friend of their flesh and blood, as one of the family. I am remembering the brothers coming home to Limerick in uniform and simultaneously thanking Roper for the Boogaloo lessons. In their hearts the aunts and cousins and friends must sense what is to come. They must know that certain cities in these United States will soon erupt in riot and race war and that in so many ways, for better and for worse, nothing will ever be the same again.

And once to South Braintree, Massachusetts to visit the family of John Bergonzi, the ghosts of Sacco and Vanzetti and to keep a blind date that begins with Sunday Mass. I cough, groan and shift in my seat until we are released to the beach. "Me white man," pale and skinny, kick sand in my own face, just to show her that I am tough and that I can at least kick sand in *somebody's* face. She stares into the distance, speaking hardly a word. I do my best, but the date is not a success. The weekend is not to be a total loss. I meet Bergonzi's sister, Lynn, and we begin a correspondence, which lasts for some months. She writes well and warmly until, in the end, the letters just seem to fall away, distance being a great fizzler.

Now, with six months to go, I am assigned to a STRAC team. Don't ask me what it stands for, but this assignment means that I can be sent to the site of any natural disaster, be it earthquake, flood, fire or whatever, to supervise sanitation and food storage and to help ensure the general well-being of the population. A mighty prestigious assignment, is this, should something happen, that is. General Patton would be proud, but now I must have all the shots and vaccinations all over again, all thirteen of them. As a consolation prize I am promoted to Specialist (E4), making me equivalent in rank to a corporal. I have become a fully trained doubly shot up killer with a No. 10 can as my principal weapon.

Nothing is left but to count down the days to freedom, to have the final booze up with the buddies and to tell war stories to my fresh-faced and very nervous replacement. I hand over the reins of the warehouse to Roper, take my discharge papers and my bag and board the plane to New York. From the beginning I have been impatient to get out. Now, to my surprise, I am emotional and sentimental as I make my way to the airport.

1966

WITH A MONTH'S PAY, some accumulated leave pay and a bunch of small denomination treasury bonds, enough to constitute a pocketful of money, I return to New York. The Draft will no longer be a persistent fear. I'm free of it.

I could have stayed in for three more years and requested a different kind of work, something more to my liking. I could have taken the re-enlistment bonus and whatever college time and tuition money were available. Army life brings order, stability and fellowship. If you want it. Mam no longer lives in Ireland, so there is no home to go back to. And I couldn't have had an easier time of it in the Army. But from what I have seen, three more years might easily lead to three more and to twenty-three more. Time would pass very quickly. A growing beer gut would be my anchor and it would soon grow and balloon into a big bag of disillusionment with only a pension at the end for comfort and reward.

Mam is living alone on Flatbush Avenue in Brooklyn. Frank is married. Malachy is married for the second time. Mike married about a year ago.

Back in New York, for my first night I crave a quiet place, a room of my own, free of noise, radios, banter, shouting and the insistent *ssshissh, ssshissh, ssshissh* of the shower shoes flapping back and forth to the showers. I can still remember the one or two evenings when there was no hot water and only a few of us took the nightly shower. Most of the two or three times a night shower-warriors were terrified at the prospect of cold water and they failed to show up. Tonight there will be hot water and privacy.

At the Commodore, on the East Side of Manhattan, I take refuge, before setting out to visit a few old haunts. Next day I call the brothers and I go to stay with Mam in Brooklyn. This is a handy arrangement for me. It will be good for her to have the company, though she can't have been prepared for this moody, intolerant, impatient man, her youngest son. Nor can she know how fervently I wish that she could have a better life or something I thought of as a regular life, and better living conditions. But I know that a regular life, for her, is impossible. It all had gone so miserably wrong, so many years before, long before I was even born.

Unable to tell her any of this, I am brisk, instead, in letting her know that I will not be staying long with her in Brooklyn. I will be moving into Manhattan as soon as I can find an apartment. Mam takes it as if she expects no better.

I am afraid that she will become dependent on me again, afraid that I will again become surrogate for my father and my brothers. My brothers are well launched on their own lives. I expect Mam to be there when I need her or when I need a place to stay, but I let her know clearly and without any warranty that I will stay only as long as I need to stay. I do it that way because there is no good way to break away. Preamble and blandishment, any attempt to soften the blow, will all come down to the moment of separation. There is no getting round it. And, of course, my own selfishness is no hindrance.

What will I do for a job? In New York City, I would guess, all the No. 10 cans are already spoken for. I don't want to work in anybody's office so I go back to Burns Detective Agency. They offer me a night job. This will allow me my days free. I am really and truly going to go to college during the day. Yes I am. With my newfound confidence and my status as a veteran, they give me a top of the line job. The New York City Ballet Theater, in Lincoln Center, is a brand new facility on the West Side of Manhattan. At two dollars an hour, the pay is well above the average.

Lincoln Center is situated in the middle of a wasteland of broken down old-time Irish saloons, in an area populated by older people who have nowhere else to go and surrounded by drug dealers and their prey. No one will go to this Lincoln Center, they say. It is a white elephant, built so far off the beaten track.

My partner on the midnight shift supports his family by working as a barber, in Harlem, during the day. His night job supports his Cadillac. Having been on his feet all day he is well content to sit in the office and wake me from my catnaps, in time for the scheduled rounds. I patrol the darkened passageways and rooms and reassure myself by calling out: "One o'clock and all is well," continuing to call out, every hour on the hour, until six o'clock. That's when the daytime workers begin to arrive and I have to stop calling out for fear of being certified as insane.

For some reason it is two in the morning, not midnight, that frames the question. No bell tolls, but still the silence always seems to ask, "Why are you here?" Every hour of every night, from left to right, I cross the always well-lit stage. The bright stage gives relief from the gloom. I am often overtaken by an urge to loosen up with a few jigging dance steps, to sing a fragment of an opera or a touch of Gilbert and Sullivan. "A Wandering Minstrel I Would Be" serves me well. Soon I am in the habit of taking the imaginary applause. With a bow and, with simulated generosity, I offer a sweep of the arm to the orchestra and chorus behind me. Reluctantly I move on, to clock in at the next checkpoint. At two o'clock one morning, I finish my dancing and singing routine and as I am taking my bow, a voice from the very back of the darkened theater cries out, "What?" or "Who?" I don't answer. I run. From then on I cross that stage almost at a trot. No more do I dance and I take no more bows.

Staying up all night through the chill of early dawn brings life to the nerve endings, causing them to tingle with the twin sensations of apprehension and anticipation. Both are soon fulfilled by the arrival of the dancers for their morning classes. By this time, the sun is well up. Apprehensions are ushered into a back seat. Blood vessels are filled to bursting and often, with the warming of the sun and the arrival of the dancers, the sun is not the only thing that's up and rampant and trying hard to poke its way through the uniform pants. But the old cap in the left hand trick comes into play, once again. I need not bother. In the uniform I am invisible.

Up at the White Horse Inn, on the west side of Second Avenue, between 88th and 89th Streets, I have a beer with Sean, the owner. By way of conversation, he tells me that they are looking for a waiter. His wife, Peggy, goes further. "We're looking for a redheaded Irish waiter. Would you be interested?" I am interested, yes I am. I need work. I will serve, in any guise. You need a redheaded Irish waiter? I'm your man. A redheaded waiter? That's me. An Irish waiter? Why not? Or just plain waiter? I am ready to go.

The following night, under Peggy's guidance, my training begins. Given my mortal fear of ever appearing to be excited or confused, it takes forever. There must be something English in my Irish upbringing that makes me believe that haste is unseemly. I can neither hasten nor hustle. Very soon, I begin to sense exasperation all round me. I catch a few stray comments: "He does seem to know it and he seems to have it. Then why the hell isn't he doing it?"

Then, one evening, apparently by consent of the governing, and in the middle of bedlam, I find that I have been abandoned. I am working alone among a mob of a thousand customers. Soon my Anglo-Celtic reserve falls away. I dive right into the confusion. Three hours later I surface, mostly intact. I have the job.

My brothers, Malachy and Mike, have been around bars and restaurants for years, as bartenders, owners and personalities. I lack their physical size, their keen intuitive wit, their warmth and their quick grasp of new and changing situations. Besides, they have always actively discouraged me from becoming involved in the bar and restaurant business.

For now, I am blinded by the easy camaraderie and the chance to have a foot in the glamorous East Side of Manhattan. And, of course, there is money, more money than I've ever seen. Tables are topped with gold. All I have to do is bring the food, take the dishes and smile at any reference to my Irish looks and accent. When they ask, "What do you really do? Are you a poet or a writer or an actor?" I must be abashed and smile with an "I'm working on it." Above all, don't dilute or spoil the illusion.

From time to time, I will get together with Joan, Sally's roommate. We have a relationship, a relationship of convenience. Should either of us feel the need, or need a friend, we get together for an evening. She had a terrible and tragic event in her family and needed company and I just happened to call her on that day. Then again I called her far more than she ever called me. Was it out of her womanly concern, that what happened to me in the Army Base Library, should never happen again? I don't know, but she never said no. We spent many a night together until, one night when I was drunk, I violated the spirit of our relationship. I called her in the middle of the night and insisted. She said yes that night, but that was the end of it.

⸎

At twenty-six years of age I am still wide-eyed and innocent. Naïve as

I am and with little self-confidence, I am too grateful for this job opportunity. I'm still worried that it won't work out, so I hold on to my two-dollar-an-hour Lincoln Center job, just to be safe. This does not allow for much sleep. My night at the White Horse begins at six. In order to be organized, I report in at five or five-thirty, limbo time in a restaurant or bar, with the day's business disposed of and the evening's festivities yet to begin.

The White Horse Inn, second home to a good many artists and writers, carries a few lawyers and Wall Street types for ballast. An episodic psychiatrist provides balance and moderation in case the artists and writers, in their hunger for attention and articulation, should accidentally capsize the ship. Bringing up the rear, are a couple of firemen and a cop. Like many a bar, the White Horse is a culture unto itself.

There are a number of young women with serious daytime jobs, which lend them the promise of a guaranteed future and a pension, in publishing or in advertising. This saloon sundae is topped by the occasional blonde-haired, blue-eyed babe, milk-washed and corn-fed. Available early in the evening or late at night, she brings with her an infinite capacity for laughter, revelry and liquor. Working her way around from writer to artist, to actor and back again, only rarely and, incidentally, is she ever seen to cross over into the world of the suits and ties.

During that summer of 1966 we are aflood with tourists venturing to the White Horse for a little diversion and a taste of New York's legendary Irish charm, and I, the most redheaded stranger, with accent still intact, can certainly fit the bill. Gladly would I have given the women a touch of the old diversion. But I soon find that too much attention paid to the women causes their dates to cut back on my share of the loot.

In his mid-fifties, Jack Donoghue is a native New Yorker. With hair a dirty grey and eyes as dead as his hair, he has what the English so aptly call a petulant mouth. A petulant mouth can be really sexy in a woman, but it is questionable in a man. Mr. Donoghue craves and receives plenty of attention. Vaguely connected as he is with movie distribution, there exists the possibility that he may know someone who knows someone. He might, possibly, be instrumental in bringing in some celebrity business.

To my twenty-six-year-old eye he is ancient, his whole persona distasteful. He bears the look of a man who has slid into the dullest of decadence, without ever showing or suffering even a hint of passion along the way. His antiquity is barely belied by his escorts, a blonde and a brunette. One on each arm, always the same two women, they are both a little bit past their prime, though they would still be good for a rub of the relic. For whatever reason, money being a strong possibility, they defer to him. Imperious in manner, he is much given to snapping his fingers and offering sarcastic asides to his two concubines. His standard quip, "Is there a waiter on duty here?" falls flat.

In such narrow confines I can't avoid the old bastard and I can't help but hear his aging sarcasms. Nor can I respond since his remarks, so typical of the impotent bully, are tossed in the air and are never aimed directly at me. And when I look into the eyes of his two companions, there is nobody home. There is no detectable sign of understanding or of human fellowship. I dread the once-weekly arrival of Jack and his awesome twosome until, one evening, while ordering his second drink, Jack begins to cough. He coughs and he coughs, a very persistent cough. I am half hoping that he will die on the spot. If he died I would have no choice but to console the blonde and the brunette. Disappointed when his coughing begins to abate, I am quietly elated when the force of his cough propels his top row of false teeth right out of his mouth, and onto the floor. Skittering across the room they come to rest very close to my shoe. With a touch of ceremony, I take a napkin and pick up the teeth. I approach his table and announce, "Sir, your teeth."

Jack and his two escorts are a constant, but by the fall the tourist traffic slows down. I enroll at Columbia School of General Studies. I attend for only a few months. Aimless and bored with first year courses, I drop out. My low-rent West Side apartment I give to my mother, so that she can leave her rapidly declining neighborhood in Brooklyn, and I move to a terrific ground floor apartment on Lexington Avenue at 92nd Street, across from the 92nd Street Y. At the rear of the apartment I have a tiny garden.

It is good to have Mam settled in an apartment in Manhattan. She had been unsettled since coming to New York and she had been isolated in her apartment on Flatbush Avenue in Brooklyn. She had lived in Brooklyn before, but that was many years ago.

· LIMERICK ·

1941

ANGELA SHEEHAN, my mother, had emigrated to the U.S. in her late teens and worked as a domestic in New York City. When I was a teenager, she told me that in one of the houses where she worked the man of the house "made advances" to her. She was not specific. She didn't have to be specific. What she said was enough to show that she was vulnerable. She had no one to defend her.

She and my father, Malachy, met in Brooklyn, where they were married and had five children, only to lose their daughter, Margaret Mary, in infancy. My mother's resulting depression matched the Great Depression, which had taken hold in the United States, forcing herself, my father and my brothers Frank, Malachy and the twins, Eugene and Oliver, to leave New York and return to Limerick.

Oliver and Eugene died in Limerick, within months of each other. Mam told me that as Eugene lay dying he kept saying, "I tan't, I tan't," over and over again. Mam believed that Oliver was calling to Eugene to come to him and Eugene was saying, "I can't, I can't." My brother Michael was born in 1936. I arrived in 1940, shortly after the beginning of the Second World War, which makes me the last of seven children born to my parents, three of whom died. Four survived.

Someone once asked me, "Were you the youngest?"

"I was," I said. "And I still am."

I was born up in Barrack Hill, in Limerick, a city drowning in damp, with no single rainy season to blame, no monsoon. Just the rain and the constant ever-creeping wet, with the jungle of damp despair kept at bay only by the people's spirit, by song and by story.

Well seasoned at eight hundred years of age, situated at the very western edge of Europe, Limerick was nobody's child. Isolated from Europe and orphaned by England, Limerick was a garrison town and only a distant relative to the other Irish cities. Yearning always toward America, she was more sister to Atlantic storm than to pleasant midland meadow.

Barrack Hill was home to Sarsfield Barracks, which housed units of the Irish Free State Army, the guardians of our wartime neutrality. A long stone's throw away, just across O'Connell Avenue, was the steepled Church of Saint Alphonsus. The church was the local headquarters of the Redemptorist Fathers, the guardians of our souls. First among Redemptorists was Saint Alphonsus. I am named after him.

⸙

My brother Malachy is named after our father, but Mam could never bring herself to say "your father" when referring to the old man. When speaking of him she always called him "your pop." According to my mother this man, my father, "your pop," was always either at prayer or at drink. When we were told that "God loves the saint and God loves the sinner; the indifferent He will spit out of His mouth" during our childhood religious instruction, I pictured my father in both roles. Saint and sinner he was, no doubt about it. For him there were no half measures in life, in work, or in drink, for that matter. And there were no half measures in his departure. He took off when I was a year old and never came back to stay.

My father had been active with the IRA, Mam said, and had to be smuggled out of the North of Ireland and away to America. Thus began his goings away. Temperament is destiny.

Mam told me that after they came back from America my father worked on the building of the Shannon Scheme, which was part of a nationwide rural electrification project begun by the Irish Free State Government in 1928. They dug a canal, built a dam and a hydroelectric plant at Ardnacrusha, loosely and fittingly translated as "Hill of the Cross," only a few miles outside Limerick City.

In my imagination the night watchman, my father, stands, alone, in the dead hours of the night, beside a rushing body of water. What does he think about as he makes his rounds? His romantic Ireland is already partitioned. His native Northern Ireland remains under British rule. Southern Ireland is free. My father, a Catholic and a fervent Nationalist, is greeted with suspicion, bordering on hostility, in the free South, because he is a Northerner. Or does he think of his life in ruins, of his wife in depression, his children living in poverty and his beloved daughter dead in infancy? Or does he think about us at all?

Born at home on Barrack Hill, as an infant I survive an attack of convulsions only with the help of a bottle of cod-liver oil poured down my throat. An ear infection puts me in the hospital for a few days causing partial deafness in my right ear. Later on, when teachers accuse me of not paying attention, or of wandering in my mind, they are only partially correct.

But partial deafness can have its compensations, most often in the church. We are no sooner baptized, it seems, than we are regularly chastised by the priests from the pulpit. They issue their hard-edged pronouncements, the harshness of their words well matched by the marble floors and stone pillars. The echo of their preachings takes a hard bounce against the walls of the church. With my unbalanced hearing, most of what they say is lost in the vaulted ceilings. Thus am I saved from castigation.

In Limerick, anyone named Alphonsus is known as either 'Phonsey or Alphie. I become Alphie. At age four, I am playing with a little girl named Claire Hannon.

"It's very hot down in hell, isn't it, Elph?" says Claire.

"'Tis, Claire," I respond.

"And they'd burn you with hot pokers down in hell, wouldn't they, Elph?"

"They would, Claire," I answer, agreeable as ever. Sitting on the sidewalk and looking up at the sky, weighty matters are these for Claire and myself to think about. And one night, I dream of top hats; tall silken shiny top hats, a dozen of them. Scattered on the ground, some are upright, some tilted over on their sides. All of them are moving. Some of them are dancing, but in the dancing there is no joy, only menace. Undertakers wear top hats.

When I was a baby, my brothers took me out in the pram so that Mam could have a break. One stood at the top of Barrack Hill holding onto the pram. The other, the catcher, was stationed at the bottom of the hill. Soon they granted me my freedom. The carriage, released, went trundling on down the hill as it gathered speed. The catcher at the bottom must have seen a penny on the ground. Or did he spot a girl passing by? Did he lapse into a dream, perhaps, a vision of a thick cut of bread with plenty of salty butter, made irresistible by a heavy sprinkling of sugar on top? It doesn't matter. Whatever he saw, or thought he saw, he was distracted. The carriage, with me still in it, flew past him, across Wolfe Tone Street and in through the swinging doors of the pub opposite, to the great surprise of the barman and the few afternoon customers. Gently to rest came carriage and me. There were no casualties.

My last childhood memory of Barrack Hill is of my pal Noel Harran and myself being lifted up onto the back of a giant dray horse. Kings of the world we are, thrilled and terrified all at the same time. Hell and dray horses, steeples and dreams, these are the threads that bound us together, in our life away from life, in Roden Place on Barrack Hill.

We move from Barrack Hill to Rosbrien, to the house of my mother's cousin, Gerard Griffin. There are goings-on in that house and we know it, Mike and I. We can hear the creaking of the bed in the loft. Frank and Malachy, my two oldest brothers, will have no part of Rosbrien and the goings-on. They go to live with my Uncle Pat. I am five years old. My brother Mike is four years older and he is badly treated. I escape punishment because I am the youngest.

Gerard Griffin's house, one of a row of laborers cottages, has a ground floor and a loft. The patch of garden in front is covered over with cobblestones. There's a meanness, a harshness, in this attempt to suppress both grass and green, but the weeds still manage to sprout their defiance.

More generous in spirit is the bit of wild at the rear where Mike and I build a fence across what had been a garden. We persuade Mam to gather a few scraps on a tin plate. We hold captive our two kittens, at the end of the wild, until Mam rattles the tin plate. In a mad scramble for the scraps, the kittens, Puss and Boots, mount a leaping charge over our makeshift fence.

For heat and for cooking there is a fireplace but little in the way of coal or turf. There is precious little food but there is a long-handled fork, handmade, of heavy-gauge twisted wire. On a good evening, when we have bread, we spear a thick slice with the fork and toast it over the open fire, toast it until the crust is blackened and slightly burned. With butter, this bread is pure gold. Slowly we savor it, while the light from the oil lamp holds off the always threatening darkness in the corners of the room.

Our outhouse is cheek by jowl with the next-door outhouse. Mrs. B., our next-door neighbor, probably uses it, but she goes unheard. Not so her husband and two sons. They sing as they go. Always the same song:

> *'Twas a down by the glen side I met an old woman (uh)*
> *A plucking young nettles she ne'er saw me coming (uh)*
> *I listened a while to the song she was humming (uh)*
> *Glory O, Glory O, to the Bold Fenian Men (oooh)*

Patriotism, sluicing and dripping, to their relief and ours, finally drops and silently we sing, "Thank you, Lord, for this relief and thank you for the Bold Fenian Men."

Much more delicate is the family a few doors down. Their children insist that their mother trim the crust from their bread so the darlings will have no roughness to contend with when they chew.

I am enrolled in Henry Street School, which is staffed by nuns and by women lay teachers. In their habits and detached ways the nuns are unknowable. Miss Matthews, our lay teacher, always wears a suit. Good looking, though with severe features, she is tailored and stern. Seamus O'Dwyer and I draw ahead of the class in reading and we are put to help the other students to read.

At lunchtime, in Henry Street School when free milk and bread are distributed to needy children, we are not needy enough. Seamus is one of a half-dozen children, but his father is working so he can't possibly be needy. My father is gone and we are half starving, but I am still not considered needy. How needy do you have to be, I wonder? Anyway, free bread and free milk, those twin badges of shame, will carry with them the seeds of begrudgery. Besides, it is always raining. Soggy bread and cold milk will bring little relief from the cold or at least that's what

I have to tell myself, as I turn away, pretending to be above charity.

At home, in Gerard Griffin's house, a few crumbs and a sometimes splash of sunshine will conjure up the afternoon mouse. He appears on the recessed windowsill, to nibble in a dish. Like a reindeer in tiny skin, prancing and pecking, he is a high tenor, lyrical in movement and graceful. Graceful he may be, but in order to survive he must be mighty gritty. This very mouse could easily leave us and go to England, join the Army, be issued two pairs of boots and two pairs of shoes and be fully fed and found. He does not. Our mouse is loyal to us and he stays. Badly off as we are, a mouse is always with us. Mam is terrified of mice.

Sometimes, in the evening, Mam sends me for a pint of milk. She will wash the can with its looped wire handle. As I set out I swing the can round and round over my head to get rid of any remaining drops of water and for the pure joy of swinging. The can, taking on a life of its own, pulls me forward and lifts me onto my toes. Like a small Greek Olympian gearing up to throw the hammer, I strain for height and distance and for greater momentum. When the can reaches the top of its arc I release the handle and allow the can to fly free. At the very last minute I jump and reach, regain the handle and keep the can from flying away altogether.

At Baker's farm, on the other side of the road and down toward Punch's Cross, Mrs. Baker pours a pint of milk and, always, a little bit extra into the can. I thank her before heading for home. Up to this point, on this one evening, I have done nothing different, except that now I completely forget that I am on my way home and that the can is full of milk. Yes, I forget. Out of old habit I swing the can, round and round again, in my usual style, over my head and faster and faster. But not fast enough. To my horror it's not the few remaining drops of water, but in a finely threaded, creamy trajectory, it is the whole pint of milk that flies out of the can.

Devastation has struck. I can't go home without milk. I kick myself for being so stupid as to throw away a whole pint of milk. Am I to explain it by saying that I swung the can just to see if I could swing it fast enough to keep the milk from spilling? Or should I say that I dropped the can and that the milk spilled out? The why doesn't matter? We desperately need the milk and I will have to do something. Shamefaced, I shuffle back to Mrs. Baker.

Living at the edge of Limerick, we are barely connected to the town. Neither do we have any footing in the countryside just beyond. The Bakers, on the other hand, are solid farmers, working their own land, rich, we think, and at a far remove from us. Now, as Mrs. Baker listens to my tale of the swinging can, she is serious to the point of severity. This is business, after all, but try as she might, Mrs. Baker can't hold back a small smile. She refills the can and sends me on my way.

Yes, Mrs. Baker is kind. She allows us boys to help out on the farm. Three of us are sent to "hunt" the ducks home at the end of the day. On the way up through the field two of the ducklings venture close to the edge and topple over the side of a small cliff and twenty feet down to their death. I'm the youngest and I am blamed for shouting at them. We all had shouted at the ducks to keep them moving. The death of the ducklings was an accident. It was no one's fault and Mrs. Baker seems to know that. She lays no blame on me.

At the end of the summer the sunshine breaks through and we help the Baker family with bringing in the hay. In the fields, with the family and the workers, we rake and pile any loose strands of hay that we can find. At noontime the women appear with tall stacks of bread and plenty of salted butter, along with cans of hot tea, well sweetened, a perfect match for the hot sun. At the end of the day, on the broad flat expanse of the hay wagon, pulled by a giant horse, we ride back to the farmhouse.

In our back garden I dig for gold. "Gold" is a lump of coal. Mam praises me whenever I find one, always just outside the back door, which makes me wonder if Mam plants it for me to find. When the men come to dig up the road in front of the house I fill their canisters with water for their tea and they allow me to scrape around with a shovel. At the end of the week I am "paid" and I'm thankful for the few pennies. But I'm even more thankful that they included me. I needed to be included, for we live in shame: shame of dirt and poverty, shame of no religion, shame of no father.

Below the level of the working class we are, unfit to be neighbors to the neighbors. Only when Mam is in the house do I feel safe and secure, but she is gone for long periods during the day, working, maybe, or trying to cadge something in the way of food. In her absence it is cold and damp and wet and bleak. Even so, Mike and I play outside in the cold and the wet. Or inside, in the damp.

❦

Play we do and yes, we do engage, but we are always hungry, always waiting for Mam to come home to light fire and lamp if we have coal and oil, and to cook, if she has found any food. In Northern Ireland they would have called us "scaldies." Like little birdies in the nest, we are, waiting for motherbird or fatherbird to return and drop food into our beaks. Above all, whatever she brings, Mam brings herself. To a child she brings the world, just by being there.

It is nighttime. Mam, my brother Mike and I are asleep in the one bedroom, at street level, when the window is smashed in from the outside. It is my father. Come the police with their sirens and flashing lights. Comes a big commotion, then a sudden quiet, and he is gone. Again. Fright gives way to puzzlement. Only later, when I grow up and find out what it is like to suffer jealousy, will I begin to understand. I almost feel sorry for him with his absolutist notions and his romantic temperament, in his rage and frustration tilting at windows instead of windmills.

When Mam refers to my father as "your pop," I know it's her way of keeping herself at a distance from him. But for all her distancing and for all her "your pops," I feel that she still has a soft spot for the old man. She must once have seen him do something extraordinary and remembered it or she must have believed him capable of doing something great. Or maybe, at one time, she had simply loved and admired him.

Embarrassed, perhaps, by what she had felt for him when she was young, it is with a touch of derision that she speaks of him now. It seems as if she is deriding my father for his foolish ways and mocking herself for her foolishness in having loved him. She has long since given up on him but I still detect a touch of respect, a shade of admiration and at least the memory of love.

Someone once asked her, "Did you love Alphie's father?"

"I did," she answered.

"So what happened?" they pressed her.

"What happened?" she repeated, and without hesitation, "Poverty flew in and love flew out. That's what happened."

❦

Soon we put the Griffin house behind us and move closer to the center of the city, to the lane behind Saint Joseph's Church. Our lane, Little Barrington Street, runs parallel to its parent, the real Barrington Street, which is a grand and proper thoroughfare up the hill and in front of us. Barrington Street is home to the shepherds of our souls, the secular priests and well do they abide in their priests' house.

Before too long, from the steps of that same priests' house, a priest will "read" my mother. He will publicly rebuke her for her sins. She had gone to the priests to ask for help for us, her children. Don't come here looking for charity, missus, he would have said. You are not a fit person to be standing here and you in your sinful state. Everyone knows that you don't even go to Mass on Sunday and that's a mortal sin. His purpose was clear, for if everyone didn't know my mother's sins before, then they would certainly know them now.

"The poor are always with us," we are told by way of consolation.

"We are, Father," we remind ourselves and the priest. "For aren't we always with us and shur who else would want to be with us?"

And "it is easier for a camel to go through the eye of a needle than for a rich man to enter Heaven." They tell us that as well, as a reassurance, I suppose. We should rejoice in our own poverty and not envy the rich man. We, at least, have some chance of getting into heaven. The rich man has none, stuck, as he is, between the camel and the eye of a needle.

To us, a camel passing through the eye of a needle is an exciting image, but it doesn't put any bread on the table. For a loaf of bread and a quarter pound of salt butter we would take our chances with the eye and the needle. Maybe even with the camel.

With Schoolhouse Lane to the rear of us, our front door and windows look out on a blank wall and on "The Chunnel." We call it "The Chunnel," this ditch that is only a few steps from the front door. Sometimes, for no apparent reason, "The Chunnel" fills with running water. We don't know where it comes from.

Our Little Barrington Street is definitely down the hill from Barrington Street. Down this same hill, as Mam tells it, my uncle Pat was chased by a gang of uniformed men in dark jackets and tan trousers. Imported by the English during the War of Independence, many of them were ex-convicts. Their dark jackets and tan pants earned them the name Black and Tans. They imposed a curfew and conducted a reign of terror in enforcing it.

Uncle Pat, having missed the evening curfew, ran down the hill toward the lane and toward home. The Tans were right behind him. My grandmother and some of the neighbor women stood at the corner, at the bottom of the hill. Waiting and worrying, they had been watching for Pat's arrival home. "Stand yeer ground, stand yeer ground," Pat shouted as he ran down the hill, all the while tugging frantically at his belt. Desperately he tried to take off his belt without losing his trousers, for his belt was the closest thing he had to a weapon. Pat was able to keep his belt and his trousers intact, to make it home and to escape a beating, or worse, thanks to the women, the witnesses, waiting at the corner.

❧

Now we are down that same hill and we are a family again: Mam, Frank, Malachy, Michael and myself. This is Uncle Pat's house now for he has continued to live there after my grandmother's death. Once again we are lodgers, but Uncle Pat is tolerant. We are more at home with Pat. Still, he has his food, and ours, when we have it, is separate. Mam dispenses our food, but when temptation overwhelms us we raid. And we don't discriminate. When necessary, we raid Pat's supply as well as our own.

Pat's house boasts electricity, but, like the food, it is rationed. The meter must be fed, a shilling at a time. No shilling, no light. When the fuse blows we learn to remove the fuse cap, to wrap it with foil from a cigarette pack, to jam the cap back on and use the fuse again.

We are still on sufferance in a house that is not ours, still feeling our way with Uncle Pat and the neighbors. I'm a little afraid of Mrs. Collins next door. She is very old in her widowhood, I think. Always dressed in black, her head and shoulders covered in a black shawl, she is righteous, upright and intimidating.

Sylvia Lyons lives down at the end of the lane and she is all that the lane is not. To my eye, Sylvia is beautiful, glamorous and full of life. Sylvia passes by one day and Mrs. Collins sees me looking at her. "That Sylvia, she's a great girl. Wouldn't she be a great girl to have up on the back of a bicycle?" so says the righteous Mrs. Collins, with a twinkle at me.

Sylvia lives with her younger sister and her mother. No husband or father is present. Sylvia's sister, Phyllis, is of an age with myself. Mrs. Lyons and my mother, both of them husbandless and both more traveled than the rest of the neighborhood women, have become friends. Sometimes they go out together, especially on this one evening when they go out, leaving Phyllis and myself to keep each other company.

Phyllis and I don't particularly like each other. Phyllis, no doubt, will be beautiful like her sister, but she is still pre-pre-adolescent. I am the round fool with the big head trying to make an impression on her. I pick up a knife and become the greatest swordsman in all France. That's me, D'Artagnan, as I thrust at the air, thrust and parry, poste and riposte, but all to no avail. Phyllis fails to recognize my greatness. Or maybe she just feels left out. Whatever the reason, she makes a grab for the knife, grasps only the blade and suffers a tiny cut. "Oh," she cries, "look what you did!"

"I didn't," I protest. "I didn't do it."

"Yes you did, yes you did!" she cries.

Even I can see that argument is useless. She's a girl and it's my fault.

I volunteer to wrap the tiny cut and stop the bleeding. That would make sense, but no, Phyllis finds a small towel the size of a potholder and spends the next two hours dabbing tiny spots of blood on the towel. When one side of the towel is covered with blood, she turns it over and completely covers the other side.

Our mothers come home. Phyllis, in her element, presents the towel and cries, "Look, Mammy, look what Alphie McCourt did to me."

A lesser woman would have fainted at the sight of the bloodied towel, but Mrs. Lyons looks at the "wound" and cleans and wraps it.

Giving Phyllis a kiss she assures her, "You'll be alright now," and I love Mrs. Lyons forever.

I love 'Melda Lyons even when she brings home the jar of soup in her handbag. This is a beef, potato and carrot soup, for isn't Ireland an agricultural country after all. Beef, potatoes and carrots are not uncommon. But there is more to this soup. Whatever perfume was in 'Melda's handbag has leaked into the soup or the soup has picked up the aroma of the perfume. It has become a beef, potato and perfumed carrot soup. I am always hungry. It would be ridiculous if anyone ever had to coax me, or any of us, to eat. But this soup is a challenge. I eat it, the beef and potato part and I drink it, the carrot part. Closing my nose, I try not to inhale it, the perfumed part. All of this I do, partly because I am hungry, but mostly so that I won't offend 'Melda, for hadn't 'Melda spared my life on the night of the blood-soaked towel?

'Melda's house has running water, and she is able to wash the blood out of the towel. But in our house, especially on winter mornings, there isn't much water. The single faucet outside the back door is fond of freezing up. Our toilet, with its broken bowl, stands outside and at the back of the house. I don't use it much. In the mornings it is much easier to get out of bed, stand at the top of the stairs and fire off out the window onto the top of the outhouse. Even better, I can often achieve a high arc and clear the edge of the outhouse, as free a feeling as I've ever had.

In days of old when knights were bold and lavatories weren't invented
They wiped their ass with a blade of grass and walked away contented

---

Uncle Pat's arm is well developed from selling newspapers in the street and delivering them door-to-door. *The Limerick Leader* is his staple. "Lader, Lader!" is his cry. "Lader, Lader, wanna Lader, last wan, last wan!" he cries, even when he still has a sheaf of two dozen under his arm. Sometimes he takes me along on his rounds, especially when he's delivering to O'Connell Avenue. The long garden pathways from the sidewalk to the front doors are too much, even for his arm and aim. And Pat has a bad leg, so I make myself useful and he always gives me a few pennies.

Newspapers, spread and layered among old overcoats and blankets, provide great insulation against the cold. And our tablecloth is a newspaper. But when we try to read books at the table, Mam despairs of us. "Yee always have yeer heads buried in a book." We persist in trying to read at the table, but she won't allow it. Such a practice is bad manners, she tells us, but we read anyway. We read the newspaper tablecloth, even upside down. Reading, a terrible addiction.

My brothers borrow books from the library. When I apply for membership, I am refused. We have a reputation for not returning books. It doesn't matter. Membership or no membership, books returned or not returned, I can taste the lack of welcome and I don't really care. I never will be comfortable in libraries. Too much literary piety, too much shush.

Reading at the table is not allowed and there is no admittance to the library but, above all, we do not eat potatoes with the skin on. Potato skins are to be fed to the pigs. We couldn't eat the skins, anyway. Our potatoes are always well encased with soil. Each pound of potatoes yields a pound of mud.

Are oo from Cork?
I ram are oo?
How're the piddayshes?
Big and shmall.
How juh ate 'em?
Shkin and all!

City boys we are and superior, we think, to the country boys. We mimic what we think of as their speech and we flatter ourselves that our speech is better than theirs. Of course we never would eat potatoes with the skin on. We would be disgraced if anyone saw us.

Mam shops for potatoes. To me, it's more like going into battle. Embarrassed, I stand back to give her room as she scrapes the mud off the potatoes. Then she will ask the shopkeeper to weigh them again. "And while you're at it, see if you can throw in a few decent-sized spuds. I can do nothing with these, tiny as they are, no bigger than taws. Nothing but mud, if you ask me. And when we peel the skin there'll be nothing left." Mam is very effective with her good clear speech. And she is careful as always, to enunciate the "ng" at the end of "nothing." The final syllable is augmented into a fine ringing sound.

There is argument, protest, coaxing, even a few mild threats on both sides. All are closely followed by appeals to common sense and to common decency. Frequent reference is made to our common ancestry and to our shared history of oppression. When all arguments have been explored and exhausted, compromise is reached.

"I'll see you next week," Mam says to the shopkeeper as she pays.

"Alright, Missus," the shopkeeper replies.

We emerge with more potatoes and less mud. Taws still predominate, but there are a few fair-sized spuds.

Butter will be needed to go with the potatoes. Up the hill and around the corner from where we live on O'Connell Street is an impressive thoroughfare, which broadens at its widest point, to form the Crescent. The Crescent is host, on one side, to the Jesuit Church and Crescent College. Directly opposite the church, on the other side of the Crescent, etched into the cement sidewalk, is a small arrow. The tip of the arrow points directly at the church. The arrow is a

Masonic symbol, we are told. We love the idea of the arrow and the Masonic mystery of it, for didn't George Washington himself belong to an Irish Masonic Lodge over in America? The arrow is said to be both symbol and warning to the Jesuits. We know that the priests of Limerick are powerful enough but the power of the Jesuits extends all over the world, so why wouldn't we be in awe of anyone brave enough to etch a challenge to the Jesuits?

In the middle of the Crescent, at the southern end, stands the statue of Daniel O'Connell. Daniel was a great orator. He organized mass demonstrations throughout Ireland in support of Catholic Emancipation and achieved it in 1829. He won basic civil rights for Irish Catholics, only thirty-some years before the emancipation of the slaves in the United States.

Daniel is known as the Liberator, and rightly so. Catholic Emancipation was a magnificent achievement, but still the begrudgers must mock him as a hypocrite. "There was a time when you couldn't throw a stone over a poorhouse wall, without hitting one of Daniel O'Connell's bastards," they will tell you. "Great Liberator, my arse," they crow. "The Great Fornicator would be more like it!"

In spite of that, Daniel remains a friendly kind of a hero and a man of the people. When we pass by his statue in the Crescent, we often feel an urge to nod in his direction, to toss him a casual, military-style salute or to offer a brief comment on the state of the city and the nation. Daniel, after all, must be kept informed, and we all commune with him.

On an evening when my brother Frank is walking uptown and toward home, my Uncle Pat is walking downtown, on the other side of the wide Crescent. As Frank passes by on one side and Uncle Pat passes by on the other, Pat, as always, must say something to Daniel. In his mind he rehearses what he will say: "Arrah, Dan," muses Pat, "and where are you now when we need you most? Isn't it lucky for you and a great pity for us that you're not around here now to see what's going on? The politicians do nothing but feather their own nests. They pay no attention whatsoever to the needs of the people. And as for the priests? The priests are no better. They're too busy filling their bellies with their English trifle and the trifle so loaded down with sherry that I'd be afraid to taste it for fear it would make me drunk. Shur the priests, nowadays, have no heart for the poor and the hungry and 'tis a cryin' shame."

That's what Pat means to say, but when he spots Frank on the other side of the broad oval that is the Crescent, he becomes distracted. All of his rehearsed speech immediately leaves his mind. A matter of much greater urgency has bubbled up into his brain. "Frankie McCourt!" Pat shouts. "Frankie McCourt, your mother said to go aisy with the butther." And, louder now, he shouts, "And don't forget!"

Pat is not shy. All of his years spent selling newspapers have given him a fine carrying voice. It carries across the broad Crescent, flying up to the windows of the Georgian houses opposite. Some of these same houses are peopled by the rich and the respectable and the aching-to-be respectable, with their ground floors and basements rented out to doctors, dentists and solicitors. A whole troop of pigeons, prayerfully perched on Daniel's head and shoulders, begins to swoop and soar. Frightened by Pat's outcry they scatter upward into flight. Frank has heard Uncle Pat's admonition, though he certainly doesn't want to hear it. In seeking to escape, Frank quickens his pace, his own muttered imprecation mercifully masked by the noisy fluttering of pigeons in flight.

At home our shortage of butter, and of everything else, continues. Our father, who art in England and absent without leave, neglects to send any money. This is not a respectable way in which to behave. He must know that our neighbors respect respectability. And our situation is aggravated by post-war rationing. We are allowed a quarter pound of butter per person per week and a quarter pound of tea and sugar.

For consolation we recite: "Isn't it a soft day thank God and sure don't we need the rain. Isn't it needed for the crops, to raise the grain to feed the beef to ship away to England. God help us. And are we not duty bound to feed them, our English neighbors, in their post-war starving so that we ourselves will suffer no shortage of rationing and be granted the blessing of a smaller Great Hunger to offer up as penance for our sins."

Our best food is shipped over to England. We can't afford it anyway. But from somewhere comes the money to buy me a new suit and new shoes for my First Communion. Before First Communion comes First Confession. At seven years of age, I must make up sins in order to bolster my confession.

I soon realize that I will never again have to manufacture sins because this First Confession brings with it a new awareness of sin and guilt. From now on I will have plenty to confess. From now on anything short of perfect resignation, anything less than total acceptance of all adversity, will be a sin. Guilt will seep into our souls like the damp that is all around us. I am totally unworthy of receiving the Lord Jesus in the sacrament. In my short pants, all big head and big knees, I am big in the knowledge that I am undeserving of new suit and new shoes and that I am even more unworthy of receiving the Sacrament.

My father knows nothing of this, my First Communion, and he is not around to explain any of the guilt that follows First Confession. But he must have sensed something. One morning I wake up in that house in Little Barrington Street and there he is. He wakes my brother Mike and myself, gives us a rare breakfast of bread and butter and tea with milk and sugar and he rushes us to get ready. I can still hear his Northern Ireland accent, "Come own, come own, ye'll be late, ye'll be late," as he sends us off to school. For once, we are on time. When we get home from school he is gone, and not for the first time.

1949

WHERE WAS MOSES when the lights went out? In the dark, you eejit! That's an old standing joke. And where is my father when the light bulb blows? I surely don't know. But I do know that I have to stand on a chair, remove the spent bulb and put in the new one. This is all to the good, so far. And when I touch an exposed wire, it is even better. Circles of electricity wind through me, coursing from head to toes, toes to head, up and down and up again.

I should have waited for Frank to come home from work. He knows about electricity, but I had changed a light bulb before and I just wanted to show that I could do the job. Now I am going away, away and further away, still going and for good, at nine years of age, when Mam grabs me and pulls me bodily off the chair and back into life.

Frank knows electricity and he's nineteen and he is our leader. Having been born in America, he is bound to be different. And he has a bicycle that I often "borrow" early on Sunday mornings, when the streets are quiet, and go for a ride. In the beginning I don't ride. Instead I place my right foot on the left pedal and push off with my left foot. I do the same thing over and over again, scooting, as we call it, just to learn balance. After a few days, comes the great moment when I put my left foot on the left pedal, push my right leg in under the crossbar and thus reach the right pedal with my right foot. Half of my lower body, my right side, is squeezed in and under the crossbar. All of my left side, upper and lower, is suspended, for balance, away and to the left. Hunched, misshapen, half boy and half bicycle, after many attempts I finally learn to "ride."

With this success comes confidence and with confidence comes more frequent borrowings of the bike. Not only do I use the bike on Sunday mornings, but I take it during the week, when Frank is at work, to scoot along Barrington Street, up by the Public Park and the Public Library in Pery Square, around the monument and back again, performing many circuits.

One afternoon, having finished my circuits of Barrington Street and Pery Square, I go hunchriding down "the hill" toward Kathleen O'Connell's shop. I'm one minute from home, just steps away from the lane, when up comes Mr. Duggan on his autocycle. Mr. Duggan owns and runs the glazier's shop at the end of our lane and he rides a motorized bicycle with a heavy frame and heavy-duty wheels. There is room to pass and to spare. I could steer to the right or to the left of Mr. Duggan and his tank of an autocycle. Instead, in my state of guilt and nervousness I am hypnotized and I run straight into him. The autocycle is intact, but my horse, Frank's precious bicycle, suffers a badly buckled front wheel. I wish for death. If I don't die now, Frank will surely kill me later.

Home I go. Leaving Frank's wrecked bike in the kitchen, I trudge upstairs and kneel down in search of an upstairs miracle. I launch into an Our Father, three Hail Marys and a Glory Be to the Father. Downstairs I go to look at the bike. There's no change in its condition. Up I go again, to repeat the prayers and downstairs again. Still no change, and so, after many repetitions I stop, leaving my prayers and, along with them, my head to be disposed of when Frank comes home. When I confess my crime, "Weren't you the fool?" is all he says and that's the end of it. My prayers have been answered.

Frank has been saving and now what we have always known would happen is coming to pass. Frank tells us that he is leaving for the U.S. He has been working from an early age. Always with a wide range of interests, he has continued to be a keen student and never wavered in his ambition to return to the U.S.

We have "The American Wake," the going-away party for Frank. In slow tempo we sing:

Now is the hour, when we must say goodbye
Soon you'll be sailing far across the sea
While you're away, oh please remember me
When you return you'll find me way-ting here

This, our anthem of farewell, the closing song of "The American Wake" will become fixed and sacred in the rubric of our emigration. Next day Mam, Frank, Mike and I board a train for Cobh, County Cork. Even as late as October 1949, taking ship for America means goodbye forever. Frank is leaving. He may never return. We cry and cry, Mike and I. Mam's tears are pure desolation. Of the seven children born to her, only four remain alive and now, Frank, the oldest, is leaving. I don't know which is worse: Frank's leaving or Mam's tears.

Mam was a fair cook and a good baker of brown bread and griddle-cakes, but housekeeping never held any interest for her. She would let things go and go until she became overwhelmed.

In her way a liberated woman, she had emigrated to New York at an early age to work as a domestic. Her marriage lasted long enough for her to bear seven children and lose three before she was left on her own to bring up the remaining four of us, in desperate circumstances. Still, by some miracle she is able to smile again, to laugh and sing again. She takes a keen interest in politics and remains a passionate Irish Republican. She loves movies and plays and is always a good neighbor.

When I was young she told me that my father came home drunk one night, on what must have been a special occasion. It must have been while they were living in Brooklyn. She had set the table with a tablecloth. My father was angry as well as drunk. Something was said and, in losing his temper, he whipped the tablecloth, dishes and all, off the table and onto the floor. I was left to believe that my father was a violent man. Years later, I asked Mam if he had been a violent man. "No," she said. "That was the only time."

Of her early days in Brooklyn she had one happy memory, maybe the only one, of an evening spent with the McAdorys and some friends, when they all went on a cruise up the Hudson River. They enjoyed an evening of moonlight and music. Mike and I used to ask her to tell us the story. When she told of that cruise, Mam would grow wistful. In the telling, her own tragic life took on the shine, the glow, of moonlight remembered. Our own miserable life in the lane, for a moment, was made a little brighter.

⸎

Now Frank is gone to America. Mam, Mike and I take the train from Cobh back to Limerick, to Uncle Pat's house. Pat Sheehan is my mother's brother. He was hit by a bus when he was young. With a bad leg and a bad limp, he is rough and ready in his ways. But he can hold a bunch of newspapers in one hand and count out change with the other. And he can do it faster than most people could do it using both hands.

Pat's sings "The Road to Raheen" and renders it, lovingly, as "The Road to Rasheen." Young Munster, "Munsters" Rugby Club is his passion. On the day of a game he puts on the long college style black and amber scarf, the sacred relic. It is said that he wore it that day, in 1928, when Munsters won the Bateman Cup, the All Ireland Rugby Football trophy. Now, more than twenty years later the amber is rust and the scarf has harbored many a moth. Even so, that is one proud scarf and Uncle Pat Sheehan, Ab, as he is called, doesn't just put on the scarf, he robes in it on the day of a game.

Pat is well known in Limerick. So is his passion for Munsters. People tease him about his scarf and insist that Munsters are bound to lose, on the day. Pat, unmoved, sets his head and his shoulders as he soldiers on to the game. Following on Frank's departure, for consolation maybe, he makes me his rugby disciple and takes me to see an occasional game.

For an important game Pat will commandeer a pony and trap and up we will sit on the sideways seats, open to wind and rain, racing a clip-clop and a clatter down through the town all the way to Thomond Park. Bursting with excitement and anticipation, throwing back the jeers and taunts of the other team's supporters, we relish our temporary superiority. For we are up, for once, and they are down.

For regular games we travel on the double-decker bus. Because of his bad leg Pat and I sit downstairs. The conductor collects fares as people board, but Pat does not pay. Instead, he informally volunteers to act as deputy conductor. We stop at a stop and people board the bus while the conductor is still upstairs. Pat makes his way to the boarding platform. "It's all right, Paddy!" he shouts up to the conductor, and bangs on the bell for the driver to drive on.

The driver drives on, the bus lurches forward and a man tumbles down the stairs. Leaping, white-faced, three steps at a time, down the stairs comes the conductor. Pat is not dismayed. "It's all right, Paddy," he says again. The conductor glares. Pat and the conductor help to right the fallen man, dust him off, and we hasten on to the game.

We don't take the bus, Mam, Mike and I. Instead, we walk downtown to Upper William Street, a commercial street with shops selling everything from bicycles to bacon to paint and wallpaper. As we stand in the shop we are among farmers, in town for the day, who pay for their goods with notes extracted from great wads of cash. And I understand, somehow, although I don't know for sure, that we are in that shop, not that far away from the lane in distance, but a million miles away in other respects, because we have vouchers. Isn't our poverty obvious, the mother and two boys in for the free food? And if it is not obvious then the manner of the man behind the counter will certainly betray it. He looks mighty uncomfortable.

Mike feels it, yes, indeed he does. Not wanting to be there, he soon wanders off outside. Mam calls after him, "My-kull. My-kull." Everyone knows that boys hate having their names called in public, especially by adults. Worst of all is to be called by your mother. And Mike certainly does not want to be called "My-kull" when plain old Michael, or Mike, would be bad enough, without the added affectation. He clenches his fists and lowers his head. With great restraint he mutters, "Nnn-Jayah!" If he were to say the name of Jesus, he would be rewarded with a bang on the head.

We live somewhere south of poverty and we shop with vouchers. Still there are rules. Other children are allowed to go outside with a great cut of bread thick with salted butter and a generous sprinkling of sugar. They will eat it slowly, as they take tiny bites, all the while griggin' the less fortunate. They will pretend not to notice the slavering stares of the rest of us as they show off their precious prize.

For us there is no eating outside. Food is too precious to be so casually consumed. Equally important, eating in the street is bad manners. And no hands in your pockets either. It looks bad and is bad for the posture. "Stand up straight, keep yeer hands out of yeer pockets and maybe yee'll amount to something," we are told. Whistling in the street is only for corner boys, standing idle on the corner, terrified of work, stamping their feet and looking to whistle up the warm in the wintertime.

There's no shortage of cold corners, inside or out. We wonder why we couldn't have lived in a warm climate where we could knock coconuts and breadfruit off the trees. We would have been happily barefoot, and happier still to wear nothing but a loincloth. Or a breech clout, as the English called it. I always wondered which was the breech and which was the clout. I didn't dare ask for fear of a snig in the bayke from Mam for being a bit too smart. It would have been a blessed relief to be savage and not have to worry about scruples, too many or too few, or sins of commission and sins of omission. No longer would we labor under the burden of having to contribute a penny here and there to saving the bodies and souls of all the babies in Africa.

Or we could be out on the Pampas in Argentina, twirling our bolos and catching wild game to be deliciously roasted over an open fire. We would play soulful music on our gaucho guitars while beautiful senoritas tempted us with sideways smiles into slow and sinless seduction. Or something. Wonderfully smiling natives we would have been and terrific gauchos.

But the sunshine is somewhere else for, like Saint Joseph's Church and Daniel O'Connell on his monument, the sun and the Atlantic keep their backs to us. America is at a great distance and Europe is way over there at the other side of the country. Ireland remains neutral and Limerick is nowhere.

❧

If our feet are dry we double check to make sure that they are still attached. But from somewhere comes a pair of Wellington boots, or

Russian boots as we call them. Designed to keep out the rain, the rubber keeps everything else in. Worn for a week without changing socks, they will create plenty of work for the tiny farmers of my imagination who labor down below, in between the toes, harvesting the crop. Some of this rich loamy soil I harvest myself. Great stuff it is, for rolling between thumb and forefinger. The aroma is fit to be bottled. It could easily and profitably be exported as essence of Irish Russian Boot.

But even Wellington boots don't last. In her despair, Mam declares that Malachy and Mike and I are hopelessly heavy on our shoes. Citing Frank as an example, she urges us to lift our feet and go easy on the shoes.

Our cousin joined the Irish Army and was issued two pairs of boots and two pairs of shoes only to desert this neutral peacetime Army and go to England where he joined the British Army. When the British Army presented him with two pairs of boots and two pairs of shoes, he changed his mind, deserted again and returned to Limerick. A rich man now, he was proud owner of four pairs of boots and four pairs of shoes.

Our cousin of the boots and shoes had little or no education and not much in the way of opportunity. I'm more fortunate. I will soon move on to the Christian Brothers Primary School on Sexton Street. Ten times the size of Henry Street School, "The Brothers" has a secondary school attached. I am in the great world of school, the first of my family to go to The Brothers. Admission is based on a written entrance examination. I know that I did well on the examination. I also know that my brothers would have done as well or better. If so, why had they not been admitted?

Ragged arsed and from the lane, I am in school now with boys from all over the City of Limerick and a sprinkling of farmers' sons in from the country. Mam does not go to Mass, a mortal sin and a great disgrace, nor is it any help that my father is absent. If he even came home once a year, for the two-week holiday in the summer, or if he sometimes sent money home, we would be halfway respectable. He does neither. Yet, somehow, I have been admitted and I will be allowed to dwell among the God-fearing. A few other boys from the lanes attend that school, but their fathers, for the most part, are accounted for and have jobs.

Classes are large with more than fifty boys in each. Our boys-only school is staffed half and half by brothers and by lay teachers. The brothers impose an iron discipline.

Young, tall, dedicated and kind is our first teacher, Brother Nevin. I am privileged, twice a day, to go outside, behind the classroom and bring in turf for the classroom fireplace. This assignment gives me a break from the classroom and I see it as a position of trust. Brother Nevin teaches us English, Irish, Arithmetic, Religion and Singing.

After school and on weekends during the month of May, we roam the fields out by Rosbrien and collect whatever flowers we can find: mostly daffodils and daisies. "Oh, Mary, we crown thee with blossoms today, Queen of the Angels and Queen of the May," a simple song for the loving mother, is our classroom anthem during the month of May. It carries no hint of the vengeful, fundamentalist Catholicism to follow.

In third class Mr. Stan Downing teaches us a poem by Seamus Sullivan:

The Piper

A piper in the street today
Set up and tuned and started to play
And away, away, away, on the wings of his music we danced
And little bare feet that were blue with cold

Went dancing back to the age of gold
And all the world went gay, went gay
For one half-hour in the street
Today.

Mr. Downing goes a step further. He insists upon proper elocution:

Ah piper in thuh street today
Set upp and tewned and stahted to play

And he gives me the starring role in a play he has written himself. The play is in Irish. My opening line is "Ta naire orm," which translates to "I am shy and embarrassed." And I am for I am playing the part of a schoolmaster, in the presence of the schoolmaster. We rehearse and rehearse, but the play is never performed.

In the next year I encounter Mr. "Baldy" O'Shea. He is acid in his approach and it is no wonder. I am more often late for school than I am on time and too often I don't have my homework done. And I miss plenty of days. One day, when I tell him that I left my homework, an essay, at home, Mr. O'Shea shocks me by designating a class Paragon to go home with me, at lunchtime, to collect the essay.

Paragon lives nearby, in Bowman Street, a real street, not a lane. He is indifferent, as we walk from the school to our lane, while I stew and sweat at the prospect of my imminent ruination. Baldy will hang me and I will be thrown out of the school for telling such a lie. What will my mother and my brothers say, and I the first of the family to go to that school?

We reach our house in the lane. I tell Paragon to wait outside. I run inside and scribble the essay in ten minutes, being careful with the pen and the ink. Any accidental blot or smudge with the nib of the pen will be a mortal sin. Down on my head will come the wrath of God and the ire of Baldy and I know which will be worse.

The essay is done and dutifully delivered to Baldy by poor Paragon. Paragon earns himself a place in pal-heaven that day. He doesn't tell Baldy that he had to wait. Later that year, Baldy proves himself to be more than fair. He is still impatient with my lazy ways, but he awards me first prize in an essay contest. The essay is titled, "A Daring Rescue." He must have known that I had rescued myself from disgrace.

⚜

I have survived to age eleven, to the age of Confirmation. With the beginning of adolescent stirrings comes the promise of real sin and a guilt which will be sharper, deeper and, somehow, sweeter. We must undergo an oral examination on our knowledge of the catechism, conducted by the bishop's deputy. Confirmed by the bishop himself, we are transformed, now, into spiritual warriors. Soldiers in Christ we are and we must behave accordingly. We must live clean lives, go to confession more often and become more frequent communicants.

And I have found a useful phrase for confession: "Bless me, Father, for I have sinned," I begin.

"How long has it been since your last confession, my child?" is the ritual response.

"Four weeks, Father."

"Four weeks?" offers the priest. He disapproves. I can tell. But I'm not surprised. I hate going to confession.

"What have you to confess, my child?" the priest prompts.

"I did not fulfill the duties of my station in life, Father."

"You did what?" says the priest.

"I did not fulfill the duties of my station in life, Father." I offer again.

Comes a noticeable intake of breath and the hint of a chuckle before the priest asks me to explain.

I tell him that on Saturday afternoon, in the Coliseum Cinema, in the dark, I stuck my foot into the aisle and tripped another boy as he was walking back toward the exit. I couldn't help it. I laughed when I did it, but I was sorry after.

"Was he hurt?" asks the priest.

"No, Father."

"How do you know?"

"Well, he got up, punched me in the shoulder, cursed at me and walked on. He wouldn't do that if he was hurt, would he, Father?"

"No, I don't suppose he would," says the priest.

"But what does this have to do with the ah…the ah? What was it that you said—the duties of your station?" and he trails off.

"Ah, yes, Father, the duties of my station in life." Now I have to shuffle: "I was late for school. I didn't do my homework and I didn't do what my mother told me to do."

"I see," the priest says. I can see that he is being drawn into my strategy. Becoming more mentor than taskmaster, he guides me through my short list of sins. I don't want to disappoint him, so I add on a few imaginary transgressions.

"For your penance say one Our Father, three Hail Marys and a Glory Be to the Father. Say a good Act of Contrition, try to do better and God bless you, my child."

My tactic will work as long as I remember to go to a different church each time and to a different priest.

When I was small we used to go swimming at a place called Sandy Bottom just beyond the outskirts of Rosbrien, out beyond Punch's Cross. It was boys only. We swam naked. It was probably a sin. Glorious little pagans we were, soaking up the scant summer sun.

Malachy, older and stronger, would swim with me balanced on his back. Soon he would go away. By the time the Mars Bar appeared in Limerick, Malachy was already a working man. He bought a Mars Bars and brought it home. Having sliced it into five pieces, he arranged the pieces on a flat rectangular piece of wood. With both hands he raised this makeshift paten to the level of his chest. Mike and myself and a couple of other boys watched closely. With our tongues hanging out, we lusted after a piece.

At Malachy's direction we lined up. Up and down the lane he led us, out to the backyard and in again and upstairs we went, to go tramping across beds, blankets and newspaper insulation and the old overcoats that served as blankets. In our passing, legions of fleas were murdered in their beds. We laid waste to their cities and razed their towns. Back downstairs we marched, down to the end of the lane and back again. Finally, the ceremony concluded, we were permitted to take our communion, one-fifth of a Mars Bar.

That was our secular sacrament. My grandmother had an old wind-up gramophone and a pile of old records. Now, both house and gramophone belong to Uncle Pat. To any young person coming to the house for the first time we pose the question: "What is the meaning of BONK?"

The only acceptable answer is: "BONK is the United Soviet Socialist Republic of Russia; Antidisestablishmentarianism."

When they have mastered the answer, we break a record over their head as token of admission. Malachy is the high priest. After going away to the Army School of Music in Dublin, he had spent some time in England. Now it is time for Malachy to follow Frank to the United States. He sails on the *SS United States*.

Frank, with his vision and his purpose, is gone. Malachy, with his sense of infinite possibilities, is gone. Mam and Mike and I are left, with Uncle Pat, in my grandmother's house in the lane.

At night the house is dark. Mam goes out more often, to play Forty-Five at St. Michael's or at the Mechanics Institute, wherever there's a large gathering of people, bright light, warmth and distraction. Sometimes, Mam and 'Melda Lyons go for a glass of cider in the snug of Stevie Coughlan's pub, around the corner on Saint Joseph's Street. Mike, four years older than I am, is usually off somewhere with his friends.

While it is light, I play outside with Tom Patterson from the first house in the lane or with Michael Moore from next door. Or a crowd of us, of all ages, play touch rugby with a ball made of rolled-up old socks and rags. Or we play kick the can and hide and go seek. In the end, we gather at the back of Saint Joseph's Church, at the top of School House Lane. Clustered on the doorstep, under the pale street light, we tell ghost stories.

Mam once had told us the story of a night in Mungret, a village outside of Limerick. My grandmother was leading a donkey. The donkey, in turn, was pulling a cart. Mam was only a young girl at the time. When they reached the gates of the graveyard, the donkey stopped dead. Mam and Grandma pushed and pulled, threatened, coaxed and implored the donkey. He wouldn't budge, even when they hit him with a stick. This donkey must have known something. Something or someone was afoot or astir in the graveyard, but Grandma and Mam didn't wait to find out. Stepping carefully out of their petticoats, they took off at a run, leaving donkey, cart and graveyard behind.

Within the circle of the streetlight, we repeat the story as we shudder in fear and delight in our fright.

Then comes the hour when the others are called in by their mothers. There is no one to call me in. I'm afraid to go into that dark house alone, but in I go. I turn on the light and hope that the shilling in the meter will hold, at least until Mam or Uncle Pat or my brother Mike comes home.

For me, my grandmother's spirit will always remain in that house. When she died, I was taken to her funeral. When her son, my uncle Thomas, died, I was taken to his funeral. Once, inexplicably, I was left in the church after the coffin was removed and after all the people had filed out. Nothing and no one remained except the image of the dear, departed coffin. For a few minutes, alone in the echoing empty church, I was lost. You can't be lost in a church, can you? There's the main altar at one end and the front door directly opposite, so you can't be lost in a church. But in my terror, I was lost. Someone came back and got me. I would always be haunted by the memory of that funeral.

Eventually, someone will come home and I will go up to bed. In the small hours I wake up. Two figures, two women, are on the landing at the top of the stairs, standing close to that very spot from which I fire off the golden stream every morning. I know that they are spirits. Spirits are all around us; spirits thrive on the darkness. Quietly they whisper. Even more quietly they laugh and I fall back to sleep.

❧

Mam revered her mother. My grandmother was spotlessly clean, according to Mam. She admired Grandma's snow-white hair. Grandma kept a wooden cask outside the back door to catch rainwater for washing her hair. But in my memory, Grandma was stern and very serious. Mam told us about the rain water, the snow-white hair and the spotlessness. "What's the use of being spotless and having snow-white hair if you never smile?" I wanted to ask Mam, but I didn't dare.

We are always reminded, "Cleanliness is next to godliness." And, of course, we should be clean. It's a practical necessity. If we don't keep ourselves clean we are more likely to get sick. That's true. But what does cleanliness have to do with godliness?

Cleanliness is good. Darkness is bad. In the dark of winter the chilblains appear at the tops of our ears and on our knuckles. Short pants give no protection against the irritation, the "ire," the roaring redness, which afflicts the exposed area where the short pants come to an end, especially around the inner thigh just above the knee.

Cold afflicts the body. Darkness downs the spirit. Darkness and sin go hand in hand, double threats to the welfare of the soul. The annual spring Mission in Saint Joseph's Church is designed to bring us forth from the darkness. And the Mission is well under way when Jackie comes home from the sea to spend a couple of weeks with his mother.

Early on that sunny, humid, Saturday afternoon, with the Mission coming to an end, Jackie may have had too many drinks. Or, more likely, he's had his fill of piety. In the middle of Schoolhouse Lane he rages aloud about religion in general and about the Mission in particular: "I'll give yee a Mission, I'll give yee a Mission!" he shouts. As he rails against hypocrisy of priests and people, he begins to take off his clothes. Jacket and shirt come first, then singlet and belt and shoes and socks. The more he takes off, the more his Christian neighbors laugh.

I don't know exactly, but I sense what he means. There's little or no love in the Mission and I am shocked that they don't help him, these adults, his neighbors. For his sake, and for the sake of his mother, why don't they stop him from taking off his clothes? And I hate them for laughing at him because I sense what he means and I can see how little anybody cares. It makes me sick. I run away. I don't want to see how far it will go.

Even this spring Mission, in the very early fifties, will bring no miracle. There is no lifting of the economic depression all round us. Emigration is our past and our present and it is our only window on the future. Most will go to England. England is close by and demands no special papers or visas. England always has room for Paddy and Mary: for laborer, soldier, barman, factory worker and housemaid.

Some Irishmen spend a lifetime in England, coming home once a year for the two-week vacation in the summer. Some, it is said, have two families: the first in Ireland and the second in England. As long as they send money and come home once a year, their Irish wives must turn a blind eye. Tales are told of London landladies whose husbands were declared missing or killed in action and never returned from the war. It is no matter. Single-handedly, it is said, these landladies create a new Anglo-Irish alliance. They take their Paddy lodgers to bed.

Some Irishmen go to Australia, New Zealand, Canada or South Africa. Thousands leave for the United States, but George Wright, from Bowman Street, goes his own way. He becomes a policeman in Bermuda. It is deemed a wise choice with steady work, regular pay, a supply of uniforms, a pension at the end and, above all, sunshine every day. As a people we are going, going and mostly gone. "Stay in school," we are told. "Do well in your exams and you won't have to leave." Mam is not so sure. She never pushes me. "Education is no load," is all she says.

For the second half of fourth class, Mr. Criostoir O'Floinn is our teacher. At maybe twenty years old, he is hawk-nosed, tall and spare. On his first day he arrives on his great iron bicycle. He is poet, playwright and Irish language enthusiast. As of yet, none of his accomplishments is known to us, but his air of dedication and discipline commands respect.

Classes are divided into sections: A, B, C and D. Ours is an A class. Everything is taught through the medium of the Irish language and largely by rote. This man adds a whole new flavor to the Irish language and to Irish history. His enthusiasm is contagious. For the first time there's music in the Irish language and Irish history takes on a new coloration.

It has always been drummed into our heads that Ireland's empire, if we have one at all, is a purely spiritual one. Be proud, we are told, that Ireland supplies more priests and nuns per capita than does any other country in the world. And we should be proud that Irish men and Irish women go abroad, especially to Africa, to spread the benefits of Holy Roman, very Roman, Apostolic Catholicism among the natives. Rarely, if ever, is it mentioned that the real Holy Romans stay at home, in Italy, drinking wine at their sidewalk cafes, watching the girls go by.

For the Irish missionaries, the hot sun in Africa must have been a blessing. The real Holy Romans have plenty of sun at home. They must be smiling at the thought of people in Ireland sending money over to the Vatican to swell the coffers of Rome while Father Paddy sojourns in the bush and on the veldt, giving his soul and risking his life.

In the same way, Sergeant Paddy, we were told, went abroad to convert the natives to the ways of the British Empire, even when they didn't want to be converted. And the natives were expected to be grateful. Our all-purpose Paddys served as Soldiers in Christ, Soldiers of Rome, Soldiers of the Queen, Me Lads, ranging and rangering all over, for the uniform and the boots. Fed and paid they were and, if they lived, they would be pensioned off. Soldier Paddy "took the English shilling" from the British Empire and his wife, or his mother, was only too happy to send it on to finance the Empire of Roman Catholicism.

We move to a new address, in Janesboro', again on the outskirts of Limerick, to a City Council house. Frank is now in the U.S. Army and he sets aside half a portion of his monthly pay to be matched by the U.S. Government. Every month we will receive a check in the amount of ninety dollars. This newfound prosperity, which will be continued by Malachy and Mike when their turn comes, combines with the move to Janesboro' to pull us up from the slum and literally across the tracks and confers on us a place among working class people.

Our brand new house on O'Donoghue Avenue, one of a row of about twenty houses, is part of the "new" Janesboro'. Some residents of the "old" Janesboro', which was built before the war, are apprehensive. They are worried, maybe, that we will tear down the banisters on the stairs and use them for firewood or that we will use the kitchen sink for storing bags of coal. We are the wild, shiftless Irish, just up out of the lanes. Barely down out of the trees we are and forever on the dole, they think. We are only a half step above the Tinkers, the Traveling People. The Tinkers, it is said, would steal the eye out of your head, and make you glad to surrender it, so charming and cunning are they.

But we are lucky in our neighbors: Costelloes, O'Connors, Fitzes, Finnans and Kellys. All of them are new, as we are. And it is lucky for us that again we have a working farm right across the street, with nothing to block our view of the fields.

It is quiet there. I swear that I can hear the dew as it falls. On crisp, cold nights, when the frost glistens on the grass, the stars are low, so low that I can touch them. In our new freedom we are released from tiny, crowded rooms with low ceilings. This brings a feeling of expansion.

There are other kinds of expansion, too, of which no one ever told me, though we have been well schooled in history, mystery and miracles. Well versed we are, in the Virgin Birth, the Resurrection and the changing of the water into wine and readily we have believed.

But history, mystery and miracles have not prepared me for this. The little fella begins to take on a life of his own, swelling up and refusing to go down. I recite from Shakespeare: "Is this a dagger I see before me, the handle toward my hand? Come let me clutch thee. I have thee not and yet I see thee still."

It's a bit like a dog chasing a car, because, God knows, if he caught it, he wouldn't know what to do with it. I'm in the same situation. Threats don't work and even when I recite four verses of authentic Gaelic poetry, all with a terrific *blas*, a near perfect accent, acquired under the tutelage of Mr. Criostoir O'Floinn, it is all to no effect. Stubborn he is, stubborn he will remain and he will not go down.

Mam is a great reader. She keeps the more temptatious books under the mattress but we know where to find them. One day when I have secretly borrowed her copy of *Absalom My Son*, I lie on the bed drinking in the charms of Livia Vaynol. The mystery, very suddenly, and of its own volition, is solved, bringing a great relief and the dawning of a new branch of knowledge.

Blissful relief and the joy of this new knowledge will soon give way to questions, confusion and to guilt. And to the certainty that such pleasure is bad. I know that I will be found out, but it doesn't take long before the guilt, while not entirely overcome, is shunted aside. Nothing is spared now. Pillows, bolsters, bathroom basin, tub, tables, garden walls, bicycle seats, magazines and footballs. All take their turn. Knotholes in fences are avoided, for fear of splinters.

Someone gives me a copy of an *English Boy Scout Handbook*. One chapter details how "every boy has in front of him a small tube" and gives some vague ideas as to when and how to use the "small tube." The information has come too late, but it is the only explanation I will ever receive. The rest I must discover for myself. It will take years.

The bathroom houses our first indoor toilet along with a tub and hand basin. Almost incidentally, the bathroom is a big improvement in sanitation. From now on, there will be no more firing off out the window and no more groanings under the stars. We have become civilized.

—⚜—

My first cousin, Peggy Sheehan, had the hard life of an orphan. She has been living with my mother's sister, my strict and demanding Aunt Aggie. When they have a falling out Peggy comes to live with us. Given her hard life, Peggy could have cried and cried, but, instead, she laughs. Very often it is nothing more than a nervous reaction, which brings her very close to tears. Other times her laugh is very merry and when she is lost in laughter we can't help but join in.

For my mother she provides much needed companionship. They become very close and will remain close for the rest of their lives. Mike and I gain a sister once removed. Peggy cheers up the house and brings a welcome female presence. Her friends come to visit and there are times when her friends, Mike's friends and a couple of my pals are all in the house at the same time. It seems to happen when Mam is not a home. We all gather in the sitting room, which is about two feet square and holds a small couch, two chairs, a radio and a fireplace.

A boy-girl game evolves. A young man or woman goes out into the hallway and closes the door. A person of the opposite sex, inside the room, calls out "meeeow." If the person outside likes the sound of it the one inside is invited into the darkened hallway. The door is closed and whatever happens is allowed to happen. Age is no barrier.

We, the younger ones, get to taste more mature fruit. There's an ocean of passion, but we never even approach the grail, or at least I don't. Time is limited and prohibition is absolute. Soon it's back to nooks and crannies.

***

Our new "gardens," front and back, provide a great outlet for frustration. Mam plants flowers under the windowsill in front. The front "garden" is nothing but clay. My friend Michael Ryan and I, in a piece of wasteland half a mile away, dig up an area of sod. Square by square we cart it home in a wheelbarrow and lay it on top of our clay garden.

The back garden we tackle with pick ax, shovel, spade and rake. Lucky, the dog, has a great time. Using his hind legs he digs right along with us, creating small mounds of earth as he goes. Lucky is Mike's dog, but Lucky and I are the same age. He has always been my pal. With his long jet-black hair he is of mixed breed, mostly terrier, but he is no mongrel. He neither whines nor whimpers and I have never seen him cower. Once, when I was seven years old, shouting and running in a group on the street, Lucky became puzzled and alarmed. Barking up at me, he leaped and nipped me in the armpit, not enough to break the skin, just enough to make me pay attention to the lone car that came barreling on down the street as we all scattered.

Lucky lives on scraps, but in the early years when there was little in the way of scraps, he learned to forage at night. He has never lost the habit. One morning, in Janesboro', I open the back door and there he is, home from his night of forage and fornication. His hindquarters are all askew, from a stroke, maybe, or from being hit by a car. I put down an old canvas bag and he lies down. At lunchtime, when I come home from school, poor Lucky is dead.

After school, in late afternoon, with pick and shovel I dig a small grave at the end of our rough garden. I wrap him in the canvas bag as I cry for him, for myself and for all of us. Picking him up I carry him toward his little grave and Lucky, my old pal, matches my tears with one more salute offering a definite reassurance that there is life after death. In tender farewell, he rains his own golden stream on my shirt, on my pants and on my shoes.

Our work in the garden continues. Tons of rocks and small stones are removed and acres of clay until we have a semblance of a garden. Ours will be a small exploratory crop, an unlikely combination of stuff, but the beetroot comes up tasty. Sean Costelloe declares our winter lettuce to be the best on O'Donoghue Avenue.

All of our neighbors have gardens and lots of young children. There is a husband and father present in every family. At thirteen, I am five years older than even the oldest of the neighboring children and younger by some fifteen years than the "man of the house" in all those houses. I can't be the "man of the house," but I become the "boy of the house" when my brother Mike leaves for the United States.

When we were young, Mike and I pretended to be gangsters and he christened me "Big Head Nolan." Mike taught me boxing, how to cover up and how to avoid and block a punch. He had never been to New York, but he taught me how to talk tough in a New York/Brooklyn accent so that I would be ready for any situation. I had been told, at an early age, that if I got into trouble outside in the street that I should take care of it myself. I could do that, but I always knew that Mike was there if I needed him. Tall and strong, Mike played second row forward for Young Munster Rugby Club. I'm proud of my big brother.

When Peggy Sheehan departs for England, to find work and a new life, Mam loses her surrogate daughter. And, when Mike leaves for America, it seems as if she has lost yet another son. I am the last one standing. From an upstairs window, I look out on the field across the street. The cows are unmoving and, on this rainy evening, no one passes by on the street below. The house is really quiet now.

1954

MEANWHILE I MOVE ON from Primary School to Secondary School at the Christian Brothers, a small triumph for the family. Again I am the first. Most of my classmates move on to Secondary School so I am surrounded by familiar faces, by Michael Magner and Michael Wallace, the resident geniuses and my friend Seamus O'Dwyer, the genius overall. Seemingly effortless in all he does, from table tennis to hurling, Gaelic football, chemistry and history and Latin, Seamus is unassuming in personality but assertive in debate. His brothers had preceded him in Secondary School, which gives him a certain status, but at the same time he is held to a higher standard.

Our school is strictly academic with an emphasis on sports and barely a nod in the direction of music. We are privileged to be in an A class. The brightest will be groomed for university scholarships, for the Civil Service and for the few good jobs available at Ranks flour mill or in the cement factory. Some will be nudged in the direction of the priesthood. Most of us will emigrate. That's a given, though it is rarely talked about. Our probable emigration is of no great concern to the powers either temporal or spiritual, although much emphasis is placed on the probable fate of our immortal souls:

For what doth it profit a man if he gain the whole world and lose his immortal soul?

On Wednesday afternoons we play hurling and Gaelic football. I play right fullback on both class teams. Brother Brady, our first-year teacher and coach, prowls the sidelines. When we are under attack he will exhort us, "They shall not pass, they shall not pass." With hands pushed deep into the folds of his cassock, all grizzled head and weather-beaten face, his air of settled purpose is a thin overlay covering an explosive agitation. When we score he walks a little faster, nodding his head up and down and chuckling to himself, all the while waving at our defense to get ready for the ball, which very soon will be coming our way. When we are scored upon, he will mourn aloud, "How are the mighty fallen, how are the mighty fallen." Brother Brady has a very slight speech impediment; his lower jaw is always thrust forward. Some mock him behind his back. Those of us who play for him will never laugh, because win or lose he makes us feel heroic.

Mr. Galvin, "the Rabbi" Galvin, our teacher in the second year of Secondary School is a kind man of quiet authority. On a rare occasion he will stop and give me a ride to school but only when it's raining. And he will exact a price by peppering me with words to spell in front of the whole class. I dare not miss.

All through my years with the Christian Brothers I have taken my share of punishment. The series of slaps on the hand with the leather strap is known as "six of the best." Slaps are the price we pay for not knowing the answer, for being late, for laughing in class, for not having the homework done, because the teacher is in a bad mood or because the moon is full. You hold out your hand for "six of the best." You take your punishment and tuck the reddened hand under the opposite armpit.

A more serious offense will bring "twelve of the best." After the first six, with the already beaten hand tucked safely away, you offer the other hand. When six more have brought that hand to a red and welted doneness, you tuck it under the vacant armpit. All the while you scrunch up your face. You hold back, mightily you struggle to hold back. We all endure it at one time or another. Blindly, you shuffle back to your seat. You hear nothing but the boding silence of your classmates. You would die before you'd cry. There is no salvation in tears, only disgrace and loss of face.

Brother Mannion served in the Royal Air Force during the war, we are told. Now he is our teacher for the third year. As always, along with the other taller students I sit in the back of the room. Brother Mannion, as do all the teachers, writes extensive notes on the blackboard. I often have trouble reading the notes and I depend on whoever sits beside me. Brother Mannion sees me asking. With a question, he pounces. I don't know the answer.

"It's on the board," he says.

"I couldn't read it, sir," I answer.

"Oh, you couldn't read it?" he mocks. "Well then, come up here."

At the front of the room, before the blackboard I stand. Brother Mannion removes his glasses, hands them to me and orders me to put them on. Feeling foolish, I do as he says.

"Can you read it now?" he asks. I can't. His glasses are strong and they make me dizzy. In silence I remove the glasses and hand them to him. Brother Mannion says nothing. We stand staring at each other until, in a flash, he hauls off and slaps me hard across the face.

"Six of the best" even "twelve of the best" are a painful but common occurrence. The leather is the accepted weapon of choice. But we are outgrowing physical punishment. Teachers rarely use it anymore. And among men, a slap in the face is an insult, a degradation that must be answered. It is more insulting than a punch to the head. A punch has some honor in it.

I am almost as tall as my tormentor. My first reaction is to take a shot at him, but respect for parents, elders, priests, police, teachers, and Christian Brothers has always been drilled into us. I am shocked, so shocked that any reaction is delayed. By the time I fully realize what has happened, it is too late. The moment has passed. The shock of the sudden slap has brought tears to my eyes. I am rooted to the spot. For a moment I stand still before shuffling back to my seat.

In the afternoon Brother Mannion gives us an assignment. I am at my desk, head down and fully engaged, when he inches up and stands beside me. Bending down so that we are head to head, he whispers in my ear, "I'm sorry for what I did to you this morning." That's all.

Not too long after, on a Saturday afternoon, Seamus O'Dwyer and I go to the Central Cinema to see *The Barefoot Contessa* starring Ava Gardner. The movie is notorious in our town, in our Catholic Limerick with its Presbyterian mores. The censor has been even more heavy-handed than usual. The movie is in bits. Even so it reeks of sex, layers and layers of sex.

The movie ends. As we are leaving the movie house, Brother Mannion and his partner are walking out on the other side. Christian Brothers travel in pairs, for protection against temptation, I suppose. Brother Mannion spots us. Abruptly, he and his partner turn left. Seamus and I turn right. We are not supposed to be at such a movie. Neither are they. Nothing is ever said.

Mam and Alice have seen the movie and they talk about it at the table. I say nothing: Alice and her husband, Paddy, are great friends of Mam. Both of them are below average height. Alice is the careful wife and housekeeper. Paddy, a terrific house painter and wallpaper hanger, is also an accomplished chess player and he plays the banjo. On weekends he plays in a dance band. I would love to learn to play the banjo. I'm often tempted to ask Paddy to teach me, but something holds me back, a feeling that I'm not worthy, maybe, or a sense that Paddy doesn't really like me.

When they come to visit, Mam makes tea, places bread and butter on the table and pours the tea. Paddy sits. Alice pours milk into his cup.

Still he sits. Alice adds sugar and stirs the tea. Paddy talks. Alice butters a slice of bread, slices it in half and arranges it on his plate. "Thank you," Paddy says. He reminds me of Robert Emmett. Only when certain conditions are fulfilled, then and only then, will he take a sip of his tea and a bite of bread.

A filler item in the evening paper offered advice on how to get rid of an unwelcome guest. The trick is to saw an inch off the two front legs of whatever chair the guest usually sits on. The guest will be forced to sit in a forward-leaning position. This will place a strain on his legs. The longer he sits, the more uncomfortable he will become. The best part is that he will never know why he is so uncomfortable.

The ritual of the milk and sugar and the bread and butter is well underway. Comes a lull in the conversation. For whatever reason, I fill the gap in the conversation with the helpful hint from the newspaper on how to get rid of an unwelcome guest. Did I want to amuse Paddy, did I want to show him how bright I was or did I just leave my mind behind? I don't know. The silence doesn't last long. Soon, Paddy nods to Alice and they finish up very quickly. In an aside to Mam, they murmur something about a phone call from their son.

Out the door they go. Mam glares at me.

"I didn't mean anything," I protest. "It was just something I read."

"Well, that wasn't very nice," Mam says. Then she laughs. Paddy and Alice don't show up for a few weeks. Mam tells me not to worry about it. When they do return, just as they are knocking at the door, Mam tells me to be quiet or, if I must talk, to stick to school, sports and the weather. I never do learn to play the banjo.

❧

With the brothers all gone, home is a lonely place and I need an escape. I have come to love Irish history, the Irish language, and what's left of

Irish culture. By losing myself in them I can forget the loneliness, the memory of the lane and the lack of a real sense of place.

On New Year's Day of 1956, Sean South of Limerick is killed while leading an IRA raid on a British Army barracks in Northern Ireland. Limerick's population is at fifty-two thousand. An estimated fifty thousand turn out for the funeral of Sean South.

Barely forty years have passed since we achieved independence from England. Sinn Fein, the political arm of the IRA, surges in popularity. It has started again. The "bloody shirt," the gun and the IRA will soon be ushered back into politics. Our next-door neighbor, Sean Costelloe, is inspired to write a classic ballad, "Sean South of Garryowen."

Garryowen, an area in Limerick City, gave its name to the great tune "Garryowen." Often co-opted by Hollywood moviemakers, the tune serves as stirring background music when the United States Seventh Cavalry rides into battle against the American Indians. Sean South did not come from Garryowen, but, in song and in story, the names Limerick and Garryowen are used interchangeably.

Along with Sean Costelloe, I become a member of a local Sinn Fein "cumann," a local political club. With a dozen men in our membership, we range in age from sixteen to fifty. In the beginning we meet in each others' houses until our chairman makes his rented garage available for our meetings. Two of our members, active IRA men during the Second World War, had been captured by the Irish Government and interned in the Curragh Camp in County Kildare. Their bitterness toward the Government of the Republic is palpable.

We must enlist the public in support of "The Oul' Cause," independence for Northern Ireland. Michael Scott and I sell *The United Irishman*, the organ of the Republican Movement, on the main streets of Limerick. To my own great delight we are always under surveillance. A member of the Special Branch, the Irish Gestapo, is always close by. My slogan, righteous and declamatory is: "Buy *The United Irishman*!

Help yourself to freedom!"

"Buy *The United Irishman*! Help yourself to freedom!" I call out to the Saturday afternoon shoppers outside Todds Store on O'Connell Street, as I look for a larger focus and a wider horizon. Putting aside, for once, the little organ, I'm peddling the Organ of Freedom, *The United Irishman*. Where do I get the cheek to exhort the poor woman? She is scrambling to buy any kind of a cheap cut of meat, to avoid the disgrace of having a meatless Sunday dinner. And, at the same time, she must hold onto a little money, so that she will have enough left to buy a new pair of shoes for her youngest, who is on his uppers.

And I exhort anybody's husband as he heads home from his Saturday half day's work in the factory. Emerging now from the pub with a large dent in his week's wages, his evening newspaper in three perfect vertical folds is neatly inserted, upright, into his right-hand jacket pocket. His tightly belted cloak of probity and sobriety is fractionally belied, then totally ripped apart by a slight stagger. Ever so quickly he recovers. His misstep is noticed by none but Organ Peddler, me, I think. But the man is duly noted, in turn, by heavy-on-the-salary, long-in-the-pension, red-in-the-neck, broad-in-the-beef Gestapo man. Himself an Organ of the State, the Special Branch man is less for law and more for order. He is in total solidarity with the priests. Police and priests, all imported into Limerick, are dispatched by our twin governments in Dublin and in Rome to tamp down any of our foolish expectations, material or spiritual or any threat to the established order.

And I call out to farmers, cash-laden, as they rush to reach William Street to buy boots and shirts, tea, sugar and salt. Desperate to get it done, they crave a little spare time for a drink and a smoke in the pub before heading back, with wife and children to the everyday cares of the farm. Rushed and harried they are. Still, for a second, these farmers break stride, in a wonder that anyone in our Limerick would dare to shout out, on a busy Saturday afternoon, puzzling the whole street and holding up traffic.

They are tempted at first to flee. Then, pulled in my direction by this appeal to their battered better nature, these farmers are briefly reined in. Hearkening, almost against their will, to some old, long-buried and long-forgotten nationalist pride, they pause in their hurrying and buy a copy of the paper.

And I call out to the men in their tweeds, in from the county. And to the twill trousers in high and highly polished boots, I call. "Help yourself to freedom! Buy *The United Irishman*!" Taken aback, they stop to take a look at me. Then, looking down, and greatly disturbed at finding themselves unhorsed and, for once, on foot, these latter-day gentry will whinny and shy away, from this shout of the rabble revived.

On Friday and Saturday nights we sell *The United Irishman* in the pubs. In an excess of sentiment fueled, perhaps, by a few pints, the men will sometimes tell us to keep the change. Now it is time for the angels to dance on the head of a pin. Is the change meant as a contribution, or are we meant to keep it? The debate is brief, lasting no more than ten seconds. Michael and I decide in our own favor and, at the end of the night, at the end of our labors, we treat ourselves to chips and coffee, at the Roma Café in Patrick Street.

❧

Fianna Eireann, a nationalist Boy Scout movement, is revived, along with the Fianna Eireann pipe band. I join the band and become a passable piper. According to our teacher, Mr. Jack McManus, I have potential. Frank Kennedy and I practice our piping at the back of our house in Janesboro'. The neighbors laugh good-naturedly at our efforts. "No fear of rats here," they chide. "Yee don't have to lead them out, for they're gone already. The sound of them pipes was more than enough to drive 'em out."

We are allowed to "play out" in parades, but only as "dummies." Drones and chanter are stuffed with newspaper for fear that we will make a noise. We balance the drones on the left shoulder and blow mightily into the mouthpiece. We puff out our cheeks and for added effect we finger our chanters. Earnest we may be, and playing our hearts out, but we can make no sound. Veteran pipers provide the music.

After a month of intensive practice, we will be allowed to play in the band. Drones, chanter and mouthpiece, all are attached to the pigskin bag. The bag is the engine room of the war pipes. The piper blows into the mouthpiece to fill the bag with air. The bag, at intervals, is compressed with forearm and elbow, causing the air to be pushed up and out through drones and chanter. The piper fingers the chanter and brings forth the melody. If we are lucky, we will make music.

The bag must be prepared. A new bag is stiff and dry. An old bag, lacking proper care, dries out with age and use. Old bag or new bag, both must be lubricated. All three drones, along with chanter and mouthpiece, must be removed and set aside. Each hole, except for the opening for the mouthpiece, is plugged with cork or with newspaper. Into the open hole we pour the lubricant, a can of treacle. The bag is rolled and rubbed and rubbed and rolled. The treacle must be evenly distributed over the entire inner surface and forced into every crevice in the skin.

Softer and softer becomes the bag, slower and slower the rhythm of the rubbing. Broad and deep is the rolling motion. Rubbings and rollings take on a life of their own. Pockets of air, inside the bag, give off sucking sounds. Between piper and pipes a special relationship will develop and, like everything else in our Catholic lives, any such relationship is forbidden.

We run dances as fundraisers, for Sinn Fein and for the band. As treasurer, I must find the hall and hire the band. No "foreign" dances will be allowed. We are restricted, in the ceilidh, to an evening of native

Irish dances. These, mostly set dances, are group affairs. Lines, with two or four people in each, will step to the music, all the time moving forward, from one end of the hall to the other. Each dancer, along the way, will engage his or her opposite number in the line facing. Everyone gets to dance with everyone else.

Ann is all flair and fire and flashing eyes. She is none of your dowdy, hang-by-the-wall, "Ax me, sister, I'm sweatin'," variety. And she engages. She engages us all, fully, in the dance. I believe, don't I know for certain, that she has a different, a special feeling for me. How do I know this? It doesn't matter. I just know it and I seek her out whenever I can.

Waves of the sea we are, as we dance the Siege of Ennis. In lines of four we advance: girls and boys, two by two. I am oblivious to those closest to me. Watching, I am, always watching and looking further down the hall. Which side of the line is she on and will she be my partner when our lines meet? We do meet. She does become my partner, if only for a minute. And she gives me that smile. I'm dumbstruck. Fortunately, there is no time for talking. We link up, I wheel her and we must move onto the next.

Fantasy it is, futile and foolish. Ann is special, yes, and even more so because she is two years older. She is also forbidden. Her boyfriend, Jimmy, a real IRA man, is on active duty and "on the run." Later he will be captured and he will achieve heroic status by being interned, by the Irish Government, in the Curragh Camp in County Kildare.

❧

To an outdoor Sinn Fein political meeting in Thomas Street comes a speaker from County Kerry. First, in ornate Irish, he speaks, then in English, as he employs the great deliberate cadences of his native county:

"A man went into a restaurant," he begins, "and he ordered a bowl of soup. There's a dead mouse in the soup. 'Waiter, waiter,' he calls out, 'there's a mouse in my soup.'

"'Very good,' the waiter responds. Taking the bowl of soup to the sideboard, he removes the mouse and returns the bowl of soup to the man's table.

"'Waiter, I don't want this soup,' the man exclaims.

"'But, sir, what do you want? You don't want the soup with the mouse in it and you don't want the soup without the mouse in it. What do you want?'

"Elections, reforms and rebellions make little difference," the speaker explains. Any real change in government is virtually impossible. We always keep the basic administrative system, even when we change the government. All we ever do is to throw out the mouse and leave the soup. We keep soup and system. He may be right. Without a great upheaval and, most of the time, even with a great upheaval, nothing changes.

Even so, on Friday night I am the fervent nationalist Sinn Feiner, made even more fervent when Ann is there. On Saturday night, I shed my nationalist skin and steal away to a dance at Saint Michael's Rowing Club. "Foreign" music is played here. Part of the ritual is to go for my first pint of stout before the dance. One pint leads to another and another, to a total of four. Later in the evening I lean back against a railing, down by Arthur's Quay and close to the River Shannon and slide all the way to the ground. I am sitting comfortably, my legs stretched out in front of me as Willie Horrigan and Mikey Ryan have a good laugh at me.

And, from Saint Michael's, we soon graduate to the Stella Ballroom. A more grown-up venue, the Stella is thought to be more sophisticated and cosmopolitan. Slow dances, close dances, bring on abrupt swellings. Our partners, at least my partners, seem to take them in stride. They may be a welcome distraction from the fumes of the pints of porter we drink before going to the dance. Legend says that one night, at the Stella, a young woman, thinking that she detected an unusual protuberance, looked down, and then further down, beyond the protuberance. Shocked and horrified, she discovered that her partner had a cloven hoof. She fled in a scream. Her partner, he of the cloven hoof, disappeared into the mists of the Shannon River. This happened at a Saturday night dance, shortly after midnight, early on Sunday morning.

I would have liked to ask her if she saw one cloven hoof or if there were two, or three, or even four. But, to priests and elders, it was no joke. One cloven hoof, even the rumor of a cloven hoof, was more then enough leverage. Forever after, when they preached about the dearth of morality among us, they invoked the tale of the cloven hoof: "Dance to the devil's music, especially in the early hours of the Sabbath, and yee'll know what to expect."

Along with the foreign dances at the Stella I take up rugby football. I must abandon the native sports, hurling and Gaelic football. Following in the footsteps of my brother Mike, I turn out to play for Young Munster. As "hooker," I am right in the middle of the front row of forwards. Arms across each other's shoulders, we bend forward, going as low as we can, almost to the point of toppling forward, headfirst. We push our heads in and under the shoulder of the opposing front row forward. The two front rows are "locked" together, for better or worse. An aerial view would reveal all shoulders, backs and behinds but no heads.

The scrum half throws the ball in so that it lands on the ground between the two front rows of forwards. Both sets of forwards push as hard as they can against each other. We are a "pack": three in the front row, two in the second row, two wing forwards and a lock forward. As hooker I must strike for the ball, with either foot, when the ball is put in by the scrum half.

All Young Munster teams train together: juvenile, under-twenty, junior and senior. In the practice scrum two "packs," with eight forwards in each "pack," try to push the other off the ball and off the field altogether. Heavy exertion brings forth some mighty heavings. Saturday night and "the rake of porter," is followed by Sunday morning practice. Pressures brought on by heavy exertions and mighty heavings will often prove to be too much. The scrum will break up. We recoil, repelled, if we are playing in front of him. We are propelled, further backward, if we are playing behind him, by the wind from a backfiring player. Stepping quickly away and holding our noses, we laugh and swear vengeance on the head of the windy one. Senior players take turns. Backfiring at will, sometimes they do it in unison and it's impossible to find the culprit.

Paddy Ahern gets married. On his first evening back after his honeymoon he turns out for training. After training, as we wash ourselves in the ditch that runs alongside the field someone asks him, "So, Paddy, how's married life?"

"Oh, not bad," Paddy replies, "not bad at all. Shur when I was gettin' up to go to work this morning didn't she turn over in the bed. 'Come back to bed, Paddy.' she says. 'Don't go to work today, Paddy. Come on, come back to bed.'"

And Paddy, poor Paddy, forever after would be known as "Come-back-to-bed Paddy."

Paddy plays on the senior team and can be of no help to us when we lose to Shannon in the final game of the Juvenile Cup competition. The following year, when we are to play them again in the final, we have a new scrum half. During practice, when our heads are down, with arms and shoulders interlocked, I hear him ask our coach Paddy Foley, "Should I put the ball in fast or slow?"

"Put it in anyway you like," says Paddy. "McCourt'll get it." I could have kissed Paddy Foley on the top of his head.

We win the Juvenile Cup competition. Munsters has never won it before. Our opponents, Shannon, an upwardly mobile working class club, have won the cup eight years in a row. They are confident. They neglect to bring the cup to the game and we have to reassemble at a later date for the presentation.

Now with rugby and school, Sinn Fein and pipe band, ceilidhs and foreign dances, my life is full. Homework suffers when girls intrude upon my concentration. The only way to meet girls is to go to a dance. Toward the end of a dance and halfway through the evening, "Would you like a mineral?" I will ask her. This is a way of saying, without saying it, "I like you, do you like me?" With any luck we leave the dance floor and adjourn for a lemonade (the mineral in question). We will spend the rest of the time together until I ask to walk her home.

The girl always lives three miles away and at the other end of Limerick, but it doesn't matter. A thousand miles wouldn't be too many. The last bus is always gone. We walk all the way, to finish the night up against the hedge for ten or fifteen minutes, until father or mother calls her in. One last kiss, one last touch, before she goes in. I am left to walk the long and lonely late-night miles home. Still burning with what went before, I am tingling with anticipation of more and a date for the following Sunday at the pictures.

It never lasts. With all my airs and aspirations, I am only a grown but still gawky schoolboy with no ambition except to go to America. At the same time, I want to be president of Ireland, a great world leader, a revolutionary, a singer and a great rugby football player. Still living on the largesse of my emigrated brothers, I take it somehow as my due, after all the years of misery, deprivation and near-starvation.

The girls lack the impossible glamour, the allure of the American girls I see in the movies. And, of course, I have no prospects, but I want them to have the glamour of a movie star. They want someone normal, someone with the prospect of a steady job, five or six days a week, good for two dates a week, and an interest in going steady. A going-steady man will appreciate a little time out so he can have a few pints with the boys on Friday or Saturday night. And in return for his company at Mass on Sunday he will be allowed time out for a rugby game with the boys. On Sunday night, every Sunday night, there will be a film together. Later still will come a family, a house, responsibility, and the slow silting down into respectability.

I wish that I could want the same. But my head is so far up my arse that all I can see are stars and stripes and the promise of America. It doesn't occur to me that I should work, even part-time. It's enough that I'm a student and that is my full-time occupation. But I have time for all kinds of diversions. So why not a part-time job? There isn't much work, but I could surely find something. So why don't I do it?

The girls seem to know me in all my shiftlessness. And I know that I don't want what they want. I would welcome a little comfort, yes. I will always yearn for the warm hearth of a real home, but it will take me a long time to grow up and show some maturity. I'm in awe of these girls. Awkward and naïve I am and a couple of years younger than my age. I'm busy, always busy, casting myself to myself in some kind of heroic mold. How will I earn a living? I will go to America and be a huge success. That's the easy part, but with no confidence in myself, I expect to be rejected by the girls. Still, on any given evening, I walk out full of hope. Later I will walk home, still at war with hope and hopelessness and filled with yearning, to that Janesboro' house now empty of brothers.

⁂

Mam stays home much more now and she expects me to be at home too. Lonelier than ever, she is. Isn't it lucky for her and lucky for me that the Costelloes live next door. Sean and Mary of the songs, and their children, become like a second family. Freely we move in and out of their house. Sean becomes surrogate father, uncle, older brother and mentor to me and Mary is both sister and daughter to my mother.

Each of my brothers, in turn, comes home for a visit, in uniform, tall and splendid and generous. All the old friends gather in the kitchen for the dancing and in the little sitting room for the singing. The house is warm. Mam is fully alive again and brimming with delight, my mother of the sorrows with three of her children long dead and three of her surviving sons away in America. One is home now in his glory, if only for a short time and she can be proud as the crowd of old friends and well-wishers keeps at bay the sorrow, the pain and the hole left in her life by children lost and husband long absent. Never was much bread in her life. Now there is just enough, but she needs a touch of circus to make it bearable and believable, to keep at bay the dogs of depression.

Invitations are very informal: "We're having 'a bit of a night' on Saturday. Frank is home (or Malachy or Mike) is home. Will yee come up?" And they all show up. On one of those nights we run out of bottled Guinness and I, the junior host, must go and deliver this news to Christy Horrigan and his compadres. Hard men they are, well used to hard physical work and well able to put away their share of pints and still be rock steady.

"We're out of bottled beer entirely," I tell them and "would yee mind having a drop of whiskey?" They slap their thighs and roar with laughter and the laughter of their thanks sails right up to the heavens.

I don't know why they're laughing. Haven't I seen them drink their pints in the pub? Haven't I seen them, when the round is ordered, turn their back on the pint, on the black body and the creamy head of "the blonde in the black skirt"? They ignore it completely, pretending that it is not there at all. Any haste in reaching for the glass, any attention paid, will be deemed unseemly, greedy or unmanly.

In the drinking of a pint of stout, no unnecessary touching is allowed: no looking, no fidgeting, no foreplay whatsoever. A man's behavior in relation to the pint is a perfect parallel to an Irishman's reputed conduct during sexual foreplay, which, at that time, and by all accounts, consisted entirely of one sentence: "Brace yourself, Brigid."

After a suitable interval and at a sign undetectable to anyone but themselves, Christy and company will turn, grasp the glass, offer a "good luck," take a good long pull and put the glass back on the bar. This action is to be repeated perhaps four, but no more than five times, until the pint is demolished. They will know, of course, that when the right rhythm is maintained, by the third or fourth swallow the backup pint will miraculously appear. God will be in his heaven, custom and protocol will have prevailed.

How, then, I wonder, can these men so readily abandon the monumental pint, the ritual "good luck" and the four ceremonial swallows in favor of a puny tot of whiskey? But they do and with obvious pleasure.

When all the songs have been sung, when "Speak, Speak, Speak To Me, Thora" and "Whispering Hope," "Some Enchanted Evening," "My Lagan Love," "O Let Me Like A Soldier Fall" and "Eileen Aroon" have been well rendered, the music winds down and the dancing must come to a halt. Spent now is the energy of the evening, but the warmth of old friendship still binds all together. We have journeyed through the night, in harmony, right up to the false dawn. Tea and small sandwiches are handed round. There's talk of early Sunday morning Mass. All begin to bid "good night" and "good morning" to each other and to my mother and "Thanks, Missus, 'twas a great night," and Mam beams. It was, indeed, a great night and two of her sons will sleep under her roof tonight.

Yes, one son has returned on the incoming tide, but the tide flows mostly outward. Most of us will emigrate. Without emigration there might be a real revolution. The English have been gone for almost forty years, but still we are not doing too well. Government needs stability in order to stay in power. All churches thrive on keeping everything the same. The Catholic Church is no different. Emigration, as a pressure valve, suits the purposes of State. The only real concern of the Church is for our immortal soul. How will our souls survive in godless England or in flagrant America? No one knows but the Church will take a chance and let us go so that they can maintain the status quo.

"Sin often enough and long enough and you will kill your conscience," we are told. We can't wait to get started. Thievery and treachery, calumny and back-stabbing, none of these will count for much. They hold no real interest for us, incidental as they are in the grand catalogue of sins. Murder receives due consideration but sex, as a sin, outshines them all. Sex is legitimate only within the confines of marriage and it must lead to conception and the birth of a good Catholic child. A place in heaven awaits those who propagate the faith. Otherwise, don't even think about sex.

In religious instruction in school we are told that Martin Luther went astray because he had too many scruples. We commit our share of sins, but we try to vary them so that we will not be repetitious. A variety of sins, we reason, is less likely to kill our conscience than will the same sin repeated over and over. At the same time, we must tiptoe on the tightrope between killing our conscience and the cultivation of too many scruples. The result is a Saint Vitus Dance of the soul.

In the Limerick Confraternity, run by the Redemptorist Fathers, membership is voluntary. Weekly meetings include the recitation of the Rosary, a sermon and Benediction at the end. Membership is voluntary but all boys, young men and adult men are expected to join. Any boy, youth or man who is not a member is considered an oddity and, possibly, a subversive threat to society. A member with too many absences from the weekly meetings will receive a visit from the prefect of his section and will be served with a "summons" from the director, a kind of writ of habeas animus. In effect the summons says: your soul is in our custody. If you want it back, then you'd better show up.

I did, once or twice, attend the annual retreat of the Boys Division. I heard the imported hellfire preacher recite the tale of the two boys who skipped a meeting during the annual retreat. They went swimming. One drowned and one was left to tell the tale. "Boys, oh, boys," brayed the preacher, "in all thy works remember thy last end and thou shalt never sin."

"What, never?" we queried, softly and in unison. "Well, hardly ever," we answered our own question.

Before too long I began to miss most meetings and paid little attention. My status as a hopeless case was confirmed when no prefect ever sought me out. The director, it seemed, couldn't even be bothered to send me a summons.

Thank God it is not all piety. For distraction, there is murder and sex, down by Sonny Darcy's. Sonny, a member of our cumann and a former internee is now, among other things, a basket weaver. His shop is down at the other end of Limerick. Michael Scott and I skip school and go to visit Sonny, on a day when he must undertake the slaughter of a full-grown sheep. He slits the throat as blood gushes. The sheep thrashes. Sonny, his head only inches from the head of the sheep, remains in close communion. Holding on tight, locked in a one-sided embrace of his victim, he gives that sheep a worthy death. Only when she stops thrashing does he release her.

Two doors down from Sonny's shop lives "Downtown" Harriet, as Scott and I will come to call her. Pretty, thin and angular, she is as willing and as hungry as I am, only I am so ignorant that it takes me many visits to figure out where everything is and forever to find the sweetness. All the gropings and the after-dance groanings up against prickly hedges, all lead to this, to this lying down, chest to breast, belly to belly and thigh to thigh. Still, with all the touching and all the fondlings, no conclusion is ever reached. Encounters always take place in her parents' house. Their at-any-time and always imminent arrival home are a trigger to great excitement, but my ignorance keeps us from any conclusion.

1959

IN JUNE WE HAVE COME to the end of schooling and we "sit" for the Leaving Certificate Examinations. All through the summer we worry about the results, which will be released in August. In the meantime, jobs are very scarce. My one offer comes from an accounting firm and only through the good graces of one of my teachers. They offer to pay five shillings a week, hardly enough money to pay bus fare back and forth. I am expected to be grateful that, without any connections, I am being offered, not a job but a position, which will give me entrée into a profession. Grateful I am not. Accountancy is not for me. I am going to America. Word comes from brother Malachy that he plans to bring my mother and myself to New York for Christmas and I know that if I go I will not be coming back.

The girl can't know or care about any of this. In the late afternoons she rides by our house. In her red raincoat she heralds the twilight. On her old-fashioned girl's bicycle, with feet at rest on the pedals, blonde hair blowing above perfect Scandinavian face, she coasts with the slow gradient. Looking neither right nor left, she drifts on down toward Ballincurra Weston. Elbows propped on the windowsill upstairs, I can't wait to trade Limerick for New York. Still, there's a touch of the old lingering loneliness. I dream for her to look, just once to look my way. But she can't know that my soul hangs in the balance; that I will be saved if she will only turn her head. She never looks, not once. She just sails on by.

In August the Leaving Certificate results come out. I have done well, though I could have done much better. In early September comes a note from Brother Kealy. Brother Kealy of the Socratic head and the rational delivery had been my principal teacher during my last two years at school. He treated us as adults. "Boys," he might have said, "you're grown up now. Do your work if you like, come to school if you feel you should, or do not, as you see fit." A learned man on the verge of retirement, he is a fine teacher. Now, in August, he has a job for me as a substitute teacher in Quay Lane, the oldest National School in Limerick.

I am to teach reading, writing, arithmetic and a smattering of Irish to a class of nine-year-old boys. My lazy morning habits quickly fall away. I'm out of bed before I am awake, on time and ready. I need to be ready. There are sixty boys in the class. Soon I will pray, every day, for early morning rain. Rain always brings a small drop in attendance. This is a boys-only school and I feel that I know these boys, at least a little bit. Most are not much better off than I was at their age, but they probably have fathers, working and living at home, and I envy them that.

The professional class is paid in guineas, each guinea the equivalent of twenty-one shillings. My check is for four guineas a week. The working class is paid in pounds, at twenty shillings to the pound. Gawky nineteen-year-old that I am, I am proud to be paid and by check. But I am sure of nothing else, except that I am going to America. It's all well and good, but the job is temporary. In two months, the absent teacher returns. I have no other job prospects in Limerick.

When I was sixteen I wanted to go to England, with friends and classmates, to work in a factory for the summer, but Mam didn't want me to go. I would have left her all alone in the house. Now, together, we are leaving for America. Soon it will be time to break the bond.

In my mind the United States, America, is in two parts. New York City is one part. Excitement, promise, yellow taxis, glamour, opportunity, New York is all of these. And, the Empire State Building. In my yearnings toward America, it was always the Empire State Building, not the Statue of Liberty, that beckoned. I had seen the Empire State Building on more than one postcard. In Limerick we have church spires. Symbols of a repressive spiritual authority, they are the past. The Empire State looks upward and outward. Beautiful in its definition and solidly rooted, it is, still, a soaring symbol of success. To grasp the essence of the Empire State Building is to feel the heart of America, in all her steel and concrete dreams.

Movies are my fantasy America, especially the Westerns. *Shane* and *High Noon* are chief among them. These are simple. Here are the tyrant and the bully, the ordinary citizens and the hero. There are no nods and no winks or sly asides here. Situations are clearly defined. In each, one man stands alone, outnumbered by bad guys. That man is a reluctant hero. "A man's gotta do what a man's gotta do. That's the law of the West." All is lost, but help will come from an unexpected quarter and the hero triumphs. He doesn't glory in his victory or wait around for accolades. On he rides and out of town.

A man could spend his life trying to reconcile these two Americas: the America of the yellow taxi in New York City and the America of the hero riding, alone, into the mountains as the voice of the little boy, thrown back by those same mountains, echoes and ricochets all around him: Shane, come back, Shane. I love you, Shane. Come ba-a-a-ck. Sha-a-a-ne.

In December come the tickets to New York. We have the "bit of a night" and close up our house, leaving it to the care of the Costelloes. Willie Horrigan comes to the railway station to see us off. What I have always wanted is now coming true but there is a wrenching in my gut as I say goodbye to Willie and to Limerick.

We sail from Cobh on the *Sylvania*, a twenty-one-thousand-ton Cunard Liner. Food is abundant, abundant and intimidating, and there are girls. Yes, indeed, there are girls: Irish, English and European, but, above all, there are American girls. In their blouses, plaid skirts and black stockings they are going home for Christmas, I hear. They're taking a break from their junior year at the Sorbonne. I know nothing of junior years and Sorbonnes, but these girls, a vision right out of the movies, are, at the same time, vivacious and unafraid, yet remote and unapproachable. I brave it and dance with the Irish girls. Reserved and a little stiff they are and who could blame them. With the forward and backward motion of the ship and my own imaginings, I am often a bit stiff myself.

The Atlantic in December is not kind and I remember Christopher, all six-foot-two of him. Broad-shouldered and strong, he lived up the hill from us on O'Donoghue Avenue. I had played rugby with him. His mother was rescued, as a child, from the *Titanic*. During one summer in Limerick, Christopher went swimming and drowned. The family never recovered.

Halfway across, the ship begins to roll. Some of the stabilizers have failed, we are told. We will have to slow down and we will arrive late in New York. Only later are we told that the sea had been so rough that the *Queen Mary* suffered broken portholes some forty feet up.

Sick we are, green and sick. Everyone, in turn, fails to appear for meals. Staying close to bunk and bathroom during this temporary death, we give back to the ocean all that the ocean has given us and mankind since the dawning of the first light. Cleansed and purified, we emerge to be welcomed back by the other veterans of the great vomit.

Frank is at the pier when we arrive in New York. Frank brings us to Malachy's apartment. Malachy and his wife and baby daughter live in a one-bedroom apartment, with a spacious deck, at 65th Street and First Avenue.

I have a slice of cold pizza, my first. It is cold but delicious. Later that day, Frank brings me to the dentist. A kindly man is Dr. Kramer and he obviously likes and respects Frank. My front teeth are already going bad but, for whatever reason, Dr. Kramer roots around in the back of my mouth. I have arrived in New York, and with my mother, no less. I've had a slice of cold pizza. And I have gone to the dentist on this, my first day in New York City. Not the usual path of the immigrant. And why is the dentist rooting around in the back of my mouth? It is clear to me, and it must be clear to him, that my front teeth need attention. But I am, literally, just off the boat. I don't ask why.

Later in the day, and with obvious reluctance, Mike shows up. I am guessing that he wants to be left alone to live his own life. We have a Christmas dinner. We are all together again, as I had hoped we would be. The Christmas-card Christmas rarely happens. There is often a certain tension.

For the next couple of months, I bunk in with a friend of Malachy's. Heir to a vast American fortune, he spends his nights in the search for enlightenment, along with his disciple, Bill. Bill is still recovering from his service in the Korean War. Magic mushrooms help them in their quest.

I sleep on the floor in the bedroom, or I try to sleep. Sometimes lulled and sometimes disturbed, I can half hear their murmurings. One night I hear a woman's voice. Then there's whispering. I can barely hear what they're saying. They are urging her to come in and join me, to bring me some enlightenment. The murmurings continue for a while, but eventually they fall away along with my disappointment.

· NEW YORK ·

1966

SIX YEARS HAVE PASSED since I left Ireland and slept on that floor. Since then I've been to Montreal, South Carolina, Chicago and Norfolk. And I took the long way round. It has taken me six years to travel from 65th Street and First Avenue, my first home in New York, to this garden apartment at 92nd Street and Lexington Avenue. From my new apartment I can walk to work at the White Horse Inn. And I will make the transition from lowly waiter to part-time bartender. I am assuming that working behind the bar will be a more straightforward job. It will save me from the brunette from Omaha, with her limpid eyes, her beautiful, friendly smile and legs from here to eternity.

In Limerick, I used to dream of women like her. She remains inaccessible and totally unreachable.

"What's an Irish burger?" she always seems to ask. In my new and exhalted position no longer will I have to shift my eyes away, for fear of falling headlong into hers.

And no longer will I have to answer, "An Irish burger? It's a cheeseburger with Irish bacon."

No longer will I have to write on my obedient little pad while she gushes, "Oh, I'll have one of those. Medium rare, but please, more to the medium-rare side of medium rare," she always seems to specify.

No more, through clenched teeth, will I have to mutter, "Yes, yes and yes," in polite reply, as I lust after her and wish for her damnation, all at the same time. Working behind the bar will lend me some added status and stature.

Women like her are always with a date. All freshened up after work, he's so fresh that even his casual attire is perfectly pressed. Coifed and betasseled in his loafers and upward bound in his "kuhrurr" at some downtown, white-shoe, super-wasp Wall Street investment firm, he is at his most patrician as he scans our simple menu of shrimp cocktail, salad, hamburger, cheeseburger, Staten Island steak and fillet of sole. With a smile reeking of privilege and private schools of tennis and girls in white sweaters he looks up at me. "What do you recommend?" is his challenge. This man can't even decide what he will have to eat. That must be a great hardship for him.

I can think only of Rudy in the kitchen, of Rudy cooking, serving and washing dishes. Last night, with his token goodnight-going-home-after-work brandy in his hand, Rudy had stopped at the jukebox. Placing his drink on a nearby table, Rudy put a quarter in the slot. His mother had just died in Cuba. Rudy could not go back for the funeral. Resting his right hand on one side, he completed the embrace by reaching with his left and grasping the upright edge on the other side of the jukebox. He made his selection and leaned in, so that he was almost spread-eagled across the jukebox display. Once, he played it. Twice. And once again. On this raft of music, Rudy sailed away home, if only in spirit and only for a few minutes. To the strains of the haunting "Guantanamera," his tears began to flow.

So, what should I recommend to this imposture of a man? What do I recommend? I recommend that you take yourself down by the East River. It's only two blocks away. Look for Gracie Mansion, the mayor's residence. The river is just behind it. Then you should go and screw yourself. When you're finished it will be easy to just topple over and into the river. Let the tides take you to the home of your ancestors, though I seriously doubt that you have any. No human person could possibly have spawned you. As we used to say in Limerick, you were probably not born at all. More likely you were fired against the wall and ripened by the sun. So, what do I actually recommend? "Well, the steak's good," is all I can bring myself to say.

John Le Carré has described it as "a waiter's anger." Indeed, and I have no excuse. I have been more or less privileged. My brothers provided for my education. I don't have to be a waiter. Doors are open to me. Fluent in the language as I am and with a good basic education, I can even pass for white. I'm in good health. Some people may look down on Irishmen, although I don't think that we have many natural enemies. Still I can't seem to gather myself up. I have fallen into the restaurant business, and at a low level. Without ever really making the decision, I have fallen into it. Now I wait. Distinction and greatness, with equal ease, will fall from the tree and into my hands. If I can't achieve real distinction then I don't give a damn. A talent for introspection is of little practical use and I surely have it in abundance. I would have attended meetings of the New York Apathy Society regularly, but I never could rouse myself.

On our nights off it is the custom for bartenders and waiters to go and visit, to "see" each other, in our different bar and restaurant habitats. And isn't it grand, boys, the ease of it, the grand entrance with drinks all round? Credentials are easy, just the name of the place where you work, or the names of one or two people you work with. The most facile introductions will follow. Everyone nods knowingly. The girls' winning smiles are abrim with welcome. The introspective has arrived.

From behind the bar your friend and compadre tops up your drink. After a few more drinks, including a tacit acquiescence in your friend's generous "buy-back" policy, you leave an exorbitant tip and move on to "see" the next one. And the next. More money is spent on taxis than ever is spent on drinks. On the night following, or the night after that, the ones we have "seen" will come to "see" us. All will go around again.

Malachy calls it "lend lease."

You know it's futile, but you must continue in your quest for one more bar, for one more friendly face. Your court of last resort is often the very place you work in, six nights a week, the same place you can't wait to get away from when you're working. By three-thirty in the morning the wound-down bar is populated only by the remaining "regulars." As the door opens, their faces moon upward in expectation. A brittle brightness, jaded at all its edges, is there to greet you, for you may be the bearer of some tidbit of news or gossip. At worst, you'll buy a drink.

As you walk in your coworker behind the bar buries his head in the washing of a glass, pushing down hard and suppressing an inward groan. Your arrival now will only delay his closing. He has been trying to close for the last half hour, but a good warrior above all, he fishes a smile from the sink, straightens himself and comes up with your drink. You have delayed him, but by the rules of the game he can show no displeasure. Tomorrow night your positions may well be reversed.

At the end of the bar farthest from the window, the lone woman closely attends the phone booth, takes a phone call and leaves in a hurry. Soon, the "regulars" will finish their drinks and leave. My friend and I are left to stack the stools on the bar, set the alarm and lock up. From the Greek coffee shop across the street, following the great breakfast of fried eggs and sausage, home fries, toast and coffee, I will be propelled homeward in a taxi. The morning newspaper in hand is a dead giveaway. "Going home with the *Daily News*," I am, a clear indication of failure. No one ever admits to going home alone, to "going home with the *Daily News*."

Sometimes, on a regular working night, we will close a little early and race to someone else's bar so that we can close that one in a hurry. In the delicious half-dark of "after-hours" drinking we will sit, joking and yarning. Always, there will be a good-looking woman, in company with one of the group. As the late night wears into the pre-dawn, she is transfigured into the absolutely most beautiful woman in the world. We must keep our distance and we do. Still, we do everything in our power to capture her attention. We don't sing "Danny Boy" because in Ireland, by custom if not by edict, the singing of "Danny Boy" is regulated. Like certain sexual behaviors, it is permitted only in the privacy of your own home and among consenting adults. But with little urging we sing to the company, though really to her, the saddest, most sensitive, shut-eyed songs ever to cross the ocean. What's the point? In the end, the beauty departs.

At five in the morning, the streets and avenues of the Upper East Side grow leaner. Gathering themselves in, they straighten their skirts and gear up for a new day. A quiet street, with its fresh morning face, will soon forget the excesses of the night.

Here they come now, though they are not many. These are the dawn breakers, these early birds. Diligent and dutiful, practical and compulsive, the very earliest of the regular working people, these are the ones who make things go. You glance at them as they emerge and they look at you. Just as quickly, you both look away. They know, and you know that they know. Nothing is left now but to go home. You are going home, not with the *Daily News* this time, but with *The New Yorker*. A feast of a short story will bring some consolation.

Nights run into days—up all night and sleep all day. A miserable, hellish continuum is this, and a pattern very difficult to change, but, by working ten or twelve hours a night, six or seven nights a week, I have managed to save some money. In March of 1967, I take my first trip back to Ireland with a detour by way of London and Edinburgh and Dublin.

Absent from Limerick for almost eight years, I am nervous about going back. I have no home there anymore. Mam lives in New York now and our Council house in Janesboro' is occupied by someone else.

Even so, I must go back to see old friends and, as always, wherever I go, I will walk the land.

In New York the smell of the subway will always remind me that I am back in the city. When I was a child the smell of cows in a byre was warm and reassuring. And the fresh aroma of horse dung, at the southern end of Central Park right across from the Plaza Hotel in New York City, is an easily distinguishable marker. Steam engines have long since been converted to diesel, but the train trip from Dublin to Limerick remains ageless and unchanging. In Limerick Railway Station the sharp tang of steam, left over from the old steam engines, still fills the station, right up to the roof and there is nothing like it. I am home.

The week in Limerick I spend with the Costelloes, easily becoming a member of the family once again, and easily resuming my old friendship with Michael Ryan and Willie Horrigan. Before I leave, we have "a bit of a night." It's a small one, with barely a minyan for the singing of "Now Is The Hour." But we sing it anyway. My Limerick isn't there anymore. That should come as no surprise, but it does, even though I am mindful of what someone once said about Dublin: "Dublin," he said, "is a city to which exiles (emigrants) return, so that they can dream of an Ireland that never was."

· DUBLIN ·

1967

THAT SUMMER, JIM MOLLOY, newly arrived from Dublin, comes to work at the White Horse. He has all the right credentials, which include graduation from the right boarding school. And he brings a bit of a superior air. He is indignant at the fact that he must empty ashtrays. I explain that this will give him an excuse to approach the tables and to be available without being intrusive. I'm inclined to resent his boarding school airs. Even so, we become friendly.

In October after many talks with Jim, I take my G.I. Bill and go back to Ireland, to University College, Dublin. I will become a barrister ho, ho, ho. And how far have we come? The unwashed will now return to the capital city of Ireland. To become a barrister, no less. Mary Callan, my good friend, gives me an introduction to her brother Paul. Paul is a barrister practicing in Dublin.

At this time, the rules and customs governing the making of a barrister would make the arcane seem progressive. A barrister, qualified to practice in Northern Ireland who wished to be admitted to the Bar in England, was required to "eat dinner" twelve times a year at the Inns of Court in London. The Paddy candidate had to show that he knew the difference between a knife and a pig's trotter.

On Dublin's Harcourt Street I find a "bed sitter," a third floor room with bathroom down the hall. I am made to feel at home by the hallway light. It's on a timer and allows only enough time to run from the front door and up the stairs before turning itself off. And I am not alone. The damp, the ever present, reassuring damp, is there to share my room and my bed.

Paul Callan advises me against becoming a barrister. Barristers are "instructed" and given their cases by solicitors. I have no family or any other kind of connection and I don't know any solicitors. Where will my cases come from? Paul urges me to become a solicitor instead. He says that I will have a better chance of being given cases at a lower level.

In order to become a solicitor, I will have to be apprenticed to a solicitor and pay that solicitor a fee. Paul recommends me to a solicitor in Limerick who agrees, delays, defers, and in the end, finds that he can't do it. I am referred to another solicitor. The second solicitor is a TD (Teachta Dála), a member of the Irish Parliament.

Before I am allowed to become apprenticed, I must be approved by the Incorporated Law Society of Ireland. When summoned for an interview by the secretary of the Society, I appear for the interview. I fully expect to sit at a table or at a desk, to tell him who I am and what I am about, in what I think of as the American way. When I open the door and walk in, the secretary is there, but he is not alone. The whole board has turned out to greet me. This is an honor, I suppose, and I should be honored to be so honored, even though I could do without such an honor. At any rate, there they are, seated on both sides of a long and highly polished conference table.

I am asked a number of questions; two in particular: "If you are attending the University in Dublin, how do you plan to spend time at the office of your master in Limerick, 120 miles and a good three-hour journey away by road or by rail?" I answer that I will go down to Limerick one day a week, during the week.

And the next question: "With no family here and no visible means of support, how do you plan to pay all your fees and support yourself?" This one comes from the man in the tweed jacket and the cavalry twill trousers, the gentleman with the veddy, veddy upper-class pseudo-English accent. He's a snob, if ever there was one, and a super snob with polished boots to match. I explain that I have the G.I. Bill and that it pays me $130.00 a month. Some of the gentlemen present are seen to wince, for isn't it well known that a true gentleman is never so vulgar as to enter into specifics about his source of funds, even when pressed. And never, ever, must a gentleman be specific as to the amount.

I go on to explain that student flights to New York are very cheap at Christmas and in the summer and that I will return to New York, during vacations to a guaranteed job there. Further, since I will be working virtually the whole summer long, I will be able to save a good deal of money. When you're working, you can't be spending, I add. Once more are they afflicted by the collective wince.

They continue in the same vein, good lawyers all, asking only the questions to which they already know the answers. They are not too subtle in badgering the witness, in fulfillment of what I feel is their assigned mission, to exclude anyone who is "not of the right stamp." I sense, also, that they will never be happy with my explanations. Don't I know it for sure, and doesn't all of Ireland know it.

Comes a pause in the proceedings and a short silence, broken by my main adversary, my tweedy, twill-clad, veddy-veddy, Anglo-Irish nemesis. He suggests to his colleagues that "we have asked him those same questions, repeatedly, and he has answered us to the best of his ability. Why don't we stop now?" The interview is over. All is lost. In a week comes a letter from the Incorporated Law Society. I have been admitted as an apprentice. I have won my first case. In my mind, I can only thank my main adversary, my veddy-veddy, Anglo-Irish friend for my salvation. How badly I misjudged him. He is the source most unlikely, yet most likely, and a decent man after all.

Almost all of my fellow students at University College Dublin are eight or nine years younger than I am. Some of them have attended private schools or a better class of boarding school. Some affect the long college-style scarf and the hair just long enough to toss when making a point. Even at my advanced age, I am a little bit intimidated by this university.

With the prescribed books in hand, I'm already into studying in my old pedestrian way, reading a chapter, picking out the essentials and making my own précis. This brings me satisfaction and a feeling that I am getting somewhere. The sparse furnishings in my room, along with rationed electricity and pervasive damp, all satisfy my need for a little hardship. A certain monkish streak goes hand in hand with my love of solitude. This love of solitude, always at war with the need for companionship, is easily tamped down. In essence, I am a terrific ascetic as long as I have blankets, a pillow and enough food, the price of a few drinks and a friend to share a laugh with.

After years spent working evenings and nights, the nights now prove to be lonely and difficult. Too often, restless at the books, I head out for a walk and end up in a pub for a few pints. Soon I reconnect with Jim Molloy. He introduces me to his running mate, Lewis, and they invite me to share a flat with them in Dartmouth Square. Within walking distance of the College and just over Leeson Street Bridge, a quiet and "refined" place is Dartmouth Square. It will be perfect for my purpose, I think.

These two, Jim and Lewis, have moved onto the prescribed courses at the Incorporated Law Society, on their way to becoming solicitors. Very social they are and well able to talk their way into or out of any place or situation. They know everyone in Dublin, from politicians to moneymen, from entrepreneurs to horse trainers, from jockeys and rugby players to models, television people and news columnists. With the right background, and having come from established families and with the right boarding schools behind them, they carry, on their wings, the dust of the old Anglo-Irish notion of what it takes to be a gentleman. Above and beyond all that, they are keen and energetic in conversation.

I will soon find out that they are fanatical about politics and always in perfect disagreement. Our flat boasts a living room, kitchen, bathroom and a garden at the back and front. But there's only one bedroom, containing three beds. At the end of a night's activity, at pub or party or dance, I get into bed, and by old habit, take up a book. They get into their beds and it is not a book they take up, but the threads of the argument left over from the night before.

Litanies are trotted out, beginning with the Rising of 1916, the Treaty, the Civil War, Michael Collins, Eamonn de Valera, the Blue Shirts, Hitler, Mussolini, Churchill and FDR; all are fully reviewed into the small hours. As the debate continues, my roommates become more passionate. Irishmen are often thick. These two are thicker, in their fixed positions, than I have ever been, even during my tirade at the Dinwiddies' house. Until, one night, Jim slips me a sleeping pill and takes one himself. At the same time he engages Lewis in hot debate and gets him rightly going. Very soon Jim drifts off to sleep. Lewis is left to debate with himself, a most cruel joke to play, especially on a voluble and opinionated Irishman.

Temptations are great. Very late nights don't make for early mornings. I lapse into my old habits of sleeping late and I spend more time at the movies and in the pubs than I ever do at lectures or in the library. At the end of the first year, having barely made a passing grade, I return to New York for the summer to start working and to put together some money. I forward a check to my master, the solicitor, to whom I am to be apprenticed. Sure enough, back to me comes the check, accompanied by a letter. I am informed by my master-to-be that he can no longer accept me as an apprentice. He has been appointed to a ministerial post in the Government. He expresses regret and offers the hope that I will be able to find someone else.

Back in Dublin in October, after the summer in New York, I am discouraged. I am not much inclined to look for another solicitor. Friends urge me to sue for breach of contract. This, for them, is a delicious prospect since my former master-to-be is in politics. A lawsuit will certainly cause some embarrassment to him and to the Government. I can see the headline:

GOVERNMENT PERSON SUED FOR BREACH OF CONTRACT BY RETURNED YANK, WOULD-BE SOLICITOR'S APPRENTICE AND SUPERANNUATED-STUDENT-WITH-BARELY-A-PASSING GRADE

It would be ridiculous. I won't sue, I tell them, but if ever again I should meet my former master-to-be, I will punch him in the face. This would make a better headline:

GOVERNMENT MINISTER PUNCHED IN FACE BY RE-TURNED-YANK-RETIRED-APPRENTICE

I can't know that I will meet him years later, when he is in poor health. He will have surely forgotten the whole matter. And I will no longer care.

I might be able to find a third master-to-be. I had really wanted to be a barrister. To me, becoming a solicitor is a poor second choice. And I can't even accomplish that.

Frank Ward and I meet at a university lecture and become friends. His family eases my pain. I spend a great deal of time in their house. Molly, his mother, is a walking saint. From morning till night she takes care of her husband, Frank Sr., and her six daughters and two sons. Harrying, encouraging, scolding and clucking she pushes them to follow their religious duties, to be upstanding and industrious, dutiful, kind and compassionate. She teaches by example. All are welcome in her house for the endless breakfasts, lunches, dinners and oceans of tea at all hours. Her own very special apple tart serves to sweeten her frequent admonitions.

Frank Ward and I "cram" together for exams. Frank brings to bear a great grasp of the facts of any given case. I'm not good on facts, but I have a grasp of the principles involved. A good team we are, studying and tossing questions, answers and analyses back and forth. "Cramming" is not good. It will get us through an exam, but, immediately afterward all facts and information, like fledglings from the nest, have a way of flying out of the mind. Worse than that is the four in the morning breakdown, when the slowing of the circulation brings on the great chill. The gods of sleep demand to be fed. We are forced to go out into the back garden for a two-man game of soccer just to wake ourselves up. Tension and lack of sleep bring on murderous tendencies. If we didn't need each other for further study, we might cheerfully kill, just for possession of the ball.

Lewis, one of my two roommate, hails from Drogheda. His family still lives there and their hospitality has often kept my spirits afloat. His father had been to sea as a radio officer for many years. His mother dreams of better things: of a house, of horses and a riding stable. Martin, Mr. Turley, of a practical turn of mind, must deal with his son, Lewis, and with his sometimes feckless ways. "You think I'm a big shit, don't you?" said Lewis in the middle of a minor argument. His father chewed on that one for five seconds and, with an impish grin, came back with, "No, but you're a bit of a shit."

And the chill of Dublin life is broken by my occasional trips down to Limerick to see our old neighbors, the Costelloes and my old pal Michael Ryan. I arrive into Limerick on the train, in the rain, on a Saturday morning and make my way up to the Costelloes' house in Janesboro'. Mary Costelloe welcomes me with a great bowl of packet and tripe and a mug of tea. I have barely finished that when she asks,

"Would you like a fry?" When I answer yes she makes the great fry of eggs, sausage, bacon, black and white pudding, bread and more tea.

Mary's husband, Sean, my old friend and mentor, arrives home for lunch. As resolute as Don Quixote on his burro, Sean does his rounds on a bicycle. Drenched in sheets and sheets of rain, he dries himself and Mary brings him the bowl of packet and tripe. Having finished the tripe, he leans back in his chair. Mary emerges from the kitchen.

"Would you like a fry, Sean?" she asks.

Sean doesn't know that I have wolfed down packet, tripe and, on top of that, a fry. He doesn't hesitate. "Would I like a fry? Indeed and I would not. What do you think I am, a savage?"

Bulbous with packet and tripe, packed to bursting with eggs and sausage and bread and tea, I shrink into my skin. I glance at Mary. She is hiding a half-smile as she looks over at Sean. But they know each other too well. Soon Sean begins to chuckle. Soon Mary lets go a laugh and it is with great relief that I can burst out laughing.

Sean slaps his knee. "A savage," he chuckles. "Well, that's a good one, now, am I a savage." And he keeps on laughing.

· NEW YORK ·

1969

I'M NOT LAUGHING when I return to New York at the end of my second year. Despite all the hospitality and the warmth of personal relationships, Dublin has presented a closed face. I could continue to pursue the Bachelor of Civil Law degree, but I am discouraged. That's one excuse. More important is the fact that bad habits die hard. I have barely made it through the second year with a passing grade before returning to New York.

The previous summer I had worked with Peter Sheehan at the White Horse. Now, for the summer, I go to work for him at The Gavel, his grand new emporium on East 79th Street. All hardwood floors and captain's chairs, it's designed to be club like, a place where "real men" will hang out. And they do. Stockbrokers all, they flourish in a rising market. Every one of them claims a share in the ownership of the place. Each one totes an iceberg blonde on his arm, for decoration. "Lay Lady Lay, Lay Upon My Big Brass Bed" and "Hair" provide the jukebox soundtrack. Carey Cadillac limousines arrive regularly and like commuter trains, they depart, in a terrific display of rampant, conspicuous consumption. This is 1969, the year of the Knicks and the Mets.

Peter is sick one night and calls to ask me to take care of the restaurant. During the evening, as people come and go, the temperature rises and rises. Even with everything turned off: ovens, fryers, dishwashers, heating system, everything, the place becomes hotter and hotter. Cooks, waiters and customers, everyone has gone home. Left alone with the sweats, I continue in my search for the cause of the overheating. In the basement, I am greeted by the molten cast-iron boiler. Looking as if it is just at the point of exploding, the boiler expands and contracts. I am hypnotized. Finally I tear myself away and from upstairs I call the Fire Department. Eighteen firemen arrive, with horns sounding and sirens blaring. In two minutes they shut down the boiler. "Half an hour more," they assure me, "and you would have been a goner."

And what a departure it would have been. Furnace and building are the property of the Cherokee Democratic Club. I would have arrived at the gates above, or below, as the case may be, on a whoosh of whiskey, brandy, vodka, gin, cognac, beer and wine. Not a bad way to go, mind you, to be surrounded by flying steaks and lobsters and in the company of whatever late-night Democrats happened to be laying down policy on the second floor above the restaurant. And wouldn't St. Peter be perplexed at such a panoply, though he would hardly be surprised.

On the following day, Peter, fearing that violations and penalites will ensue, is a bit upset, but when he realizes that he is free and clear, since the boiler doesn't belong to him, he assures me that he's glad I lived to tell the tale. Coming from the usually acerbic Peter, this is as good as a welcome home.

During that week, Lynn shows up; Lynn whom I knew from the White Horse when she used to come in on dates with her writerly boyfriends. The door of the White Horse faced east, yet the first time I had seen Lynn, the setting sun was behind her, possibly a reflection from the windows on the other side of Second Avenue. Without a hope or a prayer I was lost in her glory, beautiful and sophisticated as she was. Yes, oh yes, she laughed at my jokes, but always bringing up the rear would come one of her artistic types. All of them tall, handsome and grave, they limited themselves to a ration of one or two shots of Jameson and two bottles of Guinness. They remained quietly assertive of their Irish heritage and carried with them a strong sense of their artistic mission and gave no sign that they suffered any of the roilings and boilings with which I constantly fought and over which, too often, I lost control.

Now, at The Gavel, it is late in the evening when Lynn comes in. She is alone. Much later, we gaze into the water down by the East River, counting stars and measuring the moon. Later still, we spend some sweet time on her couch.

I will be going back to Dublin in September. For now, my main purpose is to work and save some money. Quiet, introspective, humorous and always full of empathy, even before empathy came into currency, full of good fellowship, tolerant and always for the underdog, that's how I viewed myself. As a generous person, "Go ahead, have another, go ahead, go ahead," I will urge a diffident drinking companion, yes I will. But only rarely can I spare any money for my mother on the distant West Side.

To make things worse, I grow tired of beer and start drinking whiskey. I have never been slavish, but it is good, sometimes, to be "one of the boys." Although solitary by nature, I often feel a strong urge to join in and to be part of whatever is going on. There are tensions all around. When Martin Luther King Jr. was assassinated, Robert Kennedy calmed even the most angry and helped to pull us together. Following the assassination of Robert Kennedy himself, there is no one to rally us. We are teetering on the brink of chaos, at home and abroad.

Then I meet Jane. Only two years divorced from her Park Avenue stockbroker husband, she lives, now, in the east seventies. Our meeting is only incidental, but during that summer I move in with her. Estranged from her husband and from her family she has only a tenuous connection with the world.

She's a Brooklyn Heights brownstone WASP, an excellent golfer and a fine tennis player, the tennis racket merely an extension of her arm. On the diving board she dances and dives with breathtaking grace. Water could be her natural habitat. Educated and intelligent, graduate of a "good" college, she had been cast in the role of companion to her husband's success. Isn't she truly blessed in meeting me, the unconnected? Neither one of us has much of a grip on reality.

An episodic alcoholic, Jane lives on the proceeds of her divorce settlement. For long periods she is alone with her miniature schnauzer and her depression. At some point, driven by a desperate need for human companionship or in a burst of mistaken optimism, she will dress up and go out into the world of the bars, only to end up drunk and hopeless and, the next day, even more fearful.

As the old Indian said: "The white man broke every promise but one: he promised to take our land—and he took it." When the gods made Jane, they fulfilled every promise but one. She couldn't conceive a child, the child who might have been her salvation. Then again, maybe the gods were wise.

Sometimes, Jane waits up for me and in the early morning, she will come to meet me and go have breakfast. Having this woman to come home to helps me to become more centered, while she seems less lonely. We set up a routine domestic life of food shopping and cooking and laundry and walking the dog. Or is it cooking the dog and walking the laundry? I often take him to the park for a run.

One day in the park, he challenges a big golden retriever. With fool's courage, the schnauzer stands his ground and barks at the retriever. The bigger dog takes the schnauzer by the back of the neck and shakes him. The master of the retriever, in a panic, pulls on the leash and kicks at his dog. Tighter and tighter he pulls on the leash. The retriever clamps down even harder. Drenched in equal parts sweat and panic, I can foresee the imminent death of the little schnauzer. What will I tell Jane if I have to come home without the dog? Most of the time he is a yapping nuisance but I have a certain affection for him. With both hands and with all my might, I pry open the lower jaw of this essentially good-natured retriever. The retriever releases the schnauzer. Yapless, for once, he trots quietly beside me as we leave the park.

Unable, or unwilling, to face Dublin, I don't go back in September. I will stay in New York with Jane and continue working. But my root-less ways and Jane's yen for flirtation are accentuated by drinking. Soon we decide to quit. We walk the dog and walk the city. We visit muse-ums and galleries. Ablaze now, we relish the fresh and clear insights as they are funneled into the brain by our new-found sobriety.

After nine months without having a drink, I go into a bar on Third Avenue, take a place at the bar and wait for the bartender. Busy at that moment, bringing supplies from the rear of the premises, he pays no at-tention to me. I can't wait any longer and I leave the bar. The absence of the bartender is surely a message from the gods, but I ignore it. Later in the day, I find a bar with an available bartender and succeed in having a drink, more than one in fact. Jane starts to drink again and to exercise her charms with even greater skill.

One night as we are leaving a restaurant I stop to pay the check. Jane, in an Arc de Triomphal piece of flirtation, stops to admire the tie of a man sitting at the bar. The man with the tie is a perfect gentleman. Removing his tie, he presents it to her. I am left in a quandary. What am I to do in this situation? I have no manual to go by. I know, in my gut, that a pretended indifference would be best, but I can't do it. So I take off my scarf and present it to Mr. Debonair Chevalier. He's non-plussed, for my scarf is old and very rough in texture, of his silken tie the very antithesis. I want to say something to him, but I don't. Instead, I take Jane by the arm and we leave.

Mired, we are, between the extreme poles of sober and drunk. On one of our outings, we drink probably the maximum legal limit of "stingers." A drink best taken without ice, the stinger is made up of about four ounces of brandy, preferably cognac, with just a touch of white creme de menthe. Shaken with ice, chilled and strained into a clear-stemmed cocktail glass, it will become lightly golden in color and with a light film on top. "A thing of beauty" it is but not always "a joy forever."

Memory of events may be hazy, but the number of drinks is counted as we go to "see" a bartender here and there. Toward the end of the night, in furtherance of the "lend-lease" program, we return to Second Avenue at 88th Street, to the vicinity of the White Horse.

We are drunk. Jane is slow in crossing the street. In my lunatic state I pull her, roughly, across the last few steps. A citizen, upstairs in an apartment overlooking the street and observing my behavior, calls the police. Comes a police car with siren blaring and lights flashing.

I have no quarrel with the police on a one-to-one basis, but I don't like them. I can trace my dislike all the way back to my childhood. The police in Ireland were looked on as the descendants of those who had signed the disputed Treaty with England, who gave away the Northern Six Counties and founded the Free State. Irish policemen, the "Gardai," were alien to us. They were transferred into Limerick from somewhere else.

This is Vietnam time, Civil Rights marching time, frequent-confrontation-between-citizens-and-police time. Cops are called pigs. In the sixties, the police in New York developed a bad reputation for corruption. Some are corrupt. Haven't I seen them myself at Nick and Harry's, where the two brothers, both working twelve hours a day, would serve breakfast "on the house" to a local cop and his partner. We dismissed it as a small courtesy, akin to a free drink. "Why not?" we shrugged. Didn't we all depend on them for our safety?

Harry and Nick only smiled. But when we observe a cop arriving, to pick up breakfast "to go" for himself and seven or eight others, amounting to breakfast for the whole station house, we feel that they are going too far. The face of the New York City Police Department is an Irish American face and that kind of behavior makes me cringe.

Now, with the arrival of the police car I must confront that face. It is made more frightening by the genius on the rooftop right above us. He chooses that moment to express his own political disaffection. From the rooftop comes a barrage of garbage, plants and plant pots. All of it lands in the street, very close to the police. More police cars respond to the call, "officers in trouble," all with lights flashing and sirens blaring, they scream to a stop.

They must arrest the drunken source of all this trouble. My lifelong unease, my mistrust, of priests and police, comes bubbling up in my throat. I can't help but resist. And I continue to resist. All the while I protest that I had nothing to do with the dumping of the garbage from overhead. Bent over, shoved and pushed right out of my state of rigid resistance, I am bundled into the back of a police car by a small army of men in blue.

And, of course, in continuing to resist, I must insist on having my say about corrupt Irish cops as the hail of rooftop missiles resumes. Overall, I am not badly treated. The police use only necessary force to get me into the police car, no more than that. So far I have deserved what I have got. In my drunken behavior, I am a walking disgrace.

At the precinct house, booked and put in a separate room, I am made to sit upright on a chair. My hands are handcuffed behind me and behind the back of the chair. A broom handle is threaded, at the level of the armpit, between my upper arms and along my back, extending at each side beyond my arms.

A young cop walks into the room. Ever so casually, he punches me in the face. Down I go, chair and all. When I struggle to get up he does it again. And again. A greying older cop with a friendly Irish face passes by, raising my hope of rescue. With barely a glance, he moves on and out the door. Punches continue into hazy time or until, I suppose, the rookie is properly blooded. Or did I take the better part of valor and stay down? I don't remember. I'm bruised but not visibly bloodied at all.

Jane, in great distress, called my brother Malachy. Malachy sends a lawyer to the courtroom for my arraignment the following morning. Two weeks later, I appear in court again, charged with felonious assault. I am accused of biting one of the cops in the leg during my arrest. A felony, indeed, this is a noteworthy first offense.

No mention is ever made of what happened to me in the station house, but after words have been spoken and appeals made, the charge is withdrawn. The judge gives me a stern warning: "Everyone gets one chance and you've had yours. Don't come back here again."

I owe a great debt to those cops who initially arrested me. They were fair enough. And I owe the one who agreed to drop the charge. Otherwise I would certainly have been convicted and a conviction stays with you for the rest of your life. And I understand why some cops might have wanted to beat up everybody. In defending our cities they were constantly under siege. They received about as much respect as those veterans returning from Vietnam, those men who were spat upon for having done what they saw as their duty.

With my white Irish skin and my blue-eyed Irish accent, I must have been a thorn in all their sides. They were defending our cities, trying to tamp down the war at home, while we were still engaged in an impossible war overseas. And yet they found themselves under seige by some of the very same people they were sworn to defend. Still, they didn't treat me badly, except for the one rotten bastard. I owe him nothing. His treatment was effective, so effective that I could barely open my mouth and I couldn't chew. For a few days my diet consisted of soup and mashed potatoes.

I deserved something, some kind of comeuppance. I had drifted away from my brothers: from Frank, now living in Brooklyn, teaching, writing, forging a life for himself and gaining a deal of respect but little recognition among the literati of Greenwich Village. And from Malachy. Married, now, for the second time and riding his own roller coaster of celebrity, Malachy was marching through a string of shows and movies, bars and saloons. And from brother Mike. Mike, very wisely, had moved to California.

⚜

And I have drifted away from Mam. She still lives in my old apartment on West End Avenue. She has become a great New York Mets fan and a keen Bingo player, but I know that she is lonely and hopeless. She still loves a party and is only too happy to get dressed up, to smile and shine, to bask in the recognition given to her by her sons' friends. Even at this late stage, with little urging, she will sing:

> *We are in love with you, my heart and I*
> *And we are always true, my heart and I*
> *When you are far away, each joy's a tear*
> *But it's a lovely day, when you are near*
> *May be that love is blind, when passion rules*
> *Well then my heart and I are just two fools*
> *And yet my darling if we ever said goodbye*
> *I know we both should die, my heart and I*

Never was I comfortable with Mam, after the years of living alone with her in the house in Limerick. I am wary of having her depend on me again. All my brothers are married and I am the prime candidate. I will see her, sometimes, call her, sometimes, and give her money, once in a while; she is struggling and I know it. But as a son I am as selfish as they come.

Ever since my encounter with the police, Jane and I feared another such happening. Our relationship has become strained and we are not doing each other any good. It is time for me to move out of her apartment. I do move out, and decide to return to Dublin.

In Dublin, my plan is to make up the final year, to take the final exams and to earn a degree. But I don't have enough money to hold me, and another rainy year in Dublin, when all my classmates have already moved on, is a gloomy prospect. My plan doesn't hold. After only one week, I return to New York and continue working.

Jackie "Blue Eyes" Larkin gives me a job at Joey Archer's place up on Third Avenue, a bar heavily populated by boxing wannabes. Even when ordering a drink, it seems, every customer feels it necessary to bob and weave, to punch the air, sniff, sniff and shuffle from side to side.

Jackie drinks at the bar, in company with his beautiful, leggy, southern-drawl lady. In comes the middle-aged man, flanked by his two sons. They claim that Jackie insulted or somehow wronged their daughter and sister. Jackie is half Irish and half Italian and he has easy access to either temperament. His great smile can be turned on at will. His hearty laugh bubbles up when bidden. Right now, at this moment, he seems to be hearkening back to some other ancestry. His Asian side, perhaps? He doesn't move and he gives no indication that he has heard the accusation. With perfect impassivity, he stares straight ahead. He doesn't even acknowledge the presence of the father and two sons.

Comes a push and a shove followed by another push and a poke in the ribs and soon the place erupts. All hands on deck. Shadow-punchers and bobbers, weavers and sniffers, all are caught up in the brawl. There's a pile up on the floor. I grab one of the sons in a headlock and take him as far as the door. He assures me that if I let him go, he'll cause no more trouble. I let him go as his father and his brother are pushed out the door.

Someone locks the door and I stand looking out the window. One of the sons takes a run with a police saw horse and rams it through the window in a hail of shattered glass. Little Joe, as he is known, is a five-foot-seven, well-built African American. He has had a couple of fights. Now, when I look outside again, I see that he is flat on his back on the sidewalk, being pummeled by the father. I go outside. It's easy to roll the father away from Joe. The son I had released earlier comes from behind and grabs me in a headlock. He lets me go when I promise, as he had promised. But no one anticipates Little Joe. Bending over and beginning at knee level, he launches an uppercut. The much taller man, the father, is lifted off his feet. Backward he sails. We hear his head hitting the pavement.

His sons pick him up and carry him away. I adjourn inside. Joey, the boss, arrives, along with his brother, to survey the damage. In his black overcoat and white shirt, Joey shows no emotion. With a circular motion of his cigar, he indicates drinks for everyone. The volume on the jukebox is raised. Shadow-boxers and bobbers, weavers and sniffers, all resume their shuffle. I move to California.

· MARIN COUNTY ·

1972

IN SAN FRANCISCO, I inflict myself on my brother Mike and his family for two months. Blind as usual, and heedless of their difficulties, I intrude my presence into an already difficult situation. I need to be reminded of Mike's dictum that when you go to California, it's the end. Beyond California there's no place to go but over the cliff and into the Pacific. I am definitely headed for the cliff, but I'm lucky enough not to have a car to bring me to the edge.

I am sustained by a few odd jobs here and there in San Francisco, but the restaurant and bar business is heavily unionized and it's hard to find a steady full-time job. Mike hears of a bartending job over across the Golden Gate Bridge in Larkspur, in Marin County. I apply and secure the job.

Larkspur, in Marin County, only fourteen miles from San Francisco, is another world entirely. Marin County is a very rich community. A definitely upper-middle class of people lives there. They do the daily commute into San Francisco to work. That is if they need to work at all. These commuters are counterbalanced by a population of rock bands, musicians, hippies, handymen and dropouts.

Stan, my new employer at the Lark Creek Inn, is a smart and energetic businessman. His great, wide, gap-toothed smile, like the edge of a precipice, is overhung by a black mustache. They say he carries a gun. In his velvet jacket, white-shirted cravat and the big-cuffed shirtsleeves, he carries the cultivated look of the gambler.

One day when a neatly wrapped piece of beef shows up in the garbage can outside the back door, it is assumed that an employee had hidden it there with the idea of taking it home later. With a hammer and a handful of nails, Stan nails shut all the windows on the ground floor. And he locks the rear door, the emergency exit. His fury is so great I'm surprised that he doesn't lock the front door as well and keep all customers out. If no one comes in, then no one can steal anything.

And one morning, before opening time, he and a vendor argue and shout at each other for a full five minutes. Something about a bill. The vendor storms out the door. Stan turns to me and asks for a brandy. I pour a brandy into a good-sized snifter. Stan tosses it down, turns away and smashes the snifter against the wall. "I feel better now," he declares.

Up in Madrone Canyon, on Hazel Avenue, I find an apartment. The house is owned and occupied by Mrs. Robinson, her husband and their children. My apartment is above ground level and next to the garage, with a hot plate for cooking and a first-class bathroom wallpapered with nudes. From my window I have a clear and unobstructed view of Mount Tamalpais, or Mount Tam, as they call it. I can see the head, the breasts, belly and thighs: the whole shape of the Princess Tamalpais and her mountain. Mount Tam is a strong spiritual force.

I am one of only two pedestrians in Larkspur. I meet the other, often, on my way to or from my apartment in the Canyon. The sidewalk, narrow and pitted in its disrepair, calls for negotiation on both our parts. I give way to him because he is older. Even more do I give way to him because he walks with a light but determined step.

Five foot five in height and simply dressed in short jacket, pants and shirt, he wears a hat with a feather in the hatband. His grey hair is down to his shoulders. We pass each other, once or twice a day, every day. Never once does he look at me. And why should he? How is he to know that I am always looking for my father?

⁂

Larkspur has the look of a Western town. None of the buildings on the main street is more than two stories high. Limestone is abundant and an overall adobe look completes the illusion of the Western façade.

At one end of town, the Lark Creek Inn, where I work, is new and rustic, bordering on a touristy sophistication. At the Silver Peso, the bar in the middle of town, the most notable tourists are Hells Angels. Always quick and delicious is the cuisine: a prefabricated cheese sandwich from the toaster oven.

And I really like the one-story movie house with its two-stories-high façade. Cheerfully do I maintain the illusion of my Western Town until one day, I realize that the Church of St. Patrick stands at one end of the main street and a one-story building occupied by the Sons of Italy at the other end. These are not the trappings of the Western Town of the movies and of my imagination. Where are the Mexicans, dozing in the sun, crossing themselves and ritually kissing their thumbs? Where is the throng lustily singing "Shall We Gather At The River" as they stand out in the noonday sun to celebrate the hanging?

By now I should have outgrown the movies and at age thirty-two I am an elder statesman among dropouts. I have made no conscious decision to be one. I'm over thirty and I am well aware of the saying, "Don't trust anyone over thirty." It takes me a while to gain acceptance and a little longer to gain the confidence of my fellow workers.

Two of them had been in Vietnam. They're well seasoned. I am innocent by comparison. And, because I drink and don't use drugs, I am
referred to as a "juice freak."

I am for the first time among Mormon women. Melanie, a square-
faced beauty with the air of an artist is the Earth Mother. Tascia of the
golden braids is a no-nonsense person. Like Melanie, she is spoken-
for, but she does laugh at my jokes. They are both attractive women,
but it is the Princess Audrey who takes my fancy. Tall, slender and
fair, across the room she glides. Her hazel-eyed blush is a magnet for
my attention. An aspiring actress, she is linked with Gerry, a photographer. Once or twice, at a party, in a quiet moment, we find
ourselves away from the crush and in a fierce embrace. I tell her that
the electricity between us is positive and irresistible. She doesn't disagree. Next day, when my head clears, I will wonder if I had dreamed
it or if the passion is all mine. After all, isn't she living with Gerry?
An ambitious man, he works mundane jobs in support of his art. My
mundane job is my only art.

I explain my quandary to Dan. Dan is a good listener. White,
middle class and living with his family over in Mill Valley, an enclave
of money and music, Dan is an artist. With a degree in art he could
have found work in the world of art. Instead, he works at the Lark
Creek Inn. He could at least have worked as waiter or bartender, or
even as a cook, but like Bartleby before him, he would prefer not to.
He works, instead, as the principal dishwasher. Tall and skinny, all
flannel shirt and jeans, his long dark hair complemented by a ragged
goatee and a mustache not yet fully grown in, Dan wears a hat with a
feather. He is cool. Sometimes I envy him his detachment.

❦

Dan owns an old U.S. mail van, which he bought at auction. They must love him in super-affluent Mill Valley, when he parks it on the street or in the family driveway. In the van we ride to a party in Larkspur. Dan doesn't drink and, at the party, I drink very little. We leave the party and walk up the main street of Larkspur in the direction of Dan's van.

Come the police. Officer Dunne, in his midnight shades, stops us and asks for identification. Dan manifests an almost Mandarin indifference, which I dearly wish I could muster. He shows his identification and he is free to go. I can't do it. Did I not fight my way from New York to South Carolina, on to Chicago and all the way to Norfolk, Virginia, all in defense of the Constitution of the United States? I've done nothing wrong. Why, then, do I have to identify myself to the Police? "I'll show you mine, if you'll show me yours," I'm tempted to say. But I don't.

I don't refuse to show him my ID. "My wallet is in my back pocket," I tell him. "Go ahead, take it out and have a look." Officer Dunne says no. I will have to produce it. Again, I refuse. He insists. I tell him that I work at the Lark Creek Inn, only a hundred yards away. I give him my phone number, my address and the name of my landlady, Mrs. Robinson. Still Officer Dunne insists and still I refuse. I am arrested, booked, fingerprinted and lodged in the prison at the Marin County Civic Center, a place made famous by a court house shoot-out in 1970.

I had been halfway enjoying this standoff with the overly officious officer. Reality sets in when I have to surrender my clothes and put on the prison overalls. Reality sets in even more when I am locked up in a cell, a holding pen for young desperadoes. Surprisingly or not, for Marin County, the immediate prison population is all white.

In the morning comes the breakfast of molasses topped with molasses. A good colonic cleanser, no doubt, in dried form it would be a perfect stand-in for gunpowder. As the morning wears on, my fellow inmates, each in his turn, will disappear into the tent-like structure that surrounds the toilet. I wonder what they're doing. Whatever it is it seems to be communal. I don't ask. After all, am I not Cool Hand Luke?

All day I keep myself to myself, and into the afternoon. At four o'clock I am brought to the receiving area where my clothes and belongings are returned to me. I am told that I can go. There are no charges against me.

The next day my brother Mike speaks to a lawyer in San Francisco. I am advised that I could sue for false arrest. I think about the idea and reject it. My life in Larkspur could be made very miserable if I sue. The officer had been overly officious, but I had been more than stubborn. Didn't I cause him enough trouble? He has a distinctively Irish name and Saint Patrick's Day is at hand.

With Saint Patrick's Day looming, I am off on my annual preachment about the Saint Patrick's Days of my childhood and the desecration of a fine old holiday by modern-day Irish Americans who find it necessary to turn it into a circus of green beer.

On the evening before St. Patrick's Day, Jenny comes to the Lark Creek Inn. She and I had a night once. I invite her to go for a drink with me after work. "Where would you like to go?" I ask her. "Your place," she answers and the blood sings in my ears. We walk up the canyon, among the redwoods. Jenny lives with Wally. He's an embalmer by trade. As a hobby he is building a model of the *Titanic*, a fitting hobby for an embalmer, I think. I don't ask about Wally. He must be off on a secret embalming mission. Jenny doesn't mention him.

But she does mention St. Patrick's Day, which brings on my standard harangue about the simple beauty of Saint Patrick's Day and its desecration. By the time I am finished, we have reached the door of my apartment. The door stands slightly ajar. I curse my own carelessness as I push it open and walk on in. My apartment is filled with people. It's a surprise St. Patrick's Day party. Even Wally the embalmer is there and I wonder if I might be next on his list. Maybe the party is to be a wake before dying, but, either he doesn't know, or he doesn't care. More likely, his relationship with Jenny is not what I think it is. I am guessing that they are just roommates and that makes me feel better.

An odd feeling it is to be a guest in your own house, especially when the menu is such typical St. Patrick's Day fare as tequila and beer, marijuana and Chinese food. Half the crowd stays over. They coil up on the floor or in my few chairs in search of a few hours rest. Next day, St. Patrick's Day itself, we spend on Stinson Beach. Saint Patrick's Night we celebrate in Sausalito. This is the best Saint Patrick's Day of my life.

That Saint Patrick's Day is prelude to a finale. In late spring of 1973 comes word that the Lark Creek Inn is for sale. A parade of prospective buyers ensues. Among them are the Gotti Brothers, owners of Ernie's Restaurant in San Francisco. I know who they are when they come to visit and I know why they are there. I know, also, that I should be reserved and proper and correct and careful. By their sideways look I can tell that they will not hire me anyway so I am anything but reserved and deferential, the very opposite, in fact. In dealing with them I am overly familiar and I commit the cardinal sin of bartending. I offer them a drink "on the house" after they've had only one.

In an informal vote among the employees I am voted the one most likely to be hired by the Gotti brothers. They hire everyone but me. I am offered not even a trial. I could feel insulted, but I don't. It would never have worked out. We would have been at loggerheads, the new owners and I. So I'll take it as a compliment. But compliments put no money in your pocket. At the beginning of summer, work is mighty scarce in Marin County, but I know that I will find something. As a precaution, for the first and only time in my life, I sign up for unemployment benefits. In a nice, clean office up in San Raphael, staffed by nice, polite, mellow people, I sign up. From then on, at regular intervals, a check arrives in the mail, but my benefits will last only three months instead of the full six. My previous employers in New York did not pay in the full amount.

❦

At the Lark Creek Inn I had met Kjell and Harry. Both of them Norwegian immigrants, they are well established in Larkspur. Seamen, both, they had crossed the Atlantic many times. Once, at least, they had crossed under sail. Tugboat captains now, they operate in San Francisco Bay. Harry goes to great lengths to get me a seaman's card, a federal document, which will qualify me to work as an "oiler and wiper."

The tugboat business is slow at this time and no job is forthcoming, but Harry and Kjell run a small construction business. They give me an occasional day's work, at four dollars an hour, which is decent money. In the mornings I rise early so that I can be at Mr. Scudder's donut shop in time to see Harry or Kjell and maybe catch a day's work. At worst, I get a free read of Mr. Scudder's morning paper.

Kjell, on the short side, is broad and a bit overweight. Inscrutable as he is, behind his dark glasses, I sense that he craves acceptance. I would guess that, like all of us, he wants to be cool, to be mainstream and to be admired. But his heavily accented English and, most of all, his bristly pride, tend to get in the way.

Early one morning Kjell arrives into the donut shop. He has a job for me, down in Pacifica, ten minutes south of San Francisco. As part of the job I will drive him to Pacifica every morning. His driver's license is suspended. The following morning I put my learner's permit in my pocket. We set off for work with me careening all over the road, over the Golden Gate Bridge and on down into the Valley of the Hopeless. Even in Limerick the sun would sometimes shine. In Pacifica the sun averts his face and leaves the field to the overcast sky.

Kjell drops me off, so to speak, and takes the car. I guess that he will use local streets and avoid the highway. He has supplied me with an electric wire brush about two and a half feet in diameter. When I plug it in, it rotates all over the place, like a heavy fan with no base, until I can get a good grip on it. This is a far cry from the cocktail shaker.

Layers and layers of old and encrusted black paint must be stripped from a row of metal fire escapes. By the end of every day I could double for a chimney sweep, but four dollars an hour is four dollars an hour and Kjell is decent. Promptly, at three o'clock every afternoon, he returns. We drive over to the local lounge bar where I wash up in the men's room and Kjell treats us to a couple of beers.

In the late afternoon there are a lot of women in the bar. Most of them bear a married look. I wonder at them. Where are their children? Where are their men? The men must be away fighting a war no one cares about. Or are they temporarily widowed by their husband's work? I don't have much time for speculation. We allow ourselves no more than two beers before I careen us back over the Golden Gate and into Larkspur. Luckily we are not stopped by the police.

The job lasts only a few weeks. Kjell will be killed while driving across the Sacramento Bridge. We never get the full story, but the details are not important. All that matters is Kjell is dead. His death calls for a gathering at his house.

His wife, in her mid-thirties, is destroyed by grief, and at the same time, so thin and pale is she, that she is almost luminescent. The other women, friends and members of the family are dressed in proper Norwegian black. They are nothing short of walking sadness.

Is it my own sick imagining or is there sex in the air? If that's the case it comes as no surprise to me. At age thirty-two, sex is everywhere.

Jenny is at the wake and I walk her home. As we walk in through the front door of her house, in the pitch black, I step on a large lumpy rug. It gives off a baritone growl. The rug turns out to be a very much alive Saint Bernard. But the great dog must be a forgiving sort. He is Wally's dog, Jenny tells me. I have to be careful that I don't become a passenger on Wally's doomed *Titanic*.

I have begun to smoke some. During the summer of '73 "the Great Columbo" arrives. My friend Thomas buys three lids. One he keeps for himself and he sells one each to Jack, my upstairs neighbor, and myself. This Columbian marijuana will mark my conversion from "juice freak" to part-time doper. Thomas, Jack and I gather often. Our pursuit of enlightenment begins with a beer tasting. A couple of lighter beers, an Olympia or a Coors, are followed by a "medium dark" beer and on up to the heavier Anchor Steam, "the wine of the region."

Great bomber joints of the Columbo are passed around. The Gaelic phrase for smoking, *ag ol tabac* translated as "imbibing tobacco" comes to mind. We don't so much smoke that grass as drink it. The joint is passed around, to be tasted, shared and enjoyed like a great bottle of wine.

I read Carlos Castaneda when his books first appeared. He held my interest, but he made only a small dent in my consciousness. In New York, even at the end of the sixties my head was mostly under my armpit. It seemed as if everyone in the country was tripping. Everyone, nationwide, was looking for a new consciousness, but I paid little attention to it. It didn't matter. When you're reared as an Irish Catholic, conscience is all. The uncharted territory of newfound consciousness might well be a hazard to salvation. And a macho man should never admit to any kind of consciousness. An eroded Catholic, I had only a shred of a macho, but even I could not afford to be in possession of even an ounce of consciousness. It would be akin to having committed a criminal act.

Now, in Larkspur, I grab onto a bit of a consciousness, as I go in search of a state of heightened awareness. I have always had a strong tendency to "zone," to focus too narrowly on whoever or whatever is at hand. Now I am learning to look up, look down and look all around.

Susie Parker had worked at the Lark Creek Inn. At this time, I come across the small paperback book on the practice of yoga, which she had given me. Slowly, so very slowly, I begin the practice of yoga. This will be a perfect continuum: yoga by day and, by night, tequila and jay.

And during these days, spent mostly alone and in contemplation of Mount Tamalpais, somehow, from somewhere, comes a copy of *One Hundred Years of Solitude* by Gabriel Garcia Marquez. I had never heard of it, but I enter into the magic. Am I reading the book or am I in it?

Most days are sunshine and never too hot. Mount Tamalpais is clearly visible. My state of meditation, aided and abetted by the morning jay, comes easy, especially outside my door. The little patch of green is perfect for reading and for meditation, with only the birds for company. I am more or less self-sufficient, except for the little head and the long evenings. At sundown, I must still head off down to the Silver Peso or hook up with Thomas or Joe and drive on over to Sausalito.

"Whatever it is you're looking for you won't find it at the bottom of a glass." The old barroom adage is often invoked, either by the biddy in the church-going hat or echoed by the red-faced veteran of many a dram as he drains his whiskey to the last drop. But I keep on looking, in my quest for escape and forgetfulness. Now, as always, perfectly schizophrenic, I devote my days to the search for enlightenment while my nights are passed in the quest for oblivion.

Thomas used to advise me to "store up thousands of hours of music in your head so that you can call up the music when you need it." Thomas should know. In Vietnam he had done advance reconnaissance on foot and he had spent plenty of time in solitude. I guess he had done a little time for drug use as well, and for dealing a little on the side. We spend afternoons storing up the music. For him it's jazz and blues. With his long reddish hair, bright eyes and broad grin, Thomas is all good will. But the grin barely hides a slight menace, a challenge. I would guess that he is well capable of shooting someone, if that someone messed with his wife, his family, his car, his motorcycle or his land.

Tequila and jay cannot allay the guilt, but I try my best. Soon I pass on from *One Hundred Days of Solitude* to Kazantzakis's *The Last Temptation of Christ*. Monkish daytime gives way to nighttime excess. I am marking time. Soon the rat begins to gnaw at the spirit, not in depression, but in despair's first cousin. I become convinced that, like Christ, I will not reach the age of thirty-three. Fortunately, necessity soon defeats despair. My three months of unemployment benefits come to an end and I have to find steady work.

⁂

I had known Norman as a customer at the Lark Creek Inn. His small construction company builds swimming pools, but he is wary of hiring me.

"I've hired restaurant people before and they didn't last," he tells me. I persist. Norman gives way. "Okay, I'll give you a chance." Early in the morning, six men to a truck, we ride out to the site, in convoy. The big cement mixer is driven and operated by Mr. Ben. In his fifties, he looks as if his African American body has been broken by a life of labor. Still he soldiers on. Nothing anymore will surprise his ancient eyes.

The cement mixer is hungry and he must be fed. His is a steady diet of ninety-pound bags of cement and I am his slave. Clasping each bag of cement to my chest, I totter, in desperation, to the hopper where I slit and break open each bag while I thank God for the gravity that will pull the cement down into the hopper. And I thank my stars that I don't fall in head first, along with the cement. Meanwhile I have to ignore the laughter of the rest of the crew and pretend not to notice Mr. Ben. I know why the crew is laughing. Who wouldn't laugh at a man staggering around under the weight of a ninety-pound bag of cement? I'm just the latest in a line of namby-pamby restaurant types and Mr. Ben's averted gaze is no mystery, either. He has seen it before, too many times, I imagine.

After a few days spent gaining strength, I develop a knack for the job. Now that I've learned to swing the bags and not to fight them, I feign a mild disdain as I pick and carry, slit and break, dump the cement and discard the empty sack, all with a small flourish. Comes the day when I dispose of three hundred sacks. I have arrived. That's step one. The bottom and all four sides of the excavation must be lined with cement and the cement is applied with a hose. The hose is attached to the mixer. Some of the cement will always fail to stick to the sides and will fall away to the bottom. I must shovel it up.

I have done plenty of shoveling in my life. This is different. Starting at the deep end, at a depth of nine feet, shovelful by shovelful, I must lob the excess cement straight up. It must land, precisely, on the narrow strip that runs around the edge of the excavation, where another member of the crew will skim it out with a trowel. There can be no waste.

Sick-making work it is. For the first three days I feel like throwing up. Then I settle in and begin, almost, to enjoy the rhythm of it: the gather, the swing and the precise pitch, straight up and right to the edge of the hole. The work becomes more pleasant when I am accepted and invited for an after-work beer with the crew. Now I am a full-fledged fighter jock of the cement bag and the shovel. There's a new comity with everyone except Mr. Ben. He's not unpleasant or unfriendly, but like an accusation, like the god of labor eternal he stands, unbending and apart, definitely apart, from those of us who are just passing through.

Comes the day when we ride out to an estate, in our little convoy of truck and cement mixer. We wait for an attendant to unlock the gate. Up to the excavation we ride. The excavation for the pool has been done, although the building of the house has not yet even begun. This is a first. We suffer a slight unease. Are we not putting the pool before the house?

Starting at eight o'clock we hump and lump and shovel. The morning grows warmer. At noon, three of us ride the truck down what passes for a driveway, in the direction of the nearest hamlet. We are in search of a cold drink and a sandwich. The gate is locked. We could climb over the fence, but we can't throw the truck over the fence. And we need the truck. In our allotted half hour we can't walk down and back. The two married members of the crew have brought food and drink. They laugh at us improvident fools. We curse and drink the tepid water out of the hose. Fuming in our frustration, we kick the blameless bags of cement. But our fury fuels our work and we finish early. Now we must wait for the key man to return and unlock the gate. At three o'clock he arrives and we head off for Sausalito and a few beers.

That is only a small hardship and by the weekend it is forgotten.

Weekends are still my own. On a perfect Saturday afternoon in the fall, I am sitting outside on my patch of green. I look up and there she is, the beautiful Audrey of the light hazel eyes. All elegance and grace, even when standing still, she is framed by Mount Tamalpais at her back. "Hi," she breathes. Her blush is gorgeous and I'm stunned. I can barely open my mouth. Inside, on my bed, she half sits and half reclines. I take refuge in a chair, at the same time taking note of her nervous nonchalance. Soon, in the hanging silence, I am choked by a stifled and stuttering sexual urge.

Milling around in my head are my recent terrible involvement, Audrey's relationship with her boyfriend Gerry the photographer, and all the possible consequences. She and Gerry seem to be happy enough together. I can't bring myself to make an opening move. We talk for a while before she leaves. For years after, I will wonder and regret. I console myself with the thought that she and I are better off, that it is a story with two endings. Was it only a temporary urge? Would she have been sorry later? I can rationalize, but reason brings little comfort when the dream is denied.

To make it worse I will remember my drunken and often repeated insistence on the electricity between us. She seemed to agree. Now, when I have the opportunity, I do nothing and that must be confusing to her. What must she think of my behavior? "The one sin God will not forgive is when a woman calls a man to her bed and he doesn't go." So said Zorba the Greek. That's no help to me. Surely I will be damned. Then again the bed, in this case, was mine and not hers. There may be hope for me. I'll have to ask a Jesuit.

After two months I become bored with my job on the swimming pool crew. The work is hard, but it is bearable. But even with, and maybe because of, my deaf ear, my hearing is uneven and distorted. I can't stand being on top of the noise from the gloppiter-gloppiter cement mixer. I ask Norman for a different job. Pleasant and obliging as always, he tells me that he does have another project going. "You won't like it," he tells me. I tell him that I'd like to try it. "Okay," Norman smiles. "Remember, I warned you."

❧

"You'll be working with two men, father and son. They work well together but they don't like outsiders."

"I think I can get along with just about anybody," I tell Norman.

So it is, that on a late Monday afternoon, I take the bus into San Francisco and report to an area of nearly dilapidated piers. Here are father and son. Am I now to become the Holy Ghost?

Father walks me over to a ladder. Down we climb. On an area of scaffolding, under the pier, we stand at a good height above the water. Temporary lights are strung along the scaffolding. Father hands me a paper mask to wear and a small jackhammer. It's heavy and awkward to handle. I am to remove the old and spalling concrete from a large area on the surface of the pier wall. Father and son will continue their work, in a different area, a distance away.

We start when the tide is out. When the water is a foot below the level of the scaffold we finish. For a week, I chip away. At a pre-appointed time I take a half-hour dinner break. The work and the environment put me in touch with Nature, and with myself. I've never minded working by myself, but I don't like being segregated.

A misstep will land me in San Francisco Bay. With a will of its own, the chipping hammer, first cousin to the electric wire brush in Pacifica, threatens to carry me overboard.

One evening, at father's direction, son and I must work close together and rearrange the planks on the scaffolding. We lift a brand new plank. Son slips, staggers and drops his end of the plank. I am left holding the other end. The plank begins to slide overboard. It's me or the plank. Or so it seems. Could I have held onto it? Maybe I could have. And maybe, just maybe, there's a little bit of malice in me after all. In any case I release the plank and it floats away on the tide.

"You dropped it." Son is quick with the accusation.

"No, I didn't," I protest. "You let go first. I had to let it go or else go with it."

"No, you dropped it," he insists. Back and forth we argue, until, in an attempt to lighten the situation and because I can't afford to make an enemy of him, I try to pass it off.

"What the hell," I tell him. Now comes my thickest accent, oozing with the treacle of *plámás*. "Shur and what's the loss of an oul' plank among friends." Son doesn't laugh.

"It wasn't an old plank, it was a new plank," he corrects me. He will betray me to our father who art on the other side of the pier. I don't doubt that he will. And so he does.

Father points to the rowboat tied up nearby. I had spent a fair amount of time in rowboats in Limerick and I can swim. At ease in the boat, I row and steer well enough. But as I pull away from the pier and the lights I am among the pier pilings. Sentinels against the tide, they loom in the dark and theirs is not a friendly face. Around and around I row. I don't find the lost plank, but I do come upon a plank. It's the same shape and size. Oily, slimy and old as it is, I haul it into the boat and row back to the pier. Father and son are waiting for me when I return. Are they disappointed that I didn't drown? Or that I didn't, at least, have the decency to disappear. I offer up the slimy oily plank. They make no move to accept it. Instead, they engage in a ceremonial scratching of heads and groins, followed by the great picking of the nose. Their only regret, I would guess, is that they can't perform all scratchings and pickings, all at the same time. Finally and in unison, they spit over the side of the pier. With a dismissive shake of the head, father lets me know that the plank is no good.

"Goodbye and thank you and I'm sorry," I tell the slimy, oily plank, as I heave it into the tide. I tie up the boat for the night and go back to work. In a short while, when I know that they are out of sight, I take my little bag, the chipping hammer and mask and, having climbed up the ladder, I leave hammer and mask at the edge of the pier. Will they wonder at my disappearance? I know full well that they won't. I walk up to Van Ness and catch the bus back to Larkspur.

Next day comes a call from Norman, the owner of the company. He sure is a kindly man, especially when I consider the nature of his enterprises. "I told you those two were crazy, didn't I? No one can work with them." He offers to rehire me for the swimming pool crew.

"Thanks and many thanks," I tell him, as I refuse his offer.

❦

Even Marin County is not immune to the various gasoline shortages and the tribulations of President Richard Nixon. The world, in these here United States, is surely coming to an end. Again, for me, it is time to move on. I don't know where I'll go, but I do know that each time I give up on a job or a plan it is a small suicide. I can't seem to help myself. Farsighted and resolute I am not.

The Silver Peso is owned by two sisters, Teeny and Trudy. On each bottle of liquor on the shelves the sisters have clearly inscribed the price of a shot. Their nephew, Sam, runs the place. Sam is known as Sam the Indian. On more than one occasion I have restrained myself from telling Sam that his people and my people have a lot in common, that both have suffered mightily at the hands of an oppressor.

Our twin oppressions resulted in the extermination and relocation of both populations, along with the death of our native languages. Our age-old customs were stamped out, our religion outlawed and our lands taken. The Irish and the Native American Indian, both have a propensity for alcohol. And we have a reputation for making trouble when we drink.

I tell him none of this. Sam might be offended. Besides, my cultivated Cool Hand Luke persona, in cowboy boots and faded jeans, would surely be shattered if I were to start on a recitation of Irish history and the Irish Penal Laws. More importantly, I remember the Dinwiddies of Norfolk and what I did to them, so I keep silent. My instinct proves to be correct. Sam offers me a part-time job. For once I have kept my mouth shut and I can accept without any awkwardness.

On Friday and Saturday nights I work with Jim. Jim's short black goatee matches his jet-black hair. His white shirt with no tie and black vest combination completes his El Diablo costume. He presides at the bar and brandishes his ever ready repartee. He is a cool hand with the dice cups. More often than not, when he and a customer roll the dice for a drink, Jim wins. He will drink a thimbleful of brandy with the loser. Jim will drink with anyone who will buy. The buyers, mostly the younger customers, look to impress Jim and to be accepted by him. There's worship in their gaze as they watch him down thimbleful after thimbleful. No thought is given to his liver, which will pay a hefty price for customers' boosted egos and the bar's jacked-up receipts.

The Peso's four-sided bar features a pinball machine on the side occupied mostly by the older locals. On the opposite side are two pool tables used mostly by the younger hippie group. Of the two sides remaining, one holds the jukebox. The other side presents a blank face to the restrooms. All of this is a fine example of peaceful coexistence. Various factions crisscross at any given time. "If you can't behave, then don't come back," is the simple rule. The rule applies even to the once a month bunch of Hells Angels who show up after their chapter meeting. Their arrival causes a tension among the men and brings out a touch of flirtatiousness among some of the women. But the Angels want to come back, so they avoid trouble by staying with their own group.

As junior partner I work my side of this square bar where trade is more transient. People truck back and forth to the pool tables. From to time, most will undertake the big traipse to the restrooms where, it is rumored, the white powder is traded and dispensed.

The Great Columbo and all the lesser marijuanas that came after it have been enough for me. Cocaine has no appeal. I had one experience with it. During my time at the Lark Creek, one of the hostesses invited me to have dinner at her apartment. With herself and her boyfriend. We had some wine, shared a jay and had a good dinner. Then the boyfriend put out some lines for me to try. I started to laugh. Wine, jay and coke, combined, were too much. Unable to stop laughing, I left my host and hostess in a state of puzzlement. The invitation to dinner, unlikely as it had been, and out of the blue, was probably a recruiting drive.

After two months of weekends Sam tells me that his aunts, Teeny and Trudy, are cutting back on the payroll. This will constitute a major reduction, from four employees to three. Sam is hugely apologetic. He seems to feel worse about it than I do. The Peso will always be one of my three all-time favorite bars in the world. I had been much happier there as a customer than as a worker. Sam pays me off, commiserates with me and buys me a drink. I have to feign a long face as I thank him, but I'm smiling inside for now, with a pocket full of bills, I'm back where I belong, Mr. Cool on a stool, by the jukebox.

Once again I start my days at Mr. Scudder's donut shop with a coffee and a donut and a free read of the morning paper. Poor Kjell is no more, but Harry gives me an occasional day's work. One morning I meet Laura, a New Yorker from Queens. She has a slight limp, the result of a car accident. She is suing, but her circumstances, in the meantime, are not good. We end up sharing some of what we have, in the way of food and drink. She is a puzzle to me. Even with her hard-edged intellectual front, she remains very vulnerable.

Never will I really get to know her, in her holding back, but we keep each other company in a friendly, if wary, fashion. She has the air of someone who has been taken advantage of. I sympathize but her hard edge turns me off. Like me, she is halfway into the hippie life, but unlike me, she is determinedly independent of it.

A doctor friend, in planning a trip to India, had asked her what she would like him to bring her. "A pound of hash," she replied. And he brought it. Hashish is distasteful to me, but I often spend a down-time afternoon in Laura's apartment. Sometimes we talk, more often not. She can be petulant due, perhaps, to the pain from her foot injury.

There is no sex in this almost intimate friendship. The idea of no sex and no likelihood of sex, in such a close relationship with a woman, comes as a complete shock to me. I had spent years and years in boys-only schools. Strictures were imposed on our growing up. My early encounters with women, confined almost entirely to our strictly segregated dance floors, never prepared me for such a relationship as this. I missed having a sister. She might have been able to give me some advice in my early years.

Sex is pushed away and off to the side, but it lurks, as it always does. Once, when I feel a strong stirring, I reach across to her. "What are you doing?" is her only response. Back come the shades of old late-fifties, early-sixties movies. The blonde-haired, blue-eyed high school quarterback plays the stud in the driver's seat with the beloved homecoming virgin queen by his side. He meets no resistance and is making great progress. His shy friend is in the backseat beside the girl with the "reputation." She's known around town as an easy lay. He's begging for only a kiss. Ever so tentatively, he places his hand on her knee. "What are you doing?" she cries, in a world-class burst of outrage. I always thought of it as a ridiculous question. She knew damn well what he was doing. Her outrage was ludicrous. So when I reach across to Laura and she declaims, "What are you doing?" I am tempted to answer, like all the boys of Limerick, "What the hell do you think I'm doing?" But what's the point? This simple utterance, this "What are you doing?" is well timed. Scathing in tone, a bullet to the heart of the ego, it is guaranteed to stopper the music of even the most powerful pipe organ.

And the urge is not that strong.

Hashish lacks the rounded, full-bodied, all enveloping quality of the Great Colombo. Acrid in taste and smell, it puts a bitter edge on the mood. So, to her "What are you doing?" I answer, "Nothin'," in a tone of weary resignation. That's the end of the sex, and I'm not surprised. I had told her of my earlier disastrous involvement. She told me that I was off my head.

✦

Steve is that rarity, a true son of Larkspur, a local. I met him when he worked in the kitchen at the Lark Creek. One night I run into him and we have a drink. I tell him the story of Laura. By way of consolation, he invites me to a party. In his top-down Subaru, in the pouring rain, we arrive at the party completely drenched. But I meet a girl. Much later, she offers me a ride home, for I am still one of Larkspur's two champion pedestrians.

We arrive at my apartment. A drink is out of the question. I don't keep any drink in the apartment. Coffee is a possibility, but I have no etchings with which to sweeten the offer. I have nothing, in fact, except a couple of verses, which I would be lucky to find. So what else can I offer her? I ask myself. "How about a game of chess?" I blurt out and she accepts.

After a few moves and counter moves, onto the bed we tumble. Among kings, queens, knights, pawns and all, we check and mate. At least I think we checked and mated. In the morning she is gone, but she has left a note. If I would like to finish the chess game, I should call her. A few days later I try to call her but one digit is smudged. Even when I try various combinations I have no success and I never do get in touch with her. This leaves me with a bad feeling for she is a good-hearted woman.

Winter in Larkspur, like the walk up and down the canyon, is long and wet. An unadorned diet of vegetables, potatoes, eggs, cheese, bread, coffee and tea and not much of any of it, plus the daily forty-seven-cent pack of cigarettes, all have conspired to make me lean in body and mind.

All during my growing up, America had been the Promised Land. I failed in New York. Not all of it is my fault, but I had my chances and I didn't take advantage of them. California has always been golden. In California, I hoped, I would be given a second chance. But, within six months of my arrival here, I became briefly involved with a woman. This involvement caused great damage to herself, to her husband and to their children. I am very sorry that it ever happened. It could only end badly. And it did. In some situations it is downright stupid to say you're sorry. Sorry is worse than silence.

A fugitive from my own guilt and a bit fearful of retribution, I am distracted. I have been adrift for some years. I have no way of knowing when or where my punishment might appear. With my heart still scarred, there is no place to go now but out.

In early March comes a phone call from Carl. A sometime pal from Dublin and New York he has been minding the store at the Doyle's downtown restaurant since I left. He and his brother are leaving the city. Ms. Doyle had asked him to call me to find out if I might be interested in coming back to work.

Having backed myself into a corner in Larkspur, perspective has taken flight and immediacy is all. It may well be time to go back to New York for a year, to try and pull myself together. I agree to go. A one-way ticket arrives in the mail. I insist that I will return to Larkspur in a year and Thomas, in a great Columbo vision, sees me returning to Larkspur, in triumph, this time in a '62 Corvette. And with a hood-scoop. "With a what?" I echo.

On my next-to-last day in Larkspur I must take the bus into San Francisco on an errand. At the bus stop, two young girls, also waiting for the bus, are sitting on the bench. In front of them, talking and gesturing and, at the same time, showing them something in a brown paper bag, stands my fellow pedestrian, he of the feather in the hat and the light but determined step. He appears to be trying to convince them of something, of something important, at least to him. The girls are paying no attention.

In apparent frustration he turns away and faces me. After carefully removing the contents, he tucks the paper bag under his arm, and holds up a bottle of apple juice. "Drink this every day and you will live a long time," he advises me. "Do this in memory of me," he might as well have said. I am impressed. This is the first time he has ever spoken to me. And I am impressed by his manner, by his earnestness and gravitas. I would like to talk to him but then the bus arrives. The girls and I climb on board. I will never see him again. There's a party for me, a repeat of the Saint Patrick's Day party, with plenty of jays and beer, tequila and Chinese food. I grow sentimental, even a bit tearful. Laura offers her scornful, hard-bitten side. Two days later I board the plane for New York. All my possessions are in my usual two suitcases as I say goodbye to Larkspur, my second spiritual home.

· NEW YORK ·

1974

A SANE PERSON SAVES as much money as possible and rides the bus into the city, but old New York habits die hard. I take a taxi from the airport and over the bridge of the two years that have passed since I left New York City. Or is it two lifetimes? Either way, I am back now, again for the first time, and with eyes wide open.

There's nothing like a newly minted hippie especially when he's a laid-back Mick-hippie or a laid-back hippie-Mick. More especially when this hippie-Mick, already halfway to his pension, is well past the superannuated side of twenty-one. Still fresh from the mellow land of Northern California I follow an old track and head straight into Doyle's Corner Pub on Lafayette Street in Manhattan. Lafayette runs parallel to Center Street and offers a scenic view of Criminal Court, Civil Court, State Supreme Court and Small Claims Court. Down the street and not too far away is Police Headquarters. It's nine o'clock in the evening. Still extant at the bar and at the high tables in the bar area, is a smattering of court officers, clerks, assistant district attorneys and U.S. marshals.

Paranoid I'm not. I swear that I am not. But when, as I walk in, twenty-five pairs of eyes beam in my direction, they're like fifty little flashlights and I am very uneasy. "Is this what they mean when they call them bulls?" Before I went to California, when I had worked at Doyle's for a while, I had kept my distance from law enforcement people and they had paid little attention to me. Now I am very much aware of them and, at this moment, they sure have taken notice of me.

Longhaired and much thinner than I was when I left, I'm a bit wasted looking, you might say. In jeans and boots, with my two suitcases and a guitar, I must seem like a threat. The low lighting in the bar makes it difficult for me to focus. Framed in the doorway and highlighted by the tension, I gain some small understanding of what it must be like to be a black man walking into a white man's bar. One of the court clerks recognizes me from my previous brief tenure and shakes hands with me. Only when I approach the bar and he orders me a drink does the scrutiny come to an end.

Doyle's is owned by the same couple who owned the White Horse Inn uptown on Second Avenue. Separated now, they are teetering on the edge of divorce. Next day, jet lag or no, I am back at work and the money is welcome. When I worked there, I had good relationships with vendors and customers. I have been invited back from California, on a one-way ticket, to help straighten out the affairs of the place. And it will need some straightening out. Am I a hired gun or am I a patsy? Time will tell. The location of the place is both a blessing and a curse. At lunchtime, the place fills up with judges, lawyers, assistant district attorneys, legal aid lawyers, plaintiffs, defendants, detectives, enforcers, expediters, divorcers and divorcees. I am some "hired gun." Everyone but me carries a weapon.

The juror at the bar may be an advertising executive or a belly dancer, a plumber, or a fisherman, a secretary or a writer. You never know. On the first day of jury duty, when they come for lunch, they all exhibit the same glazed look. By the third day even the belly dancer has begun to relax into her role as just another juror. There's no longer any need to explain herself. A camaraderie develops, nurtured by the affable, silver-haired banker. He's made even more affable by his two-

or three-martini lunch. The limits of this camaraderie are defined by the scribe at the end of the bar.

Some years before, my friend, Billy, was working at this same bar. When he overheard someone discussing the details of a criminal case. He told someone else the details of the case. Subpoenaed, and hauled into court, he had to tell what he knew and when and how he knew it.

Toward the end of lunch, Ms. Eunice Jennings, a lawyer specializing in drug and sex crimes, appears at the end of the bar. She is brimming with curiosity. "How many martinis did he have?" she asks, as she inclines her head in the direction of the banker at the center of the bar. We are on a first-name basis, Eunice and I. Why not answer her? But instinct holds me back. I tell her that I don't know. Again she asks, this time in a disbelieving tone.

"You don't know?" she accuses.

"He paid cash. I don't remember how many he had."

"Billy would remember, wouldn't he?" Again she accuses.

"Yes, Billy would remember," I answer in response to her accusation.

I have to agree with her. Yes, Billy would remember. And look what happened to him, I want to add. But I don't want to argue with her, so I just walk away. Ms. Jennings turns away in disgust.

I am guessing that if I had told Ms. Jennings that the juror in question had three martinis, she would have hauled me into court. I would have had to testify that the juror in question had consumed about half a fifth of gin. And at lunchtime, mind you. Ms. Jennings, devious in defense of her client, would have had herself a nice mistrial and I would be to blame.

I sure don't want any problems with good guys or bad guys, or with subpoenas and conniving attorneys, Your Honor. I'm happy to be back and working in New York. And I'm happy to see that the camaraderie among the jurors still prevails. Even Ms. Jennings and her intrigues can't infringe upon that.

For some customers, a late lunch will wear on into early evening. Judge Ramirez is careful as to how he is perceived in public. He appears strictly at night. A bantamweight boxer in his youth, now entering into middle age, the judge is short but still trim. His thin mustache is carefully curried. In a contest, his tiny, perfectly rounded paunch, would take first place in the bantam belly class. When he orders a drink he proffers no money. I am duty bound to deliver his drink. Custom demands that I go through the motions of starting a tab for him, by taking pen and bar check in hand. This always disturbs him. From under his evil little mustache, "Put it down to experience," he will hiss at me. And at a volume low enough so that no one else will hear. Carefully he sips at his drink. By the time he has almost finished it, a new patsy will have appeared and will offer to buy his next drink. With carefully modified reluctance, the judge will accept.

Judge Ramirez is still a bantam with a secretary who is twice his size. Sometimes they have a drink together. All goes well until the day when his chief assistant court officer, I am told, sent to deliver an urgent summons, knocks a cursory knock at the door of the judge's chambers. In his haste he pushes open the door and there, in full view, are the moons of the bantam cock justice, naked except for his robe, pumping away on top of his questionably blonde secretary. Hastily, the court officer withdraws. The judge's secretary never comes to the bar again.

Bantam judge is on friendly terms with William, a senior court clerk, and it is no wonder. Both are cut from the same cloth. They are constitutionally incapable of ever putting any money on the bar, except that William uses a different modus operandi. I can see him through the windows of the sidewalk café. From his Lincoln, parked in the street outside, he keeps faithful vigil. When he sees that one or two pigeons have entered the bar, most casually he will saunter in. With a show of feigned surprise he will greet everyone, especially the designated pigeons. With great good fellowship he will accept the offer of a drink from pigeon number one, possibly a junior court clerk seeking promotion. Or he may be a lawyer who needs to have his case dealt with by a particular judge. The free drink will get William's attention. A drink is fine, but his Lincoln doesn't run on alcohol, nor will it pay his mortgage, after all. The favor will cost a lot more than a drink. That discussion will come later and in a private place.

Seymour, a lawyer and a decent one at that, barely acknowledges William. That tells me a lot. Seymour is liked and well respected. He represents tenants only. He foregoes the large fees he could earn by representing landlords.

I don't need a landlord and tenant lawyer. I don't even have an apartment. During my first week back in New York I stay in a one-night-stand hotel in the Times Square area. Cockroaches keep me company and, for reasons unknown, I receive a free copy of the *Daily News* every day. On my third night there, a woman enters my dream. She is wielding a whip. Jolted awake, I can't go back to sleep, so I look through the *Daily News*, all the way to the back pages, all the way to the next day's race card. A horse named "Lady Whip," calls out to me. The next day a friend, who has a friend who knows a bookie, places a bet for me. Lady Whip doesn't let me down. She wins, and pays a hefty price.

My brother Frank and his wife, Alberta, come to visit me during my first week back. They suggest that I "house sit" their Brooklyn brownstone, the same house in which they had rented an apartment before buying the house. They will be away in Spain for the summer. The previous owner, in a fit of jealousy, had shot and killed her husband. The shooting happened in the two-room basement. I am to live in this basement for the summer. Fresh from the vibes of the one-night-stand hotel and still haunted by Lady Whip, I ask Frank where the murder took place. It happened in the back room, close to the garden, according to Frank. I select the front room as my sleeping area.

Every day, after work, the subway carries me on the short hop from downtown Manhattan to the apartment in Brooklyn Heights. In the garden, under the lilac tree, I settle in to read. Lilacs are overhead, underfoot and all around. All I need is a visit from the Princess Audrey. And I certainly wouldn't make the same mistake twice.

All grin and grass, in cowboy boots and contact blue eyes, my friend Thomas arrives from Marin. Compact in build and neatly packed, he brings an even more neatly packed bag of marijuana. Of a high quality, the grass would be enough to mellow out all of Brooklyn. Thomas takes his place in the back room in the basement. I don't tell him what happened there.

By special arrangement with the boss lady in the restaurant, Thomas comes to work with me as an apprentice. Working for tips and food he will soon learn the jargon, the drinks and the names of the regular customers. In a matter of weeks he graduates and becomes a regular full-time paid employee. In celebration we smoke it up, drink it up and paint the floor of the entire apartment. The paint will have to dry. We have painted ourselves out of the apartment. No matter. We continue our overnight celebration in the garden.

On Fridays, due to the volume of business, our day's work carries over until ten o'clock. Between shifts, in late afternoon, we adjourn to the liquor room downstairs to smoke a jay. Back upstairs we must face James Perkins, special assistant to the special district attorney for narcotics. He's a regular on Friday nights, along with his dancing troupe of assistant district attorneys. Loyalists and zealots, to a man and to a woman, they are always in tow.

James Perkins likes to flip coins for drinks. Sometimes I will beat him. "Only an honest man can beat me," he declares. Is he praising himself or is he praising me? Or is he joking? All of the above, I would guess. I smile. He's a decent sort and an honorable man and he's no zealot. Where did he go wrong, I wonder, that he should have become a prosecutor? I guessed that he needed a steady job and a pension. It seems to be a wise choice.

Every Friday night comes a full complement of court clerks, assistant district attorneys, legal aid lawyers, judges, jurors, court officers and clerks, all in search of escape and relief. On this Friday evening comes a black man. He is in his early thirties. As he wanders from table to table, he pays particular attention to the women. The court officers suggest that he move on. He ignores them. I can see what's about to happen. I approach him and suggest that he come with me. "Don't worry, we'll take care of him," the court officers chime in. "I know you will, and thank you. But for now I have to be in charge here and this man belongs to me."

Next-door is a parking lot, empty and unattended at night. Franklin Street itself is very quiet at this time of night. The court officers could have taken him there. No one would have heard anything. Instead, I walked him outside and he must have grasped the situation. "Thank you," he says to me, on the sidewalk outside. Maybe I should have thanked him. And I did, later in the evening, when I found out why he had been in court that day. He had been charged with a felony. For shooting a bartender in the behind.

❦

Thomas had come to New York to learn bartending and to see the city. Three months have passed. His training is complete and he leaves for California. I continue my evenings in the garden.

One evening I work late and Bobby Jordan and Patricia and I are having a drink before going home. Patricia tells me that Lynn is coming downtown to meet her and to see me. Lynn arrives. She is as beautiful as ever.

We have drinks and we dance. I suggest to Lynn that we go somewhere else. Just the two of us.

⚜

All that summer Lynn and I are together while Frank and his family are away in Spain. More than once I tell Lynn that she should not depend on me, that I will be going back to California the following March. "Yes, I know," she says. She knows more than I do. She talks me into buying cups and plates and cutlery, for me a very serious step. When, at the end of August, Frank and his family come back from Spain, Lynn prepares a welcome home dinner for them.

Over dinner, Lynn recounts her first meeting with Frank and his wife. Early that summer, Lynn had stayed over with me. In the early morning, I left for work. Because mine was a garden apartment the gate outside the front door was kept locked. And I had locked the inner door, which led to the stairway. Lynn did not have a key and when she set out to go to work, her only way out was through the garden, which gave no egress to the street. After climbing up the fire escape to the first floor she knocked on the window. Frank's wife, thinking it was the cat, went to the window. Seeing Lynn in all her splendor, she opened the window and let her in. Lynn hurriedly explained herself and walked through the apartment in order to get to the front door. There was Frank, in bed with the blanket pulled up to his chin.

"Good morning," he said.

"Good morning," said Lynn. And she ran. Now, over a good dinner, we can laugh about it.

And on the following Monday morning, toward lunchtime, I'm back at work when, with barely a greeting, a brand new juror walks up to the bar.

"I'll have a blum-de-blum-de-blum-de-blum, very cold, very dry, straight up. Nothing in it. Not even your finger." I can share in the joke. It is by way of telling me to belay the olive, the lemon and the onion. He is a writer, or an editor, I would guess, when he lays out book and notebook and applies himself to reading and making notes. On Tuesday, with a halfway friendly greeting, again he begins his drink-ordering recitation: "A blum-de-blum-de-blum…" I finish it for him. "Yes," I say, "I know, I know. Nothing in it. Not even my finger." He smiles, loosens up a bit and, by the time an hour has passed we have exchanged a few pleasantries. On Wednesday he even greets the juror closest to him at the bar.

The scribe and I actually discuss some matters of politics and sports, even a little personal history. On Thursday he greets me in a friendly way, spares me the recitation and the worn joke, orders lunch, eats most of it and settles to his book. Then, with a startled air, he looks up, takes a good pull on his drink, pays his check, shakes hands on a hasty farewell and strides out the door. I'm surprised, but I assume that he will be back the next day. I expect that he will, at least, finish out the two weeks of jury duty, but he doesn't come back on Friday. Nor does he appear during the following week.

A month later Lynn tells me that she had met a friend of hers for lunch. This friend had had drinks with Lynn's old boyfriend. The boy-friend told of his lunchtime visits to a bar and restaurant downtown. He had enjoyed talking to the man behind the bar, until he heard the bartender called by name. Lynn had remained friends with friends of the old boyfriend. She told them about me. Now, upon hearing my name called, the old boyfriend put it down to coincidence. But, when the same person asked, "How is Lynn?" he knew that was no coincidence and that it was time for him to go. With some regret, he left. Sometimes there is honor in retreat.

In September I move from my basement apartment in Brooklyn to Lynn's place on East 79th Street. From her eleventh-floor living room, there is a clear view of midtown Manhattan and points south. This is a serious move. Lynn is not from Ohio or California. No, she's a native New Yorker, of Russian-Polish-Jewish stock. She is close with her family.

All of my protestations have been taken by the wind. I will not be going back to California. "How would you like to be buried with me mother's people? I am tempted to ask Lynn, by way of an Irish marriage proposal. "It's time for a priest and a rabbi," I suggest, instead. Lynn doesn't disagree and I take it as a yes.

Some streak in me won't let me get married to Lynn while I'm living in her apartment. In the *Sunday Times* I find an ad. Twice as large as the average ad and printed in large type, it is written in plain English, without the usual abbreviations. There's no agent and no fee to be paid for this rundown apartment in a once well-kept building. There are high ceilings and space enough, I think, to show movies in the living room. But it doesn't really register with me that we will actually be living there. I haven't lived anywhere, for any length of time, since I left Limerick fifteen years ago.

Not only is the building in decay, so is the whole West Side. Lynn's family, disturbed at our choice of location, will ask each other, "Why is he taking her to live over there?" Damned if I know, I am tempted to reply. Why does anyone live anywhere?

Two brothers had lived in the apartment for more than thirty years. They must have liked the original dark green paint for they never repainted. They were succeeded by a young couple who used a razorblade to carve a diagonal line from top to bottom on every wall in every room. They retained the original dark green on the upper half. The lower diagonal area they painted blue in one or two rooms but mostly the lower half was painted black.

Ceilings come with small tufts of wool stuck to them. Thankfully, there are no bloodstains. In my marijuana-cum-tequila-cum-yoga state of mind I smell ritual practices, because of the tufts on the ceilings. And there are some strange diamond-like designs on the walls. But it's the candle grease all over that makes me uneasy. I am even more uneasy when I realize that we are only one block from the Dakota Building, the location for the filming of *Rosemary's Baby*.

Fortunately Lynn doesn't suffer from my Celtic superstitions. The couple who lived there before us had been evicted. Lynn suggests that they had been unable to pay the electricity bill and used candles instead. Hence the candle grease. I have to agree. I am still bothered by the little tufts of material on the ceilings, but I say no more. This is a big apartment, at a decent rent, and we want it.

"Lots of work and pay the rent," Lynn's mother says, when, for the first time, she sees the apartment. My mother is impressed by its size. Families and friends help us to plaster and paint. At Thanksgiving both of our families come for dinner and at Hanukah, and, again, at Christmas. People seek us out. Being on the verge of marriage seems to have created a magnetic field around us. Divorce is not like that. Nobody boards the sinking *Titanic*.

❧

Our friend Charlie Smith, a practicing Catholic, gives us the name of a rabbi. With some reluctance, the rabbi agrees to perform a Jewish wedding ceremony and he recommends a priest as co-celebrant. Priests and rabbis willing to perform a mixed ceremony are rare, but Father Jacobs, following a brief interview, agrees to do it.

Patricia, the maid of honor, had been instrumental in reuniting

Lynn and myself. My friend, Frank Ward, agrees to come over from Ireland and to act as best man. Lynn's brother Lewis will give her away. Best of all, the rabbi promises to bring the chuppah, the canopy held over the heads of the bride and groom during a Jewish wedding ceremony. Charlie Smith and George Byrnes, both gentiles and both in the six-foot-six range in height, will hold the two rear poles. My brother Frank, the third gentile, and Danny Cooke, the only Jewish chuppa holder, will hold the two poles in front.

The wedding will be held at a non-denominational church on West 35th Street. Because of a lack of funds and my own aversion to being dictated to by some officious factotum of a maitre d', the reception for a hundred people will be at our apartment. Tables and chairs will be rented. The food will be cooked at Doyle's, with Ms. Doyle's gracious consent, and will be delivered and served by Mr. Wong and Mr. Cho.

Our lack of furniture is a blessing. Lynn sets up two rooms, café style. Sam, the jukebox man from Doyle's, delivers a jukebox to the back room. "The Anniversary Song," with its old Yiddish melody and sung by Al Jolson, has been a great favorite in my own family. By coincidence, Al Jolson had been a great favorite of Lynn's late father. "The Anniversary Song" will be perfect as our one special request.

Frank Ward arrives from Dublin and we put him up in a hotel. On the night before the wedding, Lynn leaves me and goes to spend the night with her mother and her friend Sandy on East 9th Street. We must not be together on this night, but we will stay in touch by phone as we await the morning.

On that Saturday morning, the day of the wedding, in the small bathroom in the rear of the apartment, I set out to change a broken light switch. This genius certainly knows how to replace a light switch and knows that it is not only wise, but necessary, to turn off the power at the breaker before commencing work. For some reason, genius decides to work "live" and blows all the lights in the apartment. To make things worse, I got off on the wrong foot with Leo, the building superintendent, on the day we moved in. Leo answers my call. Sensing perhaps, that he is dealing with a lunatic, he shows mercy. Quickly he installs a new switch and restores power to the apartment.

I try to call Lynn at Sandy's apartment to report progress, but telephone service below 14th Street has been suspended. My Juliet is incommunicado and I am left to my own devices. Frank Ward picks me up and we make our way to the church. This eighth of March, 1975, is a chilly but lively day of racing clouds and blustery winds. Under a sky full of rain we assure each other that it's all for the best of luck.

Of the invited guests more than a few are old-fashioned Irish American Catholics. They might be uncomfortable in a non-Catholic church, especially at a mixed Catholic and Jewish wedding. Or they might just look at it askance. Some members of Lynn's family are older European Jews. They, also, might look askance. Two groups, both looking askance and from opposite directions, could end up at war with each other. Their askances might collide in the middle.

We're taking no chances. The more traditional Catholics and Jews are invited to the reception at our apartment. Those thought to be more accepting will come to the church wedding and to the reception.

Groom and best man, chuppa-holders and guests, we all wait. My well-attended bride-to-be waits in the church office with Father Jacobs. As yet, there's no rabbi. "Where is the rabbi, where is the chuppa?" we ask each other, as the designated chuppa-holders eagerly await their assignment. And still we wait, as a half hour stretches into an hour. Still no rabbi. Still no chuppa. An hour and a half has gone by. Lynn becomes distressed and who would blame her?

By telephone we learn that our rabbi is at the hospital, attending at the bedside of a very sick friend. He's not coming. Father Jacobs calls a hasty conference and tells us that he has a friend, a rabbi friend. He will try to enlist him. Born of a Jewish father and an Irish Catholic mother, Father Jacobs completed his service in the U.S. Navy and decided to become a clergyman, either as priest or rabbi. He chose, eventually, to become a Catholic priest. He is well versed in Hebrew and in Latin and, in the absence of the rabbi, volunteers to perform a semblance of a Jewish as well as a Catholic ceremony. Tears are dried. Hysteria is held at bay. Heart attacks are put on hold. The wedding group gathers, again, at the rear of the church.

Up the aisle and toward the altar Father Jacobs leads us. Then it comes, loud enough for everyone to hear, this high-pitched beep-beep-beep. Father Jacobs excuses himself. The wedding procession comes to a halt. Back to the church office he goes and, in a few minutes, he returns. He is smiling. The little procession again moves forward. At the altar, Father Jacobs whispers that his friend, the substitute rabbi, will meet us back at the apartment.

Bearing a passing resemblance to Woody Allen, Father Jacobs ascends the steps of the altar. Turning now to face the congregation, ever so softly I hear him breathe one word, "Woody." Is he seeking guidance from the great director? He doesn't need any. Able man that he is, Father Jacobs performs an impressive, though abbreviated, Jewish ceremony, followed, immediately by the Catholic version. We have done it the Jewish way and the Catholic way. We could have taken up the missionary position, right there and then and no one would have disapproved. We could have gone Buddhist or Hindu for a day, even Protestant, God help us, just as long as we got it done. Following the long delay in getting started and the length of the double ceremony, there is a shifting in the pews.

Say I do, say I did, say I will, say I must. Say guilty as charged, Your Honor. Say your mother. Say anything, promise anything. Whistle "Dixie" for God's sake. Sing us "Temptation." Do something, do anything. Just get us out of here. That's what I imagine I hear from our worn-out, pew-bound families and friends. In the end I kiss my bride. Once, I kiss her, for old times' sake, once more, as a promise and a third time for good luck. Down the aisle at last we go back the way we had come.

Buoyed down the aisle by cheers and good wishes and a good many sighs of relief, we make our way to the back of the church, sign the register in the church office and take refuge in one of the two waiting limousines. Back at our apartment the bar is in full swing. Peter Myers presides. Peter and I worked together at Doyle's Corner Pub. He had agreed to be bartender at my wedding if I would do likewise at his impending. Within two weeks of our announcements, Gerry Burke, the third bartender at Doyle's, had caught the fever and decided to get married. Bobby Jordan, bartender number four, left town. From matrimony he found sanctuary in Cape Cod.

Rings the doorbell, and rings and rings, as the apartment fills up. The untouchables, the more traditional Jews and Catholics, are joined by the crowd from the church. Lynn, released at last from anxiety, has begun to relax. Father Jacobs arrives and is introduced all round. His Jewish-Catholic pedigree is a great source of wonder, especially among those who had not been at the church.

After an interval the ringing doorbell conjures up Rabbi Bruce Goldman. Large, bearded and vigorous, he is clad in black hat, black suit and white shirt. He has the look of a man who has outrun his pursuers only by riding over high mountains and across miles of perilous prairie. I fully expect him to dust off his chaps with his hat. Is he wearing spurs? He is not, but I swear that I can hear them jingling.

It is clear that Rabbi Goldman has agreed to perform the wedding ceremony only as a favor to his friend Father Jacobs. It is equally clear that he is very anxious to meet my brother Malachy. "Is Malachy

McCourt here?" is his first question. I go and find Malachy and introduce the two of them.

After a hurried conference with Lynn and myself in the back
room, Rabbi Goldman appears to be satisfied. We can proceed. In the
living room Father Jacobs again performs the Catholic part. Rabbi
Goldman joins in and back and forth they go in an ecumenical tennis
match of a wedding ceremony.

In Jewish tradition, at the end of the wedding ceremony, the
groom must step on a glass and smash it. This will symbolize an end
to needless violence. In the spirit of the age and with a nod toward
feminism, Lynn and I are each assigned a glass to smash. A woman's
wedding shoes are not combat boots. Lynn has a little trouble smash-
ing the glass so we must join forces. In unison, we smash the second
glass. "Mazel tov!" rings out. Once again we are married.

Our friend, Pat Higgins, an old-fashioned Irish American Catholic, had not been invited to the church for fear that he would be
uncomfortable. Pat is introduced to Danny Cooke, the only Jewish
chuppah-holder. "Any relation to the man across in Saint Patrick's?"
Pat asks. He's referring to Cardinal Cooke. Danny starts to laugh.
Pat quickly realizes his mistake. He is at first, abashed, but Danny's
laughter puts him at ease and they end by laughing together.

Lynn's great uncle, Carl, originally from Eastern Europe and now
in his mid-seventies, is a bit bewildered at first until he too is drawn
into the spirit. His European wife, Marylin, a survivor of the Holo-
caust, is a bit tentative. I wonder if she will approve. I ask her directly.
"You'll be okay," she nods, as the noise swells. Plentiful food and
drink fuel the tide of goodwill. Or is it just relief, that after all the
confusion and delay, the thing is finally done?

Husband and wife now, Lynn and I have our first dance in the
back room, but on the jukebox, the "Anniversary Song" has somehow
become the "Anniversary Waltz," not the same thing at all. Ordinar-

ily, this might be cause for a pound and a half of dismay, but, after all that has happened, it's a minor detail.

Three days and two nights are the duration of our honeymoon. From our room at the Plaza Hotel we can see the junction of our street and Central Park West. *Desaparecidos* in the city, part of the anonymous throng, we are free to roam without obligation or schedule.

❦

By the following Wednesday I am back at work and I am reminded of what they used to say on the Upper East Side. "A swinging singles bartender makes the cash register ring." A swinging bartender I never had been and I am no longer single.

During the last year at Doyle's I have been de facto manager. As chief purchasing person, principal hirer and firer, diplomat and ambassador, I've had access to everything, it seems, except the real inner workings of the place. Married, now, I can no longer give it my undivided attention and I can't work as many hours. Soon I detect a subtle, chilling shift in the atmosphere and an inkling that I will no longer be the favorite son. It's time to start looking for something else.

My brother Malachy is between acting jobs. He calls to ask if I need any help, so I ask him to come down. We end up sharing the nighttime bartending. Malachy is terrific at entertaining customers. Sometimes it happens that an uptown saloonkeeper comes downtown on official business. He may have been summoned downtown by the Health Department perhaps, or by Consumer Affairs. Before undertaking the hazardous trip back uptown, the saloonkeeper will "stop in" for a drink. God knows he needs it, believes he needs it, or believes, at least, that he owes it to himself as payment for his hazardous trip downtown.

By old habit, or by design, the displaced saloonkeeper, down-town now, will take up, as his post, the corner seat at the end of the bar closer to the door. From this perch he can observe the faucet as it drips into the sink. And he can keep a close eye on the bartender. There's an intimacy to it. Better still, his face is to the door, his back to the wall.

Malachy is well experienced in the bar business. When Mr. Up-town Saloonkeeper insists on talking business, and only business, Malachy grits his teeth. "It's bad enough that I owned a few bars and that I now have to work in a bar," he confides to me. "Do I also have to tolerate this tiresome analysis of the Manhattan saloon business?" But he knows that he has no choice. He listens and suffers.

After an hour or so, Malachy's head begins to tilt forward toward his chest. Rousing himself, in desperation he offers a silent prayer. A second refugee comes through the door. He turns out to be the owner of another uptown saloon. He takes his place at the second best van-tage point, the end of the bar furthest away from the door. My end of the bar.

Delicacy is called for now. The newcomer knows Malachy and Malachy must give him his share of attention. Barely into his second drink, the newcomer launches into his own detailed analysis of the bar business. East 77th Street and Second Avenue is his world. Mala-chy listens and nods a comment, as needed, here and there, until he begins to droop and to weary. Each of these saloonkeepers is a foun-tain of endless cliché and a citadel of monumental certitude. Like crouching tigers of psychic destruction they lurk, one at each end of the bar. There's no escape.

Malachy's prayer is answered. Inspiration strikes. "John," Mala-chy interrupts, "do you know Paddy Lynch?" And he almost chuckles, as if it has just come to him. With a sideways nod, Malachy indicates the first refugee saloonkeeper in the far corner. "Paddy," he calls out to the corner-sitting saloonkeeper, "you know Jack Olmstead, don't you?"

The two saloonkeepers wave to each other. After some tentative and uneasy banter, the second refugee moves down and joins the first. Blessedly soon they are deep in conversation and in a very short time they will outdo each other in buying drinks for the bar. Malachy's tactic brings a triple benefit. His sanity and mine are saved. And he has drummed up some business.

Malachy doesn't stay long at Doyle's and I will miss his company.

It is the fall of 1975, in the half light of early evening. In his porkpie hat, black overcoat to the knees and white shirt open at the collar, with short pudgy steps a man advances toward the bar. His eyes are a dead stare. Very still he stands, with his eyes rolling away in his head, at a forty-five-degree angle.

"How ya doin', Chief?" he offers.

Chief is off tonight, I'm Ace, I'm tempted to answer, but I don't. There's a touch of good will and a strong hint of self-mockery in his greeting. He has stepped into the light. He is taking refuge from the dark, deserted, cheerless, downtown street. What does he want but a chance to join in the charade?

He orders a rum and coke. No money is tendered. But then again, isn't New York City, like Montreal, just loaded down with eccentric millionaires? Any request for payment, no matter how great my misgivings, could be troublesome. A badly timed request for payment will destroy even the illusion of an illusion.

From then on once a week Sidney will appear. Peggy is uneasy in his presence. I can't blame her. He's very odd. Lacking any cloak of respectability, he is the opposite of Law and Order. He just doesn't fit. Worse, while he orders the sweeter and more expensive drinks, such as Harvey's Bristol Cream and Kahlua and cream, money does not enter into the transaction. With no heart for turning him away, I have no choice but to pay for his drinks. I would guess that Sidney is Jewish, but that doesn't get in the way of his weekly dissertation on the Egyptians and their civilization. Sidney is convinced that the Egyptians were masters of magic.

From then on, Sidney appears about once a week. He invites confidence and, after a few weeks, when I tell him of my plan to open a place of my own, we discuss money. Why am I talking to him about money? He doesn't even pay for his drinks and he doesn't seem to have any money. But he invokes the magical powers of the Egyptians. "Don't worry about the money," he tells me. "You'll get what you need." When I ask him how, or where, "Don't worry, you'll get it," is all he says. Who is Sidney? How can he be so sure?

***

At this time, Thomas sends me a newspaper clipping from a Marin County newspaper. The man, my old pedestrian friend, the apostle of the apple juice, has died. I should have paid more attention to the feather in his hat. He was a Native American Indian. Maybe that's why he kept his distance. And he was ninety-four years old. Must be something to be said for drinking apple juice.

***

A senior clerk in the Civil Court has befriended Lynn and myself. When I tell him that I am planning to move on, he suggests that if I ever find a premises and decide to open a place of my own, he is prepared to put up some money. This is reassuring, for I am golden boy no more. My time at Doyle's is coming to an end.

That summer Lynn and I steal away for a week, to the island of Chebeague the Great, off the coast of Maine, where Gene Webb works on his gothic novels while his wife, Nancy, ministers to us. I'm free to walk around the island, to ride a bike and to work up a good Maine chill. The sherry in the evenings is a great and easily justified antidote. Only once does the sun appear and that's on the ferry back to the mainland. We gain a touch of color. Otherwise no one would believe that we have been away.

1976

"SHE'S WORKING ON her second," said the Irishman, when his wife became pregnant with their second child. Lynn is now working on her first. Thanksgiving comes. And Christmas. Both families come for dinner and we move on into the New Year. The baby is due in April.

Self-centered as always, I am more than a step removed from Lynn's pregnancy. It isn't really happening to me. I'm not ready. We have no money and no insurance and I wonder how we will manage. We'll manage in the same way as I always managed, I tell myself. Which is no way at all. When things became too difficult I had moved on to the next situation, the next location, the next job and I had always done it without giving it much thought.

Lynn has always worked more than one job at any given time. Among them is a position as coordinator for a group of film editors. In her role as secretary and bookkeeper to a psychiatrist, she sits in a quiet side office. She must not see or be seen. By contrast, she had enjoyed working part-time as a waitress. The job gave her a chance to be in but not a part of the singles bar scene. Besides, the money is good.

She had worked at CBS as a young executive in charge of film library services. Once, at someone's whim, she was dispatched, as part of a film crew, to Saint Patrick's Cathedral. They were to cover the funeral of Cardinal Spellman in 1967. Cardinal Cooke had succeeded Cardinal Spellman. Lynn, in her mini-skirt, was lucky enough to encounter the new cardinal, face to face. "Are you part of this circus?" he asked her.

"Yes, I am," Lynn answered.

"This is a funeral," the new cardinal told her. "This is no place for little girls in little skirts."

By the time Lynn returned to the newsroom at CBS, everyone knew about the incident. Summoned by the news director, she was told that if she planned to return to the Cathedral the next day and cover the funeral, she had better be properly attired. The following morning she reported to work in a long, drab, brown dress. "What happened to you?" a coworker asked. "You look like you're going to a funeral."

"Perfect," said the news director.

Lynn still freelances as a photographer. Always ready to go, as I begin to find out, she sleeps with a few pieces of jewelry on, just in case someone calls with an invitation to a party. Thus does she reinforce my own notion that when men yawn they are tired and that women yawn only when they're bored. A woman, if she is interested, will go for three nights without sleep. A man is hard put to stay awake for one night.

⁕

Creative and innovative and with a keen eye for color and space, Lynn now delights in setting up our back room for the baby. She gives up all her jobs except for her job with the psychiatrist.

A week before the due date a slight complication sends Lynn to the hospital for a few days. On Palm Sunday, one week before Easter, she is still in hospital. Her mother, Miriam, comes to visit. Miriam, of the Polish-Russian-Jewish stock, had stopped off at a Catholic church. She arrives now, at the hospital, bearing a sprig of palm and presents it to her daughter. It is a fine ecumenical gesture. Lynn, in her impish way, is equally ecumenical. "Your Lord was one of us," she will remind me. "And so was His mother," There's no denying it.

Lynn has been home from the hospital for a week. Late at night the pains begin. I'm cool. I don't have any pain. "Time the contractions by the clock on the wall, not by the clock in your head," they had told us at the Lamaze class. Yes, I am cool. It's after midnight. In the Lamaze class they said that the husband might get hungry at the onset of labor pains. Sure enough, the husband is hungry. In the kitchen I make myself a grilled cheese sandwich. It tastes so good that I make myself another. The pains begin to come more often and with greater intensity. The doctor, on the phone, orders us to the hospital.

Lynn is whisked away. I am consigned to the excess baggage room reserved for expectant fathers. Time and again, over the next several hours, I will leave the waiting room and ask for progress reports. "Go back and wait," I am admonished. I do as I am told. All through the night I will sit and nod, wake and ask, sit and nod, and ask again. "Be patient and wait," they tell me. "We'll let you know when there's something to report." I should have been with Lynn.

Shortly after ten o'clock, a nurse finds me. "Mr. McCourt, you have a baby girl," she announces.

"And my wife?" I ask. "How is she?"

"She's fine, yes, she's fine. She's resting."

With Lynn and Allison home from the hospital the world comes to visit. Mothers, brothers, sisters-in-law and friends all come to see the new baby. Lynn's brother, an obstetrician and gynecologist, asks about Allison's delivery.

"With high forceps," Lynn replies.

"And why was that?" he asks.

"I don't know," Lynn says. "But I do know that they didn't consider me a good candidate for a Lamaze-style delivery. I heard them say it, just after I kicked the doctor in the stomach. And I know that the doctor was in a big hurry to catch a plane to Florida. His wife was sick."

We had paid this same doctor, visit by visit, but I had to deal with the hospital bill so that Lynn and Allison would not be held hostage. I had secured their release only with a series of postdated checks.

Lynn keeps one of her part-time jobs and stays home with the baby. Allison is quiet. She rarely cries.

New York City plans a great Bicentennial Celebration for the Fourth of July. Dire are the wise in their predictions. Hundreds of thousands of people will crowd into the city. The police will be completely outnumbered. Mobs will run riot in the streets. On the day, with Allison in her baby carriage, along with a picnic lunch, we walk over to Riverside Park for a clear view. As in a dream, a Hudson River dream, an armada of tall ships sails past us. No riot comes to the city on this glorious afternoon.

Thanksgiving comes. Comes Chanukah and Christmas, with a Christmas tree and a prayer, to the tune of Tannenbaum, "O Christmas Tree, O Christmas Tree, bring all of your blessings on Lynn and Allison and me."

1977

O N WEEKENDS LYNN AND I walk around the city in search of a premises for a bar and restaurant. Through Hell's Kitchen, Chelsea, the Village, over to Murray Hill and on up to the Upper East Side we walk. Then, in January, Lynn meets Ernesto, right on our street. The next day he comes down to Doyle's to see me. He and his partner are opening a restaurant. They need a third partner to put up some money, to help in setting up the restaurant and to share in running it.

Ernesto had come to New York in the 1960s. Part of a new wave of immigrants from the Dominican Republic, he had been cook and dishwasher at the White Horse for a while. He was good at his job and we had always been friendly.

I agree to go and take a look at the new place. Right down the street, on the same block where I live, it's so close that I don't even have to cross the street. A disused plumbers supply store, it is three steps down from street level. I had walked all over the city, but I had never paid any attention to this place. At ten o'clock on Friday morning I walk down the steps, to be greeted by the unmistakable smell of fresh stucco.

Ernesto introduces me to Tony, his partner. Originally from Spain, Tony had spent some years in the Merchant Marine before settling in New York. A stern expression dominates his face, with a hint of mockery around his mouth. And the same slant of mockery lives in his eyes.

Looking taller than his six-foot-one, as tall and gaunt as Ernesto is short and chunky, Tony has the classic long jaw of the Spaniard.

As we begin to talk I find myself paying less attention to the two of them than I do to the place itself and to the feeling of the place. I don't know how or where but I know that I will find the money. This place will be a success.

Our court-clerk friend promises the money. "It will be a Mexican restaurant," I tell him and I add that I got a taste for Mexican food in California. He shows no surprise.

"Whatever it is, I know you'll make a go of it," is all he says. Sidney, the Egyptian magician, with his confident assurance that I will get the money, immediately comes to mind.

Our friend comes to see the new place. Ships lanterns hang from the ceiling, their dim light reflected on the stuccoed walls. The uneven floor, slanting like the deck of a ship, looks barely capable of supporting the formica-covered tables and the institutional, cafeteria-style chairs. Our friend is undeterred. "Very nice, very nice," he murmurs, as we walk through the short tour. "Very nice indeed."

This is nothing like his favorite Italian restaurant, where gorgeous mussels await, the lusty sauce just begging to be sopped up with crusty bread. Where waiters, dutiful and well experienced, seemingly rusting in place, will glide smoothly into action upon his arrival. Nor is it like the club of his dreams, where the jazz pianist in the corner salutes him with a precious nod of recognition and, putting aside his own song list, the pianist will play his one or two special requests, out of order and out of the ordinary. Our new premises is not like either of these. Physically it lacks a great deal. It lacks even the faded promise of a rundown Irish pub.

A Mexican restaurant, fer Chrissakes? Who ever heard of a Mexican restaurant? What have I got myself into here? Our friend may have been thinking that but, as I said, he is an old-fashioned man. A true gentleman, once he has promised, gives no sign of any doubt or uncertainty. Our friend confines himself to one more "very nice." We make our way up the steps and out the door. And he keeps his promise.

The liquor license comes through. We are cleared to open on March first, but we can't. The first of March falls on a Tuesday. Ernesto's father once told him never to start a new enterprise on a Tuesday. Our opening night party will take place on Wednesday, the second of March. Free food and free drink will lure a couple of hundred opening night guests and will bring us tons of good will.

On opening night, Mam attends, as do Frank and Malachy and their wives. Mam is happy to be among her sons and their friends. My family breathes a collective sigh of relief, I imagine, relief that I have landed somewhere and that I am becoming responsible.

On the night following our glorious opening night, Peter Myers shows up with his wife, to offer moral support. On that night, and for many nights thereafter, there is only a dribble of customers to sustain us. Tony's wife sells cosmetics. In an attempt to boost our business, she prevails on her group to hold their monthly lunch in our restaurant. Fifty women arrive for lunch. All goes well until it comes time for dessert. No provision has been made for dessert, but Tony must provide. Making his way to the kitchen, he tells Ernesto that the women want dessert. Ernesto makes no reply. Our dessert menu is limited and, with no prior notice, there will be nowhere near enough desserts to go round. We have on hand only fifteen orders of flan, our principal dessert. Flan takes a long time to prepare. In his white shirt and black tie, with black pants and shiny boots, Tony is full-blown colonizer now. Drawn up to his full autocratic height, he is masterful.

"You have flan for this party?" His Castilian locution is miraculously and meticulously transposed into English. For my benefit, I imagine. Tony is not asking a question here. He is making a demand.

Ernesto once told me that in Santo Domingo, in the time of Trujillo, the Dominican dictator, one of the dictator's soldiers had stepped on his foot. Ernesto was forced to apologize. How could he have been so careless as to place his foot under the soldier's boot? To Tony's demand, "You have flan for this party?" Ernesto does not immediately respond. There are ghosts in that kitchen, the ghosts of invaders, conquerors, armies of occupation and the memory of the barbarities committed in their name. All are resurrected.

In his little chef's hat and apron, sweltering in the heat between counter and oven, Ernesto raises himself to his full five foot six. Ernesto's agitation is betrayed only by a small but perceptible quiver of anger and by a passing glance at the meat cleaver, which lies on the counter, within easy reach of his right hand. In his strongest voice and his most determined tone, Ernesto hurls Tony's demand back in his face. "No," he declaims. And, after a brief pause he adds, "No, I have no flan for this party." A heavy silence falls. Ernesto glares at Tony. Tony glares back at him. Tony stamps out of the kitchen.

In the spring, we follow Tony's plan and lay a concrete floor in the backyard. Furnished with tables and chairs, the little patio becomes very popular and our business improves.

That summer, during the citywide blackout, the news is very bad. There's rioting and looting uptown. Tony, with a combination of prudence and understandable paranoia, insists that we close the restaurant. I don't want to close. I suggest, very gently, that we stay open and that we have a party, a blackout party. There's an abundance of candles and we sure won't need air-conditioning. People will be happy to sit outside. Tony neither agrees nor disagrees. Instead, he goes home. Ernesto and I are left to do as we see fit.

Our customers pay for warm beer and cold food and they're happy to get it. They're happy to be somewhere, anywhere, other than in their hot apartments. Above all, a New Yorker must have a good blackout story to tell. On the following morning, on the ground and under a patio table, I find a bag of what looks like weed. Alas, no weed remains. The bag of weed has been reduced to a bag of seeds and stems. The owner of the bag has a good story to tell.

Tony, in his early fifties, has other business interests and doesn't seem to need money. Ernesto is in his early forties and I am in my late thirties. We do need money. Rigid in his thinking, Tony could be a son of Generalissimo Franco. He's less than a generation older than either one of us but as the illusion of partnership deteriorates, under the stress of our summer of moderate success, he seems to grow older.

There is very little business at lunchtime. *Cue* Magazine is known for its restaurant reviews. A good review in *Cue* brings the promise of success. A woman comes for lunch and she is carrying a copy of *Cue*. Tony is quick enough to notice the magazine and he is aware of its significance. The woman attempts to order Mexican food. Tony demurs and suggests that she have steak. The woman persists. Tony insists. The woman has steak and she will never understand why.

Now in the middle of the summer Tony has gone in search of an air conditioner. He finds one, used of course, and well used. A fifteen-ton unit, it is powerful enough to cool the Empire State Building. If size mattered, this would be the king of all air conditioners. His Cuban American air-conditioning Connections, hired just for the day, muscle it down the steps and into our little dining room. Positioned very carefully along the north wall, it makes for a perfect fit and it is a short run for the hook up to the water tower on the patio. Meanwhile the cooks have emerged from the kitchen. They are eager for a sample of the new air-conditioning. The waiters, Joe and Dennis, and the busboy, Mario, stand expectantly in the middle of the dining room. Chris Smith is the son of our old friend Charlie Smith. Only sixteen and already very tall, he is working in the restaurant for the summer. With fond anticipation, he smiles down on our "new" air conditioner. Comes the great moment. They turn it on. Nothing happens.

Our founder cannot be wrong. It has to be a faulty installation. The Cuban American Connections are ordered to double-check everything, which they do, and shake their heads. All connections are in order. It must be the unit that's defective. Tony is adamant. The Connections leave.

We are swimming upstream. New Yorkers will tolerate indifferent food, poor service, weak drinks, even unpleasant surroundings. And still they will pay. But in the absence of air-conditioning they will turn right around and leave. To their credit, as they leave, New Yorkers will sometimes show a surprising sensitivity. They will do their best not to hurt your feelings. "We'll be back, yes, we'll be back," they offer, by way of reassurance. "I have to be downtown by eight-thirty. Just remembered. Sorry."

It's a good thing that Ernesto has already left for the day or the situation might become volatile. Soon our senior partner will make his exit.

Next morning, under a canopy of gravitas, Tony, Ernesto and I assemble for a meeting. Ernesto speaks English, but Tony, for some reason, must address him in Spanish. Drawing up both corners of his mouth and holding that position for as long as he can, he achieves the maximum Castilian effect and delivers an ornate brand of Spanish. Then, in his staccato brand of English, he informs us that there has been a mix-up. His Cuban American Connections must have picked up and delivered the wrong machine. He will call them and get them to straighten it out.

A fifteen-ton elephant sits in our little dining room and a very dead elephant it is, impossible to ignore. An eyesore, it rises from floor to ceiling. Ernesto proposes that we get someone to paint a mural on it. Tony is not amused. In the afternoon, after Tony has left, Ernesto and I drape the elephant in yellow tablecloths. With a ball of twine we secure the veil.

Customers ask about the elephant. It's a secret exit, a tunnel in case of a raid by Immigration, we tell them. We all have a good laugh. During the next few days we have to laugh a lot as Tony continues to ignore the monster. He doesn't even look in its direction. But, over the next few weeks we all develop a certain fondness for the relic. Customers lift the tails of the tablecloths and peer under the skirts of the monster. "Stop that," I tell them. "Do you have no decency, no respect?" Soon they will draw pictures on the draping, signing their names, even. Sometimes they leave written messages for each other.

On quiet nights the draped machine becomes a diversion, a curiosity, a topic of conversation. We can't hide it so we position a good-sized round table, with seating for eight people, directly in front of it. That table becomes the table of choice for those who brave the discomfort of sitting inside, without air-conditioning. For all that, by the end of July the temperature is intolerable. In our little dining room three steps below street level, the humidity is visible. Dampness clings to the stuccoed walls and to the carpet and it is too hot now to sit in the patio.

Tony makes no move and, given his temperament, Ernesto and I are reluctant to bring up the subject of air-conditioning. Our partnership is so shaky that even a mention of the machine may well provoke a constitutional crisis. Luckily, in the person of Victor, the gods take a hand. Victor lives in the apartment next door to me. He owns and operates a plant and flower store on West 72nd Street. Originally from South America, he has complained to me, neighbor to neighbor, and more than once, about the hard life he lives. He hates running a store. Worse, he hates plants and often takes refuge in alcohol.

Tony, likewise, has no respect for Mexican food. At least once a week, in a show of contempt, he orders Chinese food or pizza. His wife and his young son are invited to Los Panchos. Up at the bar they sit, to share the imported food. In an act of provocation, thinly disguised as generosity, Tony invites waiters and bartenders, customers even, to dip in. This is an insult to Ernesto. Tony smiles his best smile. Ernesto retreats to the kitchen.

Tony and Victor are acquainted. Each is a purveyor of that which he hates. On a Sunday night they just happen to go out drinking together. On Monday Tony's wife calls. Tony is not well. He was mugged and beaten up the night before. Later in the day I visit him as he lies in state. The bedroom walls are painted a dark green and I am reminded of the dismal state of our apartment when we first moved in.

But Tony is transformed. Gone is the gaunt Spaniard, gone the long jaw and the bitter countenance. Swollen from the beating, his face looks almost benign. Puffy and soft, his eyes are almost pleading in expression. When he asks me to take care of the business and when he says please, I am vouchsafed a rare view of Tony the human being.

"Sure I will. I'll take care of everything. Don't worry," I tell him. No sooner am I back in the restaurant than I am on the phone to the Cuban American Connections. I ask them to find me a ten-ton air conditioner, one that works. They deliver it the next day and they remove the beloved fifteen-ton monster. From our bank account I withdraw fifteen hundred dollars, deduct that amount from the checkbook and enter it as cash in our cash receipts book. After the "new" air conditioner has been installed, I pay fifteen hundred dollars to the Cuban American Connections and an additional fifty dollars for removal and disposal of the monster.

At the end of the week a gaunt-again Tony comes back to work. Immediately he accuses me of stealing the fifteen hundred dollars I had withdrawn from the bank. I explain that I put the money in the cash box, entered it in the cash ledger and took it out to pay for the air conditioner. Still, he accuses me of stealing fifteen hundred dollars from the cash box. I explain that the money was taken from the bank, placed in the cash box and taken out of the cash box and was used to pay for the air conditioner. "Money in, money out," I offer. "*Cogito ergo sum and sum.*"

Tony responds with a "Que?" He will not understand. I have "disappeared" fifteen hundred dollars. That's all he knows, but I know that he does understand. He understands perfectly well, but he has been made to look bad. Someone must pay. An independent bookkeeper is summoned. She rides in on the C train, checks the books and rides out with a quick day's pay. She is in agreement with Tony. Our partnership is ended, but we do have a working air conditioner.

Meetings follow: meetings among ourselves, meetings with lawyers, meetings with the pigeons on the sidewalk outside. Our business is shuffled into third place behind argument and intrigue. Our patio had carried us through the summer. Now, in October, the closing of the patio for the winter leaves us struggling. When Tony agrees to sell his share, we prepare to buy him out. Negotiations begin.

In late October Lynn develops health problems. A specialist, Dr. Martens, tells us that it is a life-threatening illness. Rare enough in older women, it is even more rare in a woman of Lynn's age. He will need to operate as soon as possible. When we ask about her chances of survival he assures us that he will do his best. Allison is barely fifteen months old. There is some talk of postponing the operation, of trying to conceive another baby, but there will be no more children. Lynn's life is at stake.

We have been living on a very small token salary from the restaurant. There's no money to pay doctor or hospital. "We don't want your money, Lynn. We want to save your life," Dr. Martens assures Lynn. At the hospital, on the day of the operation I sign the consent form and it is the end of the world.

Tony and I have been sharing working hours, alternating days and nights, week by week. I can't tell him that I will need time to be with Lynn. His wife has been sick for years with a range of illnesses.

Maybe I'm being unfair to him, but I believe that he will pounce on any sign of weakness on my part. When Lynn remains in the hospital for some days immediately following the operation, I have to sneak away just to go and visit her. Ernesto knows our situation and he covers for me.

After such an operation most women, I am told, will take months to recuperate. Three days after the operation, even though she is in a very weakened state and suffering a great deal of pain, Lynn wills herself to get up and to care for Allison. Friends would surely rally round. Lynn tells only two people: her friend Carol and our upstairs neighbor, also named Lynn. They come and help.

At Los Panchos, partnership wars and negotiations still rage. Mr. Gold is Tony's lawyer. "You are playing poker and you have nothing in your hand," Mr. Gold says to me. He's right. I have been racking my brain trying to figure out how I will raise the money needed for the big buyout. Mr. Gold is a man of experience and he is reading my mind. I have to muster all my bravado.

"You will never know what I have in my hand," I reply. Mr. Gold smiles his lawyerly smile.

Our business is in the doldrums of early December when friends of Lynn's family arrive for a visit. Although born and bred in New York, no sooner had they bought a car than they moved upstate. Upstate they picked up a bigger car and an even worse attitude toward the city. Then they moved to Florida. Returned, now, for a visit, they have invited Lynn's mother to go out for dinner. When she suggests Los Panchos they demur. Their demurrer drips with a strong hint that our place is not quite good enough.

In a restaurant only one block away they have dinner. They had declined my invitation to at least come back to our place for coffee and dessert. Now they walk up the street to their car. The car is not there. It has been towed. I understand their outrage and I sympathize. Then they begin to chime the old refrain, the usual disparagement of New York. I will help them find the car, but I can't resist. "Did you know that in Florida, where you live, they tow away pedestrians?" I ask.

"No, they don't," they chorus. "There are no pedestrians in Florida."

"Precisely," I insist. "In Florida, if you're dumb enough to walk, and if you have the misfortune to stop for a minute, they will tow you away. So stop complaining about New York." We recover their car and they leave.

⚜

Oro is Tony's last name. Oro means "gold." Mr. Gold is Mr. Oro's lawyer. The brilliant Seymour Forman, long on principle and blessed with humor, is very short on reverence. In representing me in the negotiations, he addresses Mr. Gold as Mr. Oro and Mr. Oro he calls Mr. Gold. Serious men are these. Men of business, they cannot be seen to laugh. They can only grind their teeth. With jokes and silly puns, and by dint of his own competence and his essential decency, Seymour wears them down. An agreement is reached on price and terms.

Soon I prevail on three friends to put up the money for the great buyout. The closing, like any closing, bears all the elements of a sacrament, with the lawyers as the high priests, the seller's lawyer chief among them. Legal secretaries, in their frequent comings and goings, in the hush of their quiet murmurings and in their attention to the underpinnings, are mere acolytes. Least among all these are the principal parties to the closing. Called upon, from time to time, to attest and to aver, Tony, Ernesto and I are little more than witnesses.

But all must make obeisance before that most holy instrument, which transcends vulgar cash, transcending even the water and the wine. It must be made available to the seller's chief priest before he even knows that he wants it. God may help the unprepared even if he is slow in presenting it, the certified check, but woe will certainly betide the one who doesn't have it, the certified grail. Outer darkness will be his lot.

On a wintry afternoon, promissory notes are signed. The check is handed over. There is some regret amongst the three of us. Even Tony betrays a trace of sentiment. Overall, we are glad that it's over.

In the early evening Ernesto and I return to the restaurant, to the quiet time between lunch and dinner. In my mind's eye, I can still see Tony coming down the steps as he used to do. Descending to the bridge, he is ready to take command of the ship. I listen in vain for the bosun's whistle. In my imagination Tony is drawn up to his full height, his jaw shining with clean shavenness, as he offers his customary "como estamos hoy," his "how are we today," which has always been uttered more in challenge than in greeting. It really means, "In what manner, and in how many ways did all of you screw up today?"

Now he's gone. Ernesto and I sit down at a table. He will retain his former position and run the kitchen. Starting at ten in the morning he will go home at five. I will have to work day and night. It will be hard work and very long hours, but we will be building something. There will be no need for any more meetings. Then again, judging by Ernesto's face, he is as apprehensive as I am, although for different reasons.

Every morning, over coffee at eleven, we discuss, "Will we or won't we?" Will we hire, fire, add or subtract? Will we buy a new freezer, a used one, or will we stick with what we have? There are no arguments. Decisions are quickly arrived at, or deferred.

Spring brings a refurbishing of the patio and we open it for business. It is 1978, some fifteen years after the inauguration of Lincoln Center. The West Side of Manhattan has begun to rumble and stir. Our customers, many of them actors and singers, writers, musicians, poets and dancers, are hungry for our large portions and low prices. They're happy to clean their plates. And we are happy to have them. There is love in the food.

In an issue devoted to outdoor dining in the city, *New York* Magazine gives us favorable mention. Two days before publication date, the reviewer tips us off. We have been given a good review and she doesn't want to disappoint her readers. We should be prepared. We double up on personnel and on food and beer and wine and sangria. On the third night of bedlam four friends of ours are waiting for a table. I send them over a drink. They wait. After a long interval I send them over a second drink. When I offer them a third they call me over. "Thank you, but no more drinks, please. We need food."

"We have run out of Mexican food," I tell them. "You'll have to have steak or shrimp. That's all that's left." They laugh. Life is hard.

Other publications follow with good reviews. Marginal friends and acquaintances begin calling me at home. "Can we get a table?" they ask and I don't understand why they're calling me. Our place is hot and I don't know it. At our prices we can't afford to take reservations. First come, first served, I tell them, but to come on over anyway and I will take care of them. Only then do I begin to realize that news of Los Panchos has percolated to other parts of the city, even to the august East Side.

And Lynn's mother, Miriam, tells me the story of the friends of the family, the same ones who would not have dinner in our place. Back again from Florida they called their daughter. A physician, she lives on Manhattan's East Side. She suggested that they meet for dinner. There's "this great new place on the West Side." They arrive at Los Panchos, to be greeted by a line. Up the steps, out the door and all the way to the corner, it stretches. There will be at least a half-hour wait for a table. Belatedly, the parents realize where they are. They ask for me and they are told that I won't be back for a while. Disappointed, their daughter has to settle for another place, down the street. I could feel sorry for them in their disappointment.

Many of my neighbors come for dinner. Most of them are well into their seventies or early eighties. Mexican food is a new experience for them, especially for the two sisters who share an apartment in my building. As they are leaving I ask if they are satisfied. "I don't know what I had," the younger sister replies, "but it was very good."

Michael Beck comes with his wife, Helen. Mike was a grown man when he went blind. Now he is well past the age when he might retire, but still active in the movie distribution business, he continues to go to work every morning. I will often see him outside our building, as he listens for the sound of his car. With his face tilted upward, he strains to catch the sunlight. On his second visit to Los Panchos, I offer himself and his wife an after-dinner drink. Mike chooses a crème de menthe.

"The green or the white?" I ask. What a question to ask a blind man. I realize that immediately, but I can't call back the words. Mike gives no sign that he has caught onto my foolishness. Instead, he tilts his chin, much as he does in the morning, goes into listening mode and comes up with a slow smile.

"I'll have the green," he says. "And thank you for the offer."

At six o'clock every evening Ernesto washes up and changes from his chef's outfit into his street clothes. In emerging from the kitchen he is not yet certain if he has a role in the front of the restaurant. At a small table for two he sits, just outside the kitchen. Solitary, at that table, he is neither owner nor customer. Nor does he have the ease of the cook enjoying his well-earned drink before going home. In the old days, at the White Horse, he would have come up to the bar, to accept compliments and to share in a bit of banter.

Something has changed. Our few early evening customers turn away from his questioning gaze. Ernesto, himself uncomfortable on his perch, makes them feel even more so. Waiters and busboys, even his cohorts, the ones who speak Spanish, seem to be on edge, with the feeling that they are being watched too closely. After a few months of his solitary gazing, I prevail on him to come and sit at the bar. This will not be easy. The barstools are high and Ernesto is not tall. He succeeds not only in mounting but in keeping his great dignity, which is always well served by his elaborate courtesies.

Time comes when the volume of business is so great that we hire someone to do the seating. It has been my habit to go home for a little while after the day's business and to return at eight o'clock. Now, with Ernesto at the bar, it is tempting to have a few drinks, all, of course, after six o'clock. Ernesto grows easily into his new role as owner of the bar, at the bar. But he remains ever watchful, and so he should.

When I am having drinks at the bar, that's what I'm doing. I'm more than well able to focus on the task at hand, but Ernesto has no compunction about getting down off his stool, and with considerable effort. He will fuss over a customer he deems to have been neglected and left waiting. I think him foolish. Too much fuss will make the customer feel awkward and make us look stupid. We shouldn't mix drinking and seating. That's my opinion. I'm wrong. People appreciate the attention.

There are those rare occasions when Ernesto and I have had too many. First-time customers are likely to be puzzled by Ernesto's behavior. He has no obvious official position, yet, alighting from his bar stool and with great, if unsteady, courtesy, he will attempt to usher them to a table. At such times Ernesto is more than usually sensitive to a rebuff. When they hesitate, he insists. If they don't go along with him, he is insulted.

"I'm waiting for someone," she says.

"Come, I will get you table," Ernesto commands.

"No, no, thank you, it's okay, I'll wait here."

When he speaks Spanish, every syllable is clearly enunciated. Now, in his equally deliberate English, "I will bring you to table," he insists. "You will wait there." The young woman, in despair, looks around and catches my eye.

What can I do? In this situation anything I do will offend Ernesto. I am saved by Phillip, the bartender. "Ernesto, this man is in a hurry," he calls out. "Any chance you could go to the kitchen and put a rush on his order? I know they'll listen to you." Ernesto moves in the direction of the kitchen. I suggest to the young woman that she sit at a table by the bar. Gratefully, she accepts. The man at the bar is happy that his food order has come so quickly from the kitchen. Ernesto is delighted with the success of his mission. The young woman is so relieved that she even manages a small smile for all of us. I resume my seat, give Phillip a thumbs-up and order two more margaritas.

Once again our meeter, greeter and seater is temporarily detained in the rear of the restaurant. A young woman walks down the steps followed closely by a group of three people. She's good looking. "Are you together?" I ask her, meaning herself and the three people behind her.

"I am," she answers smartly and I know that I should have stayed on my stool.

Tim, a waiter and a good worker, is the nephew of a well-known movie director. He has a keen eye and he manages to do his work while remaining one step above or to the side of it. I wish that he would fully embrace the job. He doesn't. He leaves and goes to work in another establishment. I ask him to stay in touch and to come back and visit. In the meantime we hear tales of the success of his new place of employment. In short order the owners have opened a second, then a third place. Tim does come back to visit. We are quick to ask him what it is like to work in the other place. Tim is a Californian. His New York skin is still developing. In his laid back way he tells us that the other place is very busy and that he is earning a lot of money. "But the owners are crazy," he adds. We ask him why he thinks that they are crazy. "They drink all the time," Tim says. President Abraham Lincoln and General Ulysses S. Grant come to mind. I ask him to please find out what it is that those crazy owners drink.

On a Friday evening a woman comes. Our little bar seats seven people with room for a few standees. The high tables in the alcove will seat eight or ten more. She offers her flowers for sale, singly or in small sprays. No one will buy. Looking studiedly away from her, they turn a collective blind eye to the beauty of the flowers. She might as well be a beggar.

Ernesto sees the situation and he is insulted on her behalf. "How much for all the flowers?" he asks her. For twenty dollars he buys her whole stock. In no time a man at the bar will ask Ernesto to sell him one. Another man, from one of the high tables, comes over to ask if he can buy a small bunch. "You had your chance," Ernesto answers. "I would not sell them to you now for one hundred dollars." And he is right. Ernesto has done a kindness and he has turned a small moral profit. Now he could very easily earn a substantial financial profit as well. He keeps the flowers. Later on he gives me a bunch to bring home to Lynn.

I will see this aspect of Ernesto again. Sometimes friends and distant relatives are only too happy to ride in on the rumor of his success. He sits with them and buys them a drink. Then he entertains the inevitable request for money. Strictly as a loan, mind you. They promise repayment, at impossible interest and in an unreasonably short time. Reasons are various. They include the startup of a small business, the loss of a job, a child's first communion or the purchase of a secondhand van so they can go into the fruit and vegetable business.

Ernesto doesn't give them a loan. When they ask for a thousand he gives them two hundred dollars. "This money is a gift, not a loan," he tells them. "There is no interest. You owe me nothing. I'm just giving you a start. Now you can go and ask four other people to give you two hundred dollars each. Soon you will have your thousand dollars."

Again he turns a nice moral profit. He saves his people from going into further debt and from their own useless promises to pay, and at outrageous interest within an unreasonable time. And he saves himself eight hundred dollars. Most important, he keeps their friendship and goodwill. I sure could have learned from him.

1981

THE LATE SEVENTIES and the early eighties bring a drastic rise in the number of homeless people in the city. People no more, "the homeless" are a new class. In our city of "bring me your poor," the homeless live a few floors below the so-called underclass. On a Sunday afternoon he comes. Is he six foot six, or is he taller? Some will say six-six. Some say seven feet tall. And wide. So wide is he that "he wouldn't come in the door for you," as they used to say in Limerick. Disheveled and confused, the man has lost his way. "I'm hungry," he says. "I want food."

Ernesto and I had agreed that we would give food to anyone who asked for it. We would give a plate of take-out food, on condition that they take it and eat it outside. This practice has worked well. But the big man has already seated himself at a table in the rear. We bring him a plate of food. Quickly he cleans his plate and when he asks for more we refill his plate. Finished, now, he stands up. "Thank you," he mumbles and lumbers up the steps and on out the door.

Earlier that day the giant had gone into another Mexican restaurant one block away and had asked for food. His request was refused and he ended up by creating a disturbance, which brought the police. Then he came to us.

❧

We must always be prepared. At home, beside the bed, a pair of pants, a heavy turtleneck sweater, a pair of socks and pull on boots will enable me to be dressed in a flash. At two o'clock on a Thursday morning in late December of 1978, I get the call: "There's a fire in the restaurant." Dressed and down the block in minutes, I find the fire fighters already inside. A minor fire, caused by the burnt-out cord on a coffee maker, has been taken care of. No one is hurt. There's no real damage except for the waterlogged carpet and the reek of smoke.

A dozen firemen are present and I give them a drink. "Happy New Year," says one.

"Oh, yeah? He won't have much of a New Year," says another. "I can't see him being open for at least two weeks."

My mouth is awake, my brain still asleep. "We'll open tomorrow. We'll be back in business at five o'clock." I announce. The firemen shrug their great shoulders. They've heard it all before.

At three-thirty I call Ernesto. "We've had a fire," I tell him.

"Okay, I'll see you in the morning" he says. He is very cordial, too cordial for a man so rudely awakened. Not much of a response from that quarter, I reflect. Ernesto thought I'd said that we'd had a fight, not a fire, in the restaurant. I find that out later.

An outfit from Queens does a good job of drying and cleaning the wall-to-wall carpet. A second call, at six o'clock, conjures Ernesto, along with a painter and a helper. They set to work at painting the entire restaurant. Most of our employees, in response to our phone calls, come to work early. All day we work on the clean up.

Our friend, Leonard Melfi had invited us to a staged reading of his "Taxi Tales." He had "bumped" two other people so we would have tickets. I will have to be there. Dozing during the readings, waking, dozing and sleeping again, I snore once or twice. Lynn pokes me in the ribs. At the end I congratulate my good friend Leonard and rush home to bed.

On Friday evening, at five o'clock, right on schedule, we open for business. I can still smell smoke. Our customers sniff the air and congratulate us on our new paint job.

Our fire is a temporary setback. Winter wears into spring and into summer. Los Panchos becomes a big success, coinciding with the revival of what will come to be known as the Upper West Side. Now it is our turn to brag. "Oh, I go to the East Side only when I'm on my way to Kennedy Airport." Our success is heralded by the call on our very public phone. The caller asks to speak to a certain high official in the Carter White House. Jokers! I think, and hang up. They call back. The call turns out to be genuine. After polling half the tables I locate the official and bring him to the phone. Celebrities are beginning to "discover" the Upper West Side.

Early on a Friday evening a van pulls up outside. The driver asks if we are interested in buying some decorations for the restaurant. Plagued, on a daily basis, by everyone selling everything, my first response is always no. Once, just to get rid of the man with the brand-new-never-out-of-the-box TV set I had asked him, "Is it hot?"

"No", he said.

"Well, then it's probably no good," I told him. That was a cruel thing I did. The man with the van full of decorations is persuasive and Ernesto is more flexible than I am.

A pony, a miniature pig, a small elephant and a burro, all inhabit the back of the van. The burro is lifelike and not too beautiful, but he does have an air. His hide, made of felt, is soft to the touch and his sad glass eyes give him character.

"Great for kids," we tell each other, neither one of us willing to admit that we are taken by the burro. Two hundred and fifty dollars later, the burro is in position, up front, right under the public telephone, just across from the bar.

She had broken our hearts in *Love Story*. In the evenings the burro awaits her arrival for dinner. She always comes in with Peter Weller. What does she see in him that she doesn't see in any of us? We could learn to hate Peter Weller. And always, on her way to the street door after dinner, Ali MacGraw will stop and stroke the burro. Behind the ears she strokes him and smoothes his hide by running her hand down the length of his back. In simple and affectionate farewell she will gently touch the top of his head. Peter Weller is forgotten. Now the burro must bear the brunt of our jealousy.

A child, even an adult, could sit on the burro. He is well built, but he is not designed for travel. So, once in a while when we must go to a wedding, First Communion, Bar Mitzvah or Confirmation I rent a car.

Wearying of rentals, we buy a car. There is an inevitability to it. First, the car. Then, the house. In Woodstock, New York, I will recreate my Larkspur frame of mind. We look at three houses. Allison is five and she is very active. In the third house she stakes her claim by settling herself, quiet and comfortable, on the floor.

Now comes another closing, another handing over of the certified check, and we take possession of the house. What do I know about houses, sublet man that I have been? But this is a new house, a wood frame with cedar shingles. I have been a wandering man for the latter part of my life, but the vibes in this house are good.

At two and a quarter acres, our land stretches almost as far as the eye can see, or, at least, as far as the fence that separates us from Glasgow Turnpike and from the neighbors on either side. On a quiet afternoon, from an upstairs window, I see momma deer, poppa deer and baby deer. Standing on the grass in front of the house they are gazing upward as if to bid us welcome. I hold still for as long as I can until they scamper away.

Ernesto spends more and more of his time in the Dominican Republic, leaving most of the running of the restaurant to me. His lieutenants are in charge of the kitchen. They do a good job, but reliable and competent as they are, it is not the same. The love is gone from the food. While Ernesto is in the Dominican Republic I am spending a good many weekends upstate. Our accountant reminds us, and he reminds us often that "no one speaks as sweetly as the owner of the place."

⚜

When Mam was in her fifties, her doctor strongly suggested that she give up smoking. She had what we called "the Sheehan chest." Respiratory ailments were common in her family. "Quit or die," said the doctor. Mam quit. Then, during the 1970s, when she was in her sixties, she suffered from emphysema. Other health problems followed and she would be in and out of Lennox Hill Hospital a number of times.

Now, in December of 1981, Mam is once again admitted to Lennox Hill Hospital. She had suffered a broken hip while playing bingo. Combined with emphysema, it was too much for her. On Wednesday I went to visit her. I tried to tell her what her presence had meant to me when I was a child. And of the warmth she brought even when we had nothing. As long as she was in the house we could weather anything. I wanted to tell her all that, but each time I started to tell her, I choked up. She didn't need me crying at her bedside. As always, she wanted "something tarty." I went out and bought her some lemon drops. On the following Sunday morning she died. Frank called to give me the bad news.

Later Frank related to me what Mam told him of my visit. Within the family I was not known for being talkative. Once, during a game of hide and go seek, by my shirt collar the brothers hung me up in a closet. I made no sound. I just waited to be found. At her hospital bedside, Mam thought I was being my usual self. "Old chatterbox was here," she told Frank. She couldn't have known how hard I had tried to tell her.

⌘

Allison is growing. Her speech is slow in coming. For a long time her only word will be "attawa." A young waitress in a Woodstock restaurant, herself part American Indian, overhears Allison say "attawa." She confirms our own notion that "attawa" may be an Indian word. Ed McCurdy, our friend and neighbor explains it differently. "Allison isn't speaking because her Hebraic and Celtic ancestors are holding her back from speaking English," he tells us.

Advice comes from all sides. A doctor friend, at our request, refers us to a speech pathologist. The pathologist, at the end of her visit, tells us that Allison needs discipline. She will have to learn discipline. She will probably have to be made to cry before any progress can be made. We can see the need for discipline. We could begin to act on it. But the tone of her report is blunt and very harsh.

Finding a school for Allison proves to be difficult. In a private school in the West 70s, the teacher is all leather skirt and knee-high shiny boots. She's half horse and half woman, delicious in contemplation. I pay more attention to her than I ever do to Allison's prospects. It doesn't matter. In a short time, we are expelled for bad behavior. In another private school, this time on the East Side, the principal bends down to talk to Allison. She puts her face very close. Allison, confused and uncertain, gives her a gentle slap in the face. Again we are expelled.

Lucky we are, to have Marta from Guatemala. With us since before Allison was born, she calls Allison her "Mamita precioso." "Dos Madres, Dos Madres," you have two mothers, two mothers, she tells Allison, in Lynn and herself. Allison sure can use dos madres. She is

· 228 ·

always in motion. Then, just to confound everyone, she will sit quietly, leafing through a book or doing a puzzle. Sometimes she will dump the pieces of three or four puzzles, mix them all together and, with little difficulty, she will reassemble each puzzle.

One morning, when I go down to move the car to avoid a parking ticket, I find that the passenger side window has been smashed in. The radio is gone. Right away I drive to the dealer over on Eleventh Avenue, to have the window replaced, swearing, as I go, that I will no longer keep a radio in the car, this being stolen radio number four.

Arriving home an hour and a half later I find that Lynn and Allison are gone. I call the restaurant. "Yeah, your wife left a message for you, something about the kid," the bartender says. It's nine o'clock in the morning. He's barely awake. In a panic I take a taxi to the nearest hospital.

Allison had been eating breakfast at the kitchen counter when Lynn turned away to answer the phone. Allison stood up on the stool and fell off. Lynn screamed into the phone. Her friend at the other end hung up and called an ambulance. Lynn, not knowing how to revive Allison, put her fingers down her throat. Allison woke up, gagged and threw up. Lynn threw on a raincoat. In the ambulance, Allison threw up again, this time on Lynn's coat. When they reached the hospital, Lynn was given a hospital gown to wear instead of the soiled coat. Allison was brought in for examination. When I arrive I think that Lynn is the patient until she tells me what happened.

A doctor approaches. She introduces herself as a pediatrician. Her user-friendly Irish name does nothing to allay her crisp, highly calculated but somehow less-than-professional manner and there's an overlay, maybe even a hint of pride, in her own medical prowess. There's a metallic edge to her voice. She seems to be proud that a quick and very precise diagnosis has been arrived at.

Losing no time she tells us what the x-ray technicians have discovered. Allison's brain is growing and her skull is not. Soon her brain will run out of room. Which leaves us with the question, "And?"

"It won't be good," the pediatrician says.

"When will we know?" we ask.

"Oh, when she starts falling, falling frequently." Almost casually she adds, "Then you'll know."

We sit down. I want to smash my own head against the wall. We sit and wait. Soon, two important-looking men appear. They join the technicians and the pediatrician in another room. After a half hour the two doctors emerge. Neurologists, both, they are grave as they approach us. There has been a mistake. The technicians misread the x-rays. Allison is fine, but they would like to keep her overnight for observation.

After the transfer to another hospital we stay in the room with Allison. In the middle of the night they come to examine her. Waking her abruptly, they use, not a penlight, but a full-sized flashlight, shining it first into one eye, then into the other. Cruel and unusual punishment, this. Early in the morning, over the protests of the hospital staff, we sign her out. This time we have plenty of insurance. No hostages will be taken and neither hospital ever sends us a bill.

That pediatrician has planted the seed. We will remain watchful and uneasy for a long time.

At Los Panchos, with an open door, we must always be watchful. Anyone can walk in, be it a panhandler, a giant seeking food, someone needing to use the bathroom or, worst of all, the man with the briefcase.

When the man with the briefcase asks to see the books we refer him to the accountant. Armed with the accountant's phone number, he will soon leave. That's easy. But when the man shows badge or shield, and asks to see the manager or the owner, that means trouble. It will usually involve a tour of the premises. Immigration came, once. One of the men working in the kitchen ran down into the basement. Rigid, he stood. With his back against the basement wall, he thought himself invisible. He would not be found. Found he was and taken away to be deported. A few months later he returned.

Health Department Inspectors, when they're "on," are great writers. Each box ticked, every line of writing, brings a fine. One inspector invites me into the ladies' room and I conclude that at that year's Health Inspectors' Convention, the ladies' room was touted as the room least likely to be bugged. Citing hardship and a growing family, the inspector tells me that for fifteen dollars he will stop writing. That's a long time ago, but even then fifteen dollars was not a lot of money. The man must be desperate. I almost feel sorry for him, almost. But I am wary. I pretend not to understand. Again he asks me and I pretend ignorance. Exasperated, he demands to see my partner.

From time to time the Fire Department comes to inspect. In their practical, straightforward way they show an understanding of the difficulties involved. They also issue plenty of cautions, offer lots of good advice and write citations as necessary. In a few weeks they will return to ensure that we have done what we promised to do and that will be that. There are no threats and no demands. They know their business and they are in earnest.

Our business is doing well. Our accountant insists that with such a thriving business we need to open a second restaurant. Expansion will be good for us. Some of the people working for us need to spread their wings and to take on more responsibility. Two years pass, but we can't seem to get moving on the expansion until, incidentally, I pay a visit to an old pal. Moss Cooney owns a restaurant and bar and half a block of priceless real estate on the East Side.

Moss tells me of a building for sale. It is downtown, on Dominick

Street. "A great deal at a great price," as Moss puts it. He puts me in touch with a real-estate agent. Money is tight, but I make a perfunctory phone call. When the agent persists in calling me back I have to tell Ernesto about the building and we make an appointment to go and see it.

Ernesto already owns a house in Queens. With his eye on a piece of land near his house he once invited me to come and take a look. His wife served us a magnificent breakfast of scrambled eggs, platanos, champagne and strong, sweet Dominican coffee. Ernesto never did buy the land, but he always keeps his eyes open for a good opportunity.

Now we are faced with this downtown property. There are people who can easily and intuitively grasp the connection between a rise of one quarter of one percent in the rate of interest and the size of the mortgage payment. I have no interest in mortgages and interest rates. Ernesto has the talent. More important, he enjoys the game.

The rear windows of the building look right down on the entrance to the Holland Tunnel. We are met by Tony Capone. He and his brother and sister share in the ownership of the building. Wistfully he tells that he and his brother and sister had been reared, supported and sent to school on the proceeds of the ground-floor lunch counter. He quotes us what seems to be a fair price.

"Let's do it, we have to do it," says Ernesto, in the taxi, on the way back uptown. Our partnership is shaky and I'm not so sure that we should do it. I am coming to resent his frequent absences in the Dominican Republic. Even more do I resent the fact that, since I live just up the street from the restaurant, I can't seem to escape. Except by leaving town. For a few years our place had been "hot." Now it has cooled. I had enjoyed building, coaxing, nurturing and pushing to make it a success. Maintaining the restaurant, as our success has begun to wane, has brought its own problems. I have begun to lose interest.

When our place was "hot" I had been able to recruit waiters and bartenders from Columbia University and from the ranks of budding actors. Now it has become more and more difficult to find the right people. Ernesto, for his part, has no trouble finding people. His brothers, half brothers, cousins and friends are an endless parade. Outnumbered, now, I have less and less in common with waiters and bartenders, so many of them Spanish speaking. I am becoming what I had never been: a foreigner.

I should have done something, initiated something. Perhaps I should have bought Ernesto's share or sold him mine. Or sat down with him and tried to work out our problems. But that's difficult when the main problem, if it is a problem, is, that he can more or less run the kitchen even when he is gone. His brother and his brother-in-law had done a decent job in his absence. Now they too have left, to open a place of their own. If I buy Ernesto's share I will have trouble running the kitchen. I might have to bring in another partner and end up back where I started.

Allison is attending a special school in Bergen County, New Jersey, twenty-five miles from the city. I must drive her out every morning and pick her up in the afternoon. It comes out to a hundred miles of driving, every day, five days a week. My daily routine is a handy escape from any decision making on my part. Living in a constant state of suspension, between working and driving, I am too preoccupied to deal with any drastic changes.

The following week, in spite of myself I am drawn into this new downtown venture. We get off to a good start. The Capone family offers to supplement the nominal rent paid by their uncle. Tall and amazingly strong, he's ninety-two years old. He is also the uncle of Carmine De Sapio. We agree to let him live in peace, in his apartment upstairs, for as long as he lives. Later on we are happy that we didn't accept any supplement to his rent. Six months after we take over the building he dies. We rent out one of the two upstairs apartments with little trouble and at a good rent. The second apartment we keep vacant for refurbishing.

❧

An occasional weekend away upstate is both respite and further escape. One weekend Lynn's friend Sandy and her friend, Richard, come to visit us in Woodstock. I have found out that Willie Nelson will be performing up at Hunter Mountain and I get tickets for the concert. Sandy and Richard are mildly enthusiastic about going to the show. On that Sunday evening the rains come. There's no room inside the tent, so we stand outside. I don't care.

Willie Nelson always stood outside. He broke rules and suffered at the hands of the IRS. He has thrived in the world of country music without ever catering to the redneck element. Still he survives. And survives very well. Lynn is dressed for the weather. She doesn't complain.

Then comes heavy thunder. Lightning follows. People begin to leave. We make our way inside the tent and find seats. I am elated at being in the presence of this brilliant and lyrical wise man. Like Willie, my heroes have always been cowboys and his rendition of "Blue Eyes Cryin' In The Rain" is a complete journey.

Bursts of thunder and flashes of lightning become more frequent and frightening. I will stay to the very end. The steep mountain road is all curves, each curve following immediately upon the one before. Heavy fog leaves no visibility. I can feel Richard continually shifting in his seat. He's nervous. He urges me to turn on the high beams. I explain to him that the high beams will only be reflected back at us by the fog. Again, he asks and again I must refuse. We make it back to Route 28, the main road, and to Woodstock without incident. Sandy explains to us that Richard's father had been in a very serious car accident.

At the new downtown site, the restaurant space on the ground floor needs demolition, a new design and rebuilding. Ernesto's brother finds two contractor candidates for us. Alarm bells sound in my head. All my instincts tell me to say no. But, once again, as in the days of Tony Oro, the partnership is in a delicate condition. I don't say anything that might cause a bigger rift.

Our two candidates are customers of Ernesto's brother at his new restaurant on Eighth Avenue. They represent themselves as a partnership. The tall and suave Dominican offers, by way of credentials, a business card and a dented BMW. He would have it repaired, he avers, "But it's less likely to be stolen as long as it is dented." This, to me, is a dead giveaway. Don't I have a car of my own with a similar dent and haven't I often used the same rationale. The truth is that I never seem able to find the time or the money to have it fixed and, I suspect, the same is true of him.

His partner is Corsican, God bless his eyes. One eye faces east, the other one west. The two partners agree to demolish the existing restaurant space and to build a new one. And they do. As evidence they leave tons of debris. There's no mention of removing any of it. And, during the demolition the Corsican has moved into the vacant apartment. Along with his Doberman Pinscher. The Pinscher roams free among the debris, the biggest, best and most private toilet this unfortunate dog has ever enjoyed.

"Demolition is complete," the partners declare, by way of demanding money. Demolition will be complete when all debris is carted away, we insist.

Clowns they are. That's obvious. I've sensed that from the beginning. They have no money for dumpsters. And I would bet that cocaine has played a part here. Now we have to get rid of them. We'll rent the dumpsters and get rid of the debris, we tell them. Let's just call it quits. After a short argument they agree. The dented BMW man is weary of the situation and to his credit he is embarrassed.

Not so the Corsican. He's still living in the apartment. The Doberman still roams free. One of Ernesto's henchmen proposes that "we should go down and throw him out of the building, him, and his dog."

The Corsican's partner concurs. Their partnership must be at an end. "Yeah, let's just throw him out in the street," echoes the Dominican.

"We will, yes, we'll do just that. We'll throw him into the street. While we're at it, why don't we just give him the building? He will own it in the end, anyway," I tell them. "And further, he'll find an enterprising lawyer, or an enterprising lawyer will find him. He will sue us for wrongful eviction, public embarrassment, slander, discrimination against cockeyed Corsicans and God knows what else. A jury will view our Corsican friend in a very sympathetic light.

"People in New York City care about the eviction of a human being, yes, indeed, they care," I tell them. "They may even protest, but after a while they forget. The protest will wither away. But just try to evict a dog, especially when that dog is a member of the Doberman clan, a much-maligned breed. You'll be a tabloid headline in no time."

"Try offering him a little money," suggests my lawyer friend, Seymour Forman. We agree on three hundred dollars. For a very small fee, Seymour draws up the papers. The money is handed over. Corsican and Doberman move out and the debris is removed.

Six months later we sell the building at a 50 percent mark up. Of course we have sold too soon. The area is changing fast and for the better. Ernesto, to his credit, had wanted to wait, but I couldn't wait. We had drained the restaurant to finance the building and we were fighting a war on two fronts. Most of all, I hated being a landlord.

❧

Ms. Peggy Doyle calls me. She's in search of a job for someone, a young Irishman. "Not much good as a waiter or bartender," she says, "he's an executive type." His sister is a friend of Ms. Doyle and she would like to help him out.

"Okay, send him up," I tell her. By appointment he arrives. Well dressed and soft-spoken in his deference, he laughs at my jokes and thankful he is when I offer him a job as daytime bartender. He will do the setting up and answer the phone, take deliveries and serve the odd daytime customer. It will be good for him and good for me. He can't do too much damage in that position and he does prove to be dependable.

The new man shows little interest in bartending or in waiting on tables but he certainly is knowledgeable about business. Quickly picking up on the nuances of the New York bar and restaurant business, he soon proposes that we should open a place together. I'm listening. I'm miserable in Los Panchos. Most of the people I hired are already gone, all the bartenders and waiters I used to talk to and depend on. An unpleasant atmosphere prevails and I am reluctant to hire new people.

My prospective partner tells me that he can raise money through his family in Ireland. I find what seems like a likely place and I pay a visit. The afternoon sun shines in, catching the shine on the wooden bar, which is being polished, at that moment, by a tawny woman in high boots. It's all very charming and I am in need of a change.

Ernesto's sojourns in the Dominican Republic become longer in duration. My trips to Woodstock are becoming more frequent.

I come back on a Monday morning to find that our beloved burro is gone. I am told that a man sat on him and broke his back.

That can't be true. The burro was well built. Over the years, I had seen more than one adult sit on his back and with no ill effect. Even if his back had been broken it could have been repaired. "Where is he?" I ask. No one will tell me. For the moment all I know is that he is gone. This is bad news. The burro with no name had come to us when our partnership was strong and the restaurant flourishing. Now, the partnership is failing, the restaurant not doing well and our burro is gone.

As in the time of Tony Oro, Ernesto and I have meetings. In our own restaurant we have meetings and upstairs in the office. In the coffee shop down the block we have meetings, in the restaurant across the street, on the Staten Island Ferry, on the jitney to the Hamptons. On the verge of divorce, for the sake of the children, our employees and customers, we must do our best to put a good face on it. Negotiations must be conducted in a friendly way. We are, after all, in a business that demands a smile at every turn. I agree to sell my share to Ernesto.

My last day at Los Panchos comes on October 15, 1986. I'm now in an awkward situation. I must pass by, every day, sometimes a few times a day, and not go in. I often cross the street to avoid meeting customers and employees and to avoid questions.

In partnership with the Irishman now, I am co-proprietor of a place on Eighth Avenue, near the Fashion Institute of Technology. My new Irish friend imports his brother from Brooklyn to work for us. He insists, meanwhile, that Lynn be involved in setting up the place. On a small budget, Lynn transforms the drab bar and dining area into a place of welcome. Most of the money I received from the sale of my share of Los Panchos is invested in this new place.

We shorten the bar and add more tables. A new neon sign in the window proclaims that Allison's is open for business. Our customers are faculty members, mostly, from the Fashion Institute around the corner. No students are allowed. The legal drinking age has recently been raised from nineteen to twenty-one. Desperate as I am, I know this to be true, but it has not really registered with me. Business is okay for a year or so. Then, in 1987, the Stock Market collapses and our business goes into decline. Not long after, my Irish friend and I decide to part company. I will have to buy his share and assume payment of the promissory notes due to the previous owner.

"Dance with the one that brung ye," is an old saying. My new Irish friend has clearly forgotten it. Or he may never have heard it. All business now, he insists that I pay him the balance of his money. He does give me a little extra time, but I do have to pay him, which causes me to fall behind in payment of rent, notes, liquor and food bills. I can't even pay the wages of the employees who remain.

Every morning I ride the subway downtown. I rush to be on time to open for lunch but for all my haste I hope that the train will break down, that I will be late, that I won't have to go there at all. I am living in a swamp.

Allison has been away at a "special" summer camp in Connecticut for four weeks. In all that time, we have not been allowed to see her. Now, on a Friday, we plan to use this first opportunity to go and visit her. I have rented a car. I will go to work first and pick up the rental car in the afternoon. Still mired in a swamp of indecision, I start out late. I'm in a hurry. I take a taxi. The driver, instead of heading downtown toward the restaurant, turns right and begins to drive in the opposite direction. I am slow to say anything. Taxi drivers can be testy. But when he continues in an uptown direction I suggest to him that he is going the wrong way.

Whipping round in his seat, in a hoarse voice he warns, "If you don't shut up I'll blow your fuckin' head off." The pistol in his right hand is pointed at my head. He seconds that by demanding money. I surrender the twelve dollars from my pocket. It's not enough. Now he wants credit cards. The gun has tilted downward. Listing at a lazy forty-five-degree angle, it is pointed at my groin.

In his agitation, the driver's gun hand shakes. I re-imagine my old Pappy telling me, "Better in the head than in the jewels." I hand over my wallet. At a slow crawl now, the driver steers with his knees. Using his left hand he extracts my driver's license and my one credit card. It's still not enough for him. He demands jewelry. I don't have any.

Still moving forward and looking straight ahead, he keeps the gun, his gun hand as shaky as ever, pointed at me. Again I tell him that that I have no jewelry. It may be a cultural thing, I'm tempted to tell him. Limerick men are not well known for wearing chains and earrings. I have to open two buttons of my shirt to show that I have no chains. I don't even have a wedding ring. The first one I broke and I lost the replacement. There's no point in burdening him with the details. He looks barely strong enough to hold up the gun, which, again, has drifted downward. The muzzle oscillates in the vicinity of the real jewels.

As naked as I was when I came in, that's how I'll go out, I want to tell him. I don't give a damn about jewelry. Jewelry is a nuisance, more of an impediment than anything else, but there's not much point in telling him any of that. Should I apologize for being such a poor robbery victim? What effect would that have on him? All I know is I must have my license and my credit card.

The driver's hand shakes even more now. Is it nerves or is it frustration with the idiot in the back seat who wears no jewelry. In his condition, he just might shoot me by mistake. I reason with him and for good reason do I reason. Without my license and my credit card I will not be able to go and see Allison. I can't fail to go and see her. I tell him to keep my few dollars and no hard feelings, but that I must have my license and credit card.

He is not happy. "Keep the money," I tell him. "But I must have my credit card and my license." There's not much point in telling him why. In his opening statement, he had threatened to blow my head off. Since then he has said little. Now he is silent. Still pointed downward, at a spot well below my belly button, the gun speaks for him. "I must have my license and credit card," I tell him again. He's had enough. With the gun still pointed at me, he pulls over to the side and stops the taxi. My wallet, license and credit card are tossed into the back seat. I scramble to pick them up before jumping out.

"He has a gun, he has a gun!" I yell, as I take refuge behind a giant concrete flowerpot. Three people are standing at the corner. They back away from me, as if I am the one with the gun. The taxi moves off. I walk to the subway. Grateful to have a token, I am even more grateful to take my place among the crowd, even in a crammed subway car.

⁂

Every morning at eleven-thirty I open for lunch. Every two or three days, in the middle of lunch, the air-conditioning will fail. Half of the lighting in the bar and dining area will go with it. Without fail, some wag at the bar will chirp, "What happened, you didn't pay the Con Edison bill?" In my precarious financial position he is too close to the truth. When it happens, I must go down to the basement and, without benefit of a fuse puller, remove the blown 20-amp fuse and put in a new one.

Because we have a jukebox on the premises we are required to make a token payment to ASCAP, every six months. "To every cow her calf and to every book its copy," is the old Irish law of copyright. I believe in that so I pay ASCAP without complaint. Then comes the man from BMI. He demands that we must pay his company for music rights. I tell him that I already pay ASCAP. BMI represents a different list of singers, musicians and composers, he tells me. I will have to pay BMI as well.

"I'll think about it," I tell him.

"I'll be back," he threatens.

Two weeks later the air-conditioning fails again, along with half the lights. Temperature and humidity are rising. I will have to run out and buy yet another 20-amp fuse in order to hold our increasingly restless customers. Or should I just open the front door for ventilation? An open front door bespeaks no air-conditioning, a mortal sin and a fatal error. The world will know that we have no air-conditioning. Or should I leave the front door closed, don my pith helmet, button up my shirt and pretend that everything is, or soon will be, normal. It's not safe to keep on replacing the fuse. Constant overheating has to be doing serious damage to the wiring and frequent blowouts will damage the air conditioner itself. I badly need an electrician. Where will I find the money? I deliberate.

In comes Mr. BMI in suit and tie. For good measure, in his role as defender of the creative artist, he wears his black FBI-style shoes and he plants himself at the end of the bar.

"Have you made your decision?" he demands.

"I can't talk to you now," I tell him.

"You have to talk to me," he says.

"I can't right now," I respond. "The air-conditioning is gone. We're sweatin' in here and the lights are out." I'm trying to appeal to his good sense, to enlist him in our common humanity, if he has any.

"Maybe so," he says, "but I must have an answer. I'll need a check as a down payment or we will sue."

I have been besieged by partners and tax men, suppliers and note holders, bureaucrats and landlords. Not to mention the daily parade of homeless people, including the very large homeless man who hustled his way into the men's room, spent some time in there and very neatly stripped all the wallpaper off the walls. I've been fending them off for years, all of them. I'm broke. I can't even pay the people who work for me. Now this idiot with the briefcase is threatening me. Has he ever sung or played a note of music in his life? Should I strangle him? Or should I just throw him through the front window?

Lynn had been doing the seating. Now she comes up to the bar. Seeing my face, she advises the fool that he'd better leave. "The air conditioner is blown," she says. "The lights are blown. And he," she points to me, "he is about to blow. He doesn't very often, but when he blows, he really blows. I know. I saw it happen once." Mr. BMI picks up his briefcase and trudges out the door.

He is not to be my last official visitor. A uniformed New York City policeman will soon lead the parade. Presumably he is there to keep the peace and to hold back the bribery. The policeman is followed by the Fire Department. Bringing up the rear is the Buildings Department.

I can't help asking, "So, what brings you all here?"

"We are the Mayor's Taskforce," the policeman responds.

I am dumbfounded, but I still can't help it. "So, we have the Police Department, the Fire Department and the Buildings Department, all in a little place this size. I suppose we should feel honored." There have been episodic scandals involving the Health Department. There have been indictments for bribery and corruption. I can't resist. "So, where's the Health Department?" I ask.

The policeman, with a straight face, manfully volunteers that the Health Department Inspector has been called away. The Mayor's Taskforce issues a few minor tickets before departing. They promise to return in two weeks. We remedy the conditions complained of. In the end, only the Fire Department comes back to check.

In mid-August I make a pilgrimage to Bayside, Queens, to deliver a payment to the note holder. I am still two months behind in the payments, but after a drink together, our parting is cordial. One week later I take the subway to work, ready to open for lunch, as usual. Very quickly I am shifted from the misery of the swamp to the mercy of the cliff. I arrive to find that the place is padlocked. A City Marshall's Notice, posted on the door, proclaims to the world that I have been evicted by the note holder.

When I call the note holder, he claims that his lawyer insisted on the foreclosure. The lawyer expresses his regret. "You can get back in for ten thousand dollars," he offers. I consider the possibility. Geoff is a banker and a very good friend, and he offers to advance the money. An upright man, he needs and expects full disclosure and a clean slate. He offers to put up enough money to pay off all debts so that I will have a fresh start. In return he wants a share and a good deal of control and oversight, for his sake and for mine.

During two weeks of calling back and forth, we discuss the possibilities. We are close to reaching an agreement, when one day, the absurdity of the situation becomes clear to me. I will have to disclose far more than I've ever wanted to disclose. Maybe I can deal with that, but I have little or no hope that I will ever get out from under. I will have to slave forever, just to keep afloat. We are friends, Geoff and I. And our families are close. There is a lot more at stake here than money.

Geoff is traveling. His wife, Joan, calls and asks if I have made any progress and I tell her that I've decided to abandon the whole idea. There is a stunned silence at the other end of the phone. I tell her that our friendship and the friendship of our two daughters, both named Allison, is very important to me. I know for certain that if we go through with this arrangement, our friendship will wither away.

"I'm very surprised," she responds, "but I understand. And, well then, we'll see you soon," she sighs, as she hangs up the phone.

The "soon" is Geoff's fiftieth birthday and a party at Lutèce. Lynn and I are invited, as are the president of Citibank, the chairman of Lincoln Center and the former chairman of the Federal Reserve. Lynn has found a job as office manager for a building management company.

And I have found a suit in my closet. Yes, and a shirt and tie to wear to the party. With twenty dollars to my name and a pile of debt, I am approaching age fifty and freshly unemployed. At the party, with each course, comes a different wine. Soon I'm "well oiled" and suffering little discomfort. We are introduced all round. Isn't this New York, after all? Isn't there always hope?

Every day I go walkabout, stopping in here and there, in restaurants and bars to offer my services. But my hair had turned white on Eighth Avenue, not much help when you're looking for work. I respond to ads in the paper and continue to fill out applications and to call the few people I know in the business to tell them that I am available. They can't know how desperate I am and I can't be too specific. This is a delicate matter. I can't impose an obligation on them by spelling it out too clearly.

Eamonn Doran owns a few restaurants. By returning my call he shows his goodwill. "There's a place for sale on the Upper East Side. I can get you in for a hundred thousand," he tells me. I almost laugh. Eamonn is hard working, intelligent and highly successful. Neither he nor anyone else can be expected to grasp the depth of my disaster. They had seen me riding high during my years at Los Panchos. That was my time "to reap and stash." I had done so, to an extent, but, by now, all my money is gone; gone into the house upstate and swallowed by the new business. Broke, and heavily in debt, I can't consider a new business. It's a job I need.

The lawyer for the note holder calls to say that I will be given a one-time opportunity to enter the premises and recover my personal belongings and effects. The appointed day is Halloween, October 31st. I fill two large garbage bags with accounting books, checkbooks, small tools and one or two pictures. Emerging into heavy rain, I have no money for a taxi. On the stairs to the subway I struggle with my two giant garbage bags. The porter mopping the steps takes notice and he startles me by offering to help. I thank him for this extraordinarily kind offer, but I manage, by myself, to board the train. Flanked by my twin bulges, I sit down.

At Penn Station the train stops and the doors open to the sound of gunfire on the platform. A mob of rampaging teenagers storms into the carriage. In self-defense, I hold my umbrella, my token weapon, with the sharp end pointed toward the ceiling. This is war. I will have to abandon my precious garbage bags. Comes a siren, followed immediately by another siren, and the crackle of walkie-talkies. A small detachment of police appears on the platform. They arrest the shooter. The rampaging mob of my imagination had been running to escape the shooter. That was the last day of my restaurant career on Eighth Avenue.

1990

Officially, and to tell the truth, thankfully, I am out of business and unemployed. As are our few remaining employees, among them the two Chinese men who ran the kitchen. They are owed the most money. Only two days before the eviction, in good faith, I had borrowed money at high interest and paid them a good deal of what I owed them. Now I will have to pay back the borrowed money. At the same time, I will have to find a way to pay the balance of what I owe them.

I continue my daily walks around Manhattan in the hope of finding some kind of restaurant work, but I am hampered because I have no money. I lack the "entrance fees," which would allow me to drop in, ever so casually, on people I know. So, walk I must, in the hope of running into somebody in the street, anyone who may know of something.

Friends who have heard the bad news call me, as do customers who had become friends. All are rendered partially homeless by the closing. "What happened?" is both refrain and chorus.

"Oh, just a case of isolation and preoccupation, too many briefcases with suits attached, my own lack of prudence, too much booze, a malaise de cuisine, bad timing and terrible location. Add an overdose of pie in the sky and plain stupidity on my part. And that's only the beginning," I could have told them. The truth is that in my rush to get out of Los Panchos I had lost my mind.

A few people call to say that they have some money put aside. They would love to invest with me if I decide to reopen or to find another place. I thank them. What I want to tell them is, "Look, I just got thrown out into the street. I've lost everything. Can't you see that I'm ruined and disgraced? And still you want to invest money with me? What are ya, crazy?"

Up on Ninth Avenue, in a Mexican restaurant owned by Ernesto's brother, I find a part-time job on Sunday and Monday nights.

Years have passed since I was an employee. I am reminded of the evening in Los Panchos, when the whole place suddenly filled up and we were not prepared. Phillip, the lone bartender, was at the point of being overwhelmed when I stepped in to help. "Phillip, I'll give you a hand with washing glasses and taking the cash," I told him.

"Okay, boss," Phillip shrugged and I went to work. A man at the bar ordered a margarita, "straight up." I assembled, in the mixing glass, the ingredients for a margarita. I'd made thousands of margaritas. A snug fit was the can on top of the mixing glass and I shook it vigorously. It had been a while and it felt good to be involved until, for no good reason, mixing glass and can parted company. I was left holding only the glass. The can, no longer in my control, had flown through the air. In a very nice elliptical trajectory, the can made a soft landing on the curve at the lip of the bar. With a tip and a drop the contents of the can spilled sideways, right into the lap of the man who had ordered the margarita. "I'm all wet, I'm all wet," he cried, as he left the stool and leapt to his feet.

In case of any mishap, mine or anyone else's, I would always provide a towel, offer a drink and pay for the dry cleaning bill. As Mam would have said, "Anything for a quiet life." That had always been a good and workable policy. The airborne margarita was definitely my fault. There's no doubt about it. I cursed my luck. Still, when a man sits at a bar and orders tequila, that most macho of drinks, in any form, shouldn't he be expected to show some fortitude, maybe a little style, a modicum of grace, even? Above all, shouldn't he have a sense of humor?

I was embarrassed. And I was angry that the drink had to land in the lap of a whining man. "Take care of this man, will you?" I asked Phillip and I left the bar. Phillip shrugged and smiled his usual "okay, boss." I abandoned ship and stepped outside for a smoke. Phillip, I don't doubt, was glad to be rid of me.

At my new place of employment the margaritas are machine-made. No shaking is necessary so there is little chance of a mishap, but I will miss the rhythm of the shaking. There's very little business at the bar, but very soon I will discover my real job. At intervals of an hour and a half, I must set up a round of drinks, mostly shots of tequila, for my friend, the owner and his friends. And always one shot for myself. We drink to the ritual toast, "Salud, amor, y dinero, y tiempo para di fructardlo." At the end of my second night's work, when I'm paid, I see that it's not much money, but I'm very glad to get it. And the boss gives me a ride home.

⚜

The piano from our restaurant has been stored in the basement, to be collected when I am ready. I go to visit Dennis Rice at Kaspar's Restaurant, on 27th Street, and ask him if he will take the piano and keep it for me. He already has a piano and doesn't have room for another one.

Dennis and I know some people in common, mostly people from the East Side. "Listen, Dennis," I say seriously, "you know that I am out of business. If you hear of anyone looking for someone, would you let them know that I'm available?" He will keep it in mind. Later that evening he calls and asks me to come and see him. On the following Friday he offers me a job as meeter, greeter, seater and late-night bartender.

Kaspar's is a handsome place, serving great food under high ceilings, in a great expanse of open space punctuated by pillars. The strip-oak wood floor is good looking but does little to absorb sound. A wonderful if occasionally erratic system sends out the sounds of the Modern Jazz Quartet, Coltrane, Brubeck, Vivaldi's *Four Seasons*, Mozart and Haydn, with Wynton Marsalis on trumpet.

Comes a couple. In their late fifties to early sixties, they are just barely in the door and have yet to spend ten cents in the place. Heavily engaged in the struggle to remove hats, coats, scarves and gloves, still they find the energy to complain. "The music is too loud. Can't you turn it down?"

I know what he will say and, for pure devilment, I relay the complaint, verbatim, to Dennis. Dennis is working in the kitchen. As he raises his head from the dacquoise he is preparing, his jaw locks. The tip of his beard points up and forward. "Tell 'em this from me," says Dennis. "Tell 'em if it's too noisy in here maybe they should go have dinner in a fuckin' morgue." Back I go, to lower the volume on the sound system. Very soon I will raise it again.

Every evening, a little before five o'clock, they come sailing in, while the kitchen crew is still preparing for the night's business. At their arrival, even the pillars seem to groan, to shift position and lean a little away from them. All to the beige, in raincoats and matching rain hats, spotless and slightly bow-legged, they could be twins. Mr. and Mrs. Call are well preserved, as they say. Polite and soft-spoken and in their early seventies, their good manners only make things worse. They can't eat this and won't eat that. They are, in essence, "a waiter's nightmare," as Lynn once described someone she knew.

I have no direct dealings with them, but Al, the Moroccan waiter ancient and ageless at fifty, easily analyzes their behavior, "The Calls?" he says, "I know what's wrong with those two. All day long they sit at home and fight with each other. All day long they fight, until at four-thirty in the afternoon she decides, 'That's it, that's it. I've had it! I'm bored. I'm fed up. It's no fun fighting with you anymore. Let's get dressed and go to a restaurant. Let's go fight with a waiter for a change.'"

They are polite, at least. What the Calls want is a good meal. They don't follow slavishly on the heels of restaurant reviewers, in this the age of the restaurant reviewer. From the Staten Island Star to the Okinawa Bugle, restaurant reviewers are locked in the throes of gustatory orgasm. Desperately do they try to keep their knees together as they brave the line between mastication and masturbation. Massive restraint is called for, especially when faced with the newest sensations, the fava beans and mesclun greens.

But even a reviewer will sometimes enjoy a meal. The "foodies" are devoted more to the discussion of food, than they ever are to the eating of it. Food is subjected to the most minute and exacting examination. Their analysis, extending beyond their own food, will extend as far as the reduction on their neighbor's plate. Without a reduction on the plate there is only disgrace. An infusion, any old infusion, will reign supreme. And pity the poor veal chop, product of tortured calf. It must be pummeled well beyond an inch of its life, and flattened, so that it fills the whole plate.

"Foodies" have come into being at the same time that homeless and hungry people become commonplace in the city. Is there some connection? "Feed the homeless…to the hungry" was one wag's solution. It might make more sense to feed the "foodies" to the hungry.

Food, and the idea of food, is ever present. Allison, by this time, is in a new school in Flushing, Queens. The school caters to children with disabilities. Because Allison's "behaviors" are erratic they propose a program of behavior modification with food as the principal tool. The program will last only six to eight weeks. The man who administers the program is expert and experienced. That's what they tell us. As Allison's behavior improves, the use of food as a behavior modification tool will be gradually discontinued. Against our better judgment, we agree.

Morsels of food and crumbs of treats are used to induce good behavior on Allison's part. We are very uneasy. Again we are told not to worry. The program will work. The man in charge really knows what he is doing. But when Lynn and I go on a field trip, a picnic, with Allison's class, we are disturbed by what we see. Allison is fed, one morsel at a time. It is cruel and unusual punishment. Then, to make matters worse, one month into the program the man in charge leaves the school. The consequences will persist.

Twice a week Allison stays late and attends an after-school program. Twice a week I drive to Flushing to pick her up, bring her home and race downtown to find a parking space before going to work at Kaspar's. By special arrangement with Dennis I start work on those days, not at my usual five o'clock, but at six. This means that I must simultaneously park the car, legally—not a minute before six. And be at work at six. It's a twice-weekly miracle.

Every evening, in the kitchen, I pick up a list of the evening's specials and I do my best to memorize it. It would be déclassé were I to be seen reading from the list. Everyone would know that I don't know what I'm talking about. So I memorize: soup, appetizers and main courses. I can never be sure, but I think I can get through it.

On those two evenings when I arrive to work at six o'clock, when customers already await, there is no hope for me. With no time to memorize, I must read the palm of my hand, or scratch my ear and recite as best I can. Above all I must not deviate from the prescribed order or I'll be lost entirely. God forbid that anyone should ever interrupt with a question. If I am interrupted, I will lose my thought and my place and, possibly, my mind.

Soup and appetizers are easy enough but, halfway down the list of six main courses, the question comes. "Where does the salmon come from?" Shades of the old White Horse. In her mid-twenties, she is luminescent and gorgeous. If I look at her I will be lost completely, lost on all fronts. I have no idea where the salmon comes from. I don't know where anything comes from, except for the beetroot and the winter lettuce I once planted in our back garden in Limerick.

"From his mother," I whisper. "The salmon comes from his mother." But I have to stop that. I am an employee once again and, when you're over fifty, jobs are not too easy to find. Fortunately, she hasn't quite heard me.

"What did you say?" she asks.

"From the Atlantic," I answer. With feigned assurance and a pretense of concern for her welfare, "The salmon comes from the Atlantic," I offer.

Eyes brimming with appreciation and gratitude, she offers up her full regard. "Thank you," she breathes. I am her hero forever, only I know better. "I'm allergic to salmon," she says, "but thank you anyway." I stumble through the rest of my recitation.

And there are the discriminati, the ones who always feel called upon to ask the most searching questions. The discriminati must impress their guests or their host with the range and precision of their curiosity. They must appear to be more discriminating than thou, and more knowledgeable than anyone else at the table.

"This reduction of oak leaves; the oak leaves, are they European or Asian?" echoes in my head. Sometimes I am tempted to give them my mother's answer: "If yee were hungry, yee'd ate it."

I'm on the late-night bus going up Eighth Avenue, on my way home. Potatoes infused with sarsaparilla invade my reverie. "Domestic sarsaparilla is it, or is it imported?" Damned if I know. And damned if I care, in my dreams I declare, but in reality I can't do that. Instead, I ask them to wait while I go and ask Dennis. Dennis knows everything.

Intense and meticulous in his dedication to food, Dennis makes fabulous desserts. And he knows his wine. If the questioner is young and pretty or if someone has a legitimate question, Dennis will hasten to the table and deliver what I refer to as "Dennis Lite." He will offer a sympathetic, concise and very clear description of the item in question and a sound recommendation.

But if, on the way to the table, his antennae detect one or more discriminati, he takes a different tack. Dennis's genius becomes my revenge. What Dennis knows, he really knows. Faced with one or more discriminati, he fires on all cylinders. At the conclusion of a fifteen-minute discourse on the pedigree of the sarsaparilla, the armchair discriminati will beg for mercy. "Bring it, please," they will plead with me. "Bring it, just bring it, bring anything. Please."

In the late evenings I work at the bar. "Do you have asparagus?" she asks.

"No. Not tonight."

"Oh," she sighs, crestfallen. And "oh" again.

I laugh. A decent woman and a regular customer is Christine. By profession a successful and well-traveled dress designer, Christine has a good heart. Attractive, and of a generous nature, she is in her mid-thirties now, and battling her weight. "What's so important about asparagus? I ask her.

"Oh, it's a great diuretic."

"Well, then, why don't I just give you two large pitchers of water? That should do the trick. You'll be able to go pee-pee to your heart's content."

"Oh you," she laughs. "You're impossible. Just order me a salad, please."

⊰❈⊱

By custom, and in self-defense, before closing up at the end of the night, I have a few drinks. It is February of 1991, at a crucial stage of the Gulf War. I watch it on television, this massive fireworks display. Bright streams of tracers crisscross each other all over the night sky. Matter-of-fact, yet barely able to conceal their excitement, the commentators speak in hushed tones. This is a docudrama, a reenactment, a staging of some long ago event? It is not. Immediate, now, this is a circus of the real: beautiful, dramatic, dynamic and tragic. Above all, for the viewer, it is a spectacle. There is no pain and no sense that there will be any consequences. Nonetheless, it is war. Again. We have learned nothing.

I have a couple of goodnight drinks while I close up Kaspar's. Before going home I turn the corner and go into Delta 88, a few doors down, on Eighth Avenue, for a few more. The musicians are putting away their instruments. The bar is at the point of closing. No one asks me, but I oblige, anyway, with a couple of sad and soulful shut-eyed Irish songs. Just to cheer everybody up and send them home happy.

Soon, the barmaid, waiters, and musicians, along with the few remaining customers, all have clustered at the opposite end of the bar. Or are they backing away? And it dawns on me, just then. Maybe my particular brand of Celtic alcoholic melancholy does not blend well with the vestigial vibes of that night's Delta blues. So I leave and take a taxi home. I accuse my wife and her mother (who is staying overnight), of being indifferent not only to the war but to the state of the world and the plight of humanity. I disrupt all their sleep, including that of my fifteen-year-old daughter and do violence to a couple of chairs. Then I leave the apartment.

In a short time I'm on Route 80 in New Jersey and heading west, with two hundred dollars in my pocket and no credit cards. The car is a rental. I'm driving in a heavy snow fall, moving along in the outside lane at eighty miles an hour.

I was thirty-five when I got my first driver's license and I have always been very careful about drinking and driving. Now I'm drunk and I'm on my way to see Willie Nelson. He can be found at his home in Abbott, Texas, rocking and strumming on his porch. Or so I've been told. If I can find Willie Nelson and talk to him maybe I can make sense of it, this latest and most senseless of wars. I am determined. The snow thickens. An angel lands on my shoulder. I pull over into a rest area and go to sleep. That was my angel. That was Saint Valentine's Day.

"Someone was praying for you," my mother would have said. Mam was not religious, but she believed in such things. In Limerick, people believed strongly in the power of prayer. People from the North of Ireland are said to be more practical.

My father was not practical. At any given time, he could be lost in prayer, or drunk, or he could be completely obsessed by his vision of Irish Independence.

This Gulf War has taken my mind. As usual, there is barely the space of one generation, between the end of the last horror and the beginning of the new one. My mind was with the war, I was drunk and headed to see Willie Nelson for advice. It was supremely important that I discuss with him a matter over which I had absolutely no control. And I left my family in a shambles. My father could hardly have done it better.

❧

Back in the city, back at my weekend job at the Mexican place, I don't fit in anymore. After my performance at home and my little trip on Route 80, there will be no more tequila for me, no more drinks of any kind. I have frightened myself. And I have become uneasy at the comings and goings to the office downstairs in the Mexican place. Men arrive and disappear downstairs. They reappear at the bar to have a token drink with my friend, the owner. Then they leave. Something is going on.

I consult with a retired police sergeant. Mike is an old customer of mine and he is also a former narcotics cop. "What would be my situation if the place is raided?" I ask him. "Would I be arrested?"

His answer, rendered with a deep-throated chuckle, is simple and to the point. "When the whistle blows, everybody goes." That's enough for me. On the following weekend, with little regret, I say thank you for the job and hang up my shot glass at the Mexican place.

⚜

For nearly twenty years we have lived in our building in relative privacy. Now, as the building becomes "upscale," we have a doorman. One evening the doorman buzzes to say that a man in the lobby wants to see me. He has a package for me, from Ireland. In the lobby, "the man" turns out to be a lawyer. I remember him. He is trying to serve me with a spurious summons having to do with our defunct restaurant. The matter had already been resolved in court. This lawyer lost the decision and now he's trying to start again.

He pushes the papers at me. "You've been served," he taunts. I take a step toward him. He takes a step back. I take another step forward and again he steps back. We repeat the exercise, until he turns and walks quickly out the door of the building. I follow fast. He starts to run and I run after him. Still running, he turns left onto Central Park West. It's six o'clock. The crowd from the subway station, heading home after work, comes face to face with a thirty-five-year-old man being chased by a white-haired fifty-year-old man.

The crowd from the subway is only mildly disturbed. Chaser and chasee are both white, so the crowd can assume that no crime has been committed. Something else is going on here. I know that I can't catch him. He knows it too. Slowing down, he glances back over his shoulder a couple of times. He's nervous, I can tell, but he wears a manic grin. And so he should. Who ever chases an ambulance chaser? And if I caught him what would I do with him? After a few blocks, I give up the chase.

More legal business follows. Our car is repossessed for non-payment. The Woodstock house is in foreclosure. We refuse to pay the mafia-like rates of interest demanded by a number of private lenders. We lose the house. Sobriety ain't easy.

I rent a twenty-dollar-a-day van. Lynn and Allison and I, with the help of a few friends, clear out the house. Furniture and furnishings are distributed among friends in New Jersey and in Ulster County for safekeeping. When it's done, when everything is gone, we return to the city. It is late on a Saturday afternoon, heading into twilight. Lynn and Allison have gone upstairs. Alone I sit, in the rattletrap van. There is no air-conditioning. Parked outside our apartment house, the van reeks of heat, humidity and the stink of failure.

I'm smoking a cigarette and thinking about all that has come and gone in our lives. Glorious success and bitter failure have led to this. A man approaches. In his early thirties, he is well dressed in Saturday-casual, dressed-down garb. He and his affluent tribe have replaced our regional riff raff of musicians, actors, singers, dancers and writers. I flick a cigarette ash out the window of the van and into the street. "Don't you have an ashtray in that thing?" the man demands.

I am hot and very sweaty. I open the door of the van. Feeling a deal of stiffness, after all the lifting, moving and driving, slowly I climb down. Very directly I look at him. "What did you say?"

"I asked you if you have an ashtray in that thing."

"Yes I do. I do have an ashtray in that thing."

Seeing my face, he steps back. "Okay, okay," he stutters. Turning abruptly, he steps quickly away. It's not his fault. It was I who lost everything. I'm to blame, not him. But he should mind his own business.

Lynn and I have been working and doing our best, but we are far behind. Our financial situation at home is dire. Facing eviction now, we are in danger of losing our apartment. I have to go to court close to twenty times to stave off eviction. On Christmas Eve, a stipulation is arrived at with our absentee-investor-landlords. They are a husband-and-wife team and they are not happy.

I don't blame them. In the courtroom, following the stipulation and the end of the proceedings, I try to catch their eye. They look away. I make the approach and offer, "It's Christmas, we should have peace."

"Yes, peace is what we want," the husband says and we shake hands on peace. In accordance with the stipulation, we will have to pay an impossible amount of money in rent arrears, in addition to our regular rent.

I can't borrow the money, but I am offered a job in a large, limited income co-op complex, which has been in existence for more than thirty years. It is situated directly across the street from what had been Allison's Restaurant and I had come to know the assistant manager, Brendan. They need someone to go through the whole property, apartment by apartment, he tells me. They need someone who can assess the conditions of habitability in each apartment. I have common sense, I think. I can see and hear, set up charts and keep records of the work. I'm qualified for the job. It won't pay much, but it will be enough to allow me to pay off our rent arrears. To visit each of the three thousand apartments will take me about six months.

On a bleak day in February of 1993, at eight-thirty in the morning, I report for work. When I look around it seems as if only the general manager is older than I am. Yet, once again I am the new kid in town. Following a tour of the property I am hired, documented and introduced all round. At forty-thirty in the afternoon, I am set free with just enough time to get to work at Kaspar's by five o'clock.

❦

Many of the apartment owners are elderly, most of them are women. When they do allow me to enter they are house proud, showing me everything, sometimes showing me more than I ever want to see. Thankfully, it is mostly small leaks and cracks. I'm lucky to have Ike with me, as mentor and tour guide. In his fifties, Ike is African American. Originally from Panama, Florida, Ike, like myself, has seen better days. He is well seasoned and shows a tough exterior.

We ring bells and knock on doors. In answer to the query "Who is it?" Ike answers in his great booming bass. "With that voice you must be able to sing 'Old Man River,'" the woman offers. She doesn't know Ike and she doesn't know me. This may be just a stab at good fellowship, but it creates an awkward moment, rife, possibly, with race and condescension. Comes a second of silence. Ike is slow to answer. There's a tensing in his neck muscles. Maybe it's a prelude to "Old Man River." If it isn't, then God knows what Ike will say.

I can't take a chance so I jump in. "No, ma'am," I tell her, "Ike does a really great job on 'Danny Boy.' 'Ole Man River' is my party piece." The woman looks at me, back at Ike and back at me again. She says no more.

In the beginning, such a novelty am I, that some of the women congregate in the hallway to await the arrival of "the Inspector." And I'm an officious bastard. Officiousness is a good defense. At a relatively late age I am in uncharted territory, a territory mined with questions to which I don't know the answers. I have no experience for this kind of a job. The development is governed by a board of directors and democracy runs rampant among the population of some seven thousand people. My big foot could easily end up in my big mouth.

The man with the clipboard can get in anywhere, says John Le Carré. With my clipboard as both badge and shield and with a pen as my baton, I conduct the proceedings. I have become the man with the badge, but it's a very small badge and there's nothing punitive about my visits. And I make sure not to carry a briefcase.

Each apartment is its own world. Most of the work is routine and the vast majority of the apartments are in good order. A few people refuse to admit me, one in particular. "It's not you, you know, it's nothing personal. It's that sonofabitch on the board. He didn't answer my phone call seven years ago. I said it then and I say it now. Until he answers my call, this board will get no cooperation from me."

"But aren't you bound by the rules of the co-op?" I ask. "Don't you have to allow an inspection, even if he never calls you back?"

"I never heard of that, I'll have to check with my attorney."

"Okay," I say. "By the way, what was that board member's name again?"

"Oh, Milton Carstairs." I check my list of board members. "Mr. Carstairs is not on the list of Board members," I tell him.

"Doesn't matter," he says and then adds, "you'll be hearing from my attorney. He's standing by, right now, waiting for my call."

"Most successful lawyers are busy people," I offer. "You must have a special relationship with this lawyer." Then I mutter under my breath, "Your attorney must be really good, if he has nothing better to do than to hang around waiting for you to call."

"What was that?"

"Oh, nothing." Then I fabricate. "This man, this Mr. Carstairs, the one who didn't return your call? I heard that he died. Seven years ago."

"Died?" he says, with surprise. "Well, it doesn't matter. It's the principle of the thing. Somebody had better call me back."

"Good enough," I tell him as I make my exit.

❦

February wears on into March, then into April and May. By the month of June the hallways are warming up. The humidity hangs in the air. To my great relief, an assistant is found for me. Desperately in need of moral support as I am, I welcome him in. With his middle-class Long Island background, he has a smile for everyone. As we set out to inspect apartments, David persists in addressing the women as "Miss."

"'Miss' is no good," I tell him. It sounds like a caricature of a Macy's saleswoman. 'Ma'am' is better. Try it." And he does. Polite to a fault, he punctuates every phrase with a smile and a "ma'am."

"Ma-am" works well until we encounter the one woman. She seems to want war with anyone who comes to her door, especially anyone who comes on official business. She doesn't want to let us in. She argues and from time to time, polite as always, David interjects with a respectful "ma'am." The argument drags on. The hallway grows more humid. In the end, she grows tired, tired of talking and tired of listening, even to herself. The thread of her argument has slipped away from her.

"Ma'am," David begins again.

"MA'AM!" she shouts. "DON'T MA'AM ME!" And continues, "Stop ma'aming me. Go home and ma'am your mother!" She slams the door and David and I burst out laughing.

In the interest of speed and efficiency and as a hedge against any further hilarity, we split up. I go, alone, to the next apartment. All the windows are covered with plastic. Some are boarded over on the inside; to keep out the cold, I suppose. But the apartment is in good shape and not at all untidy. "I'm sorry about the state of the apartment," the man says. In his forties, he is dark haired, thin faced and intense. On the couch lies an old woman. Covered with a blanket, she is just barely there. Skeletal, she is, and she is not breathing, as far as I can see. "When my mother was around she kept the place in better condition," the man offers.

"Yes, I see," I reply. But I don't see. What I see is an ancient woman, dead on the couch, with her son keeping her company, long past the end. I don't want to be there.

"Do the best you can," I tell him, as I move toward the door. "Let us know if you need any help."

"I've been doing it all myself." I'll bet you have, I think to myself. I'll bet you have, you lunatic, but then he adds, "I've been taking care of my grandmother, ever since my mother went." Now it becomes clear. The mother is dead. The woman on the couch is his grandmother.

And is your grandmother dead as well? I want to ask. Just then, the woman on the couch, the grandmother, stirs and moans. I jump. "Good enough," I stammer, as I move quickly toward the door. "Take care of yourself," I call out to him. I am bound to report the situation to the social-services people. And I do. They must have contacted the grandson. A few months later I meet him in the street.

"How dare you interfere in my affairs, how dare you report me!" he shouts.

"I thought you could use some help. You seemed so isolated."

"I can take care of my own business," he shouts. "And you should mind yours."

"Okay," I say. "I'm sorry." And I walk away.

❧

By October I have substantially fulfilled my contract. Some of the holdouts I will have to deal with later, but most will be handled by social-services people and by lawyers. But, every month, I am told, as people move up to a bigger apartment, or move out altogether, each apartment must be prepared for the new people moving in and now I am offered a new position. I am to be Chief of Restorations.

I am assigned a crew of eight and a number of contractors are immediately available to me. I am to supervise and coordinate the restoration of each vacated apartment and bring it up to "move-in condition." My workday begins at seven o'clock. I rise at five-thirty, at a time when I used to go to bed.

Early to bed and early to rise? I will wait and see.

I've always been a one-man band. How, now, will I learn to function in this bastion of democracy and, at the same time, learn to tiptoe through layers of bureaucracy. I am thinking out loud. Jimmy overhears me. He's from County Leitrim. He's a contractor. "Say nothin'. And keep sayin' it," he offers.

"Is that the Leitrim way?" I ask.

"Say nothin'. And keep sayin' it," is his only response. It's a start.

For twenty years, in the course of my work, I've had to make decisions, sometimes in consultation with a partner, very often not. Now I must take direction from superiors little more than half my age. It is difficult but, on the good side, I am not alone anymore.

There are layers of protection. I can consult with people when I have to make a decision or when I need help with something. No longer do I have to worry about men with briefcases. Lawyers and consultants will deal with them. And there is a certain camaraderie among my fellow supervisors, the contractors and the other employees.

There will be no briefcase for me, no five-seventeen train to the suburbs, to Manhasset or Syosset. I have always wanted to stay close, if not to the means of production, then at least to the basics of urban life. If I am to be in the city I will be of the city.

In Limerick, my education had been strictly academic, but with the bit of gardening, with the shovel and the spade, I had made a connection, however tenuous, with the soil and with physical work. That was at the beginning. Little did I know that I would live a number of lives and end up in close proximity to faucet installation, tile and flooring replacement and electrical overhaul. And that, within the confines of a defined working day, I would find a degree of freedom.

Allison has settled in at school. She is doing a little better and, for now, her story is her own. Lynn is again working full-time. Her work brings her into contact with artists and with people who run art galleries. There is a certain fulfillment in that.

In this new job I am sometimes taken to task and it is embarrassing. I could leave, as I have done so often. Too many times have I walked away, too many times have I quit. At this stage, embarrassment is a luxury I can't afford. I have to soldier on. "What's the use of being Irish if you can't be thick?"

⊰❈⊱

The old inspection job still lingers. A few people are still holding out. The general manager requests that I take time from my new position to go and visit one particular holdout, to see if I can persuade him. It's ten o'clock in the morning. A sixtyish man opens the apartment door. I know him by sight.

"Oh, it's you. So you're the inspector? Well, I'm not going to let you in. I don't have to, as long as my apartment is in good shape, which it is."

"Probably so," I say, "but I'm supposed to inspect every apartment in this complex."

"What for?"

"For general conditions of habitability. Or is it conditions of general habitability?"

"That's a mouthful," he says.

"You're right in that. Don't know how I managed to say it with a straight face. You're the first person to ask, so you're the first to have heard it."

"That's reassuring. What's your name?"

"McCourt."

"Irish, eh?"

"Yes, I am."

"Tell you what, my Irish friend. Why don't you come in? I have a nice bottle of cognac. We'll have a drink and you can see the apartment. You just can't inspect it. What do you think?"

"You mean I'll have to leave my clipboard outside?"

"No, no, you can bring your clipboard with you. Go ahead, bring it in. Just don't write on it. We'll have a drink and a chat. That way you'll know there's no hard feelings."

"Listen," I tell him, "I'm working. It's ten o'clock in the morning. And you want me to start drinking?"

"You're Irish, aren't you? You can handle a couple of drinks any-time, right?"

"Maybe I can. Maybe I can handle ten drinks. Maybe I'll finish the bottle. It wouldn't be the first time. Then you'll sing a different song, because when I start I'm not likely to stop. But I'm not looking to get fired. I need this job."

"Suit yourself," he says. "What a pity. The Irish ain't what they used to be."

"You're right. We're not what we used to be. Maybe we never were what we used to be, or what you thought we used to be. Then again maybe we were. Is anyone what he used to be? Who knows anymore? Should I go on?"

"No, no. Please, please. That's enough. It's okay." He's a little ner-vous now. "Just felt like a drink and a bit of a chat. Maybe next time?"

Now I'm sorry that I opened my mouth. "Yes, yes, maybe next time. I'll see you then. And good luck."

I have another appointment and I set out on the ten-minute walk to the other end of the property. The tension of the exchange is gone. In the end, we both left the door open. I can visit him again. A bridge, for once, is left unburned. I'm learning.

· NOTHING WORSE THAN A CONVERT ·

Secure and safe, my daughter and my wife are in their beds,
my brothers, more or less, have found their way.
All night, and into early morning, it has rained.
Behind a wall of fog, the Empire State stands tall, in quiet anticipation
of the dawn.
My namesake church of Saint Alphonsus, taken by the sands of
change,
from downtown is long gone.

But, back in Limerick still standing and still reaching
is the spire of the church of my patron saint.
There's hope in that
And hope, maybe, that somewhere, in a lane leftover,
A boy will dare a bite, for once will taste the forbidden
In the peel, the skin, of a good-sized spud.

And if I listen close I'll hear: "They shall not pass, they shall not pass,"
in an exhortation rising with the wind
Is it Brady, Brother Brady, Brady of the grizzled head
his hurley stick a walking cane?
Has he come again to cheer me on, to tramp once more
The shifting sidelines of my wandering mind?

Marin is left behind, in memory both good and bad.
It's Arizona now that calls and Colorado
with an enticing song
Man, am I tempted. Will I venture one more time, just one more new
beginning?
But no. Like all my other frontiers and escapes, the West will have to
wait its turn.
Too much to leave behind, this time.

Born into rain, my runoff lives all funneled into this
Like the Empire State I'll stand and do my best.
Trapped into routine morning, defined by early coffee and ritual scone
in hand
I'm taken by a small self-mocking smile, a pin prick to remind me.
There is nothing worse than a convert, nothing worse!
Have I not said it a hundred times, a thousand, to anyone who would
listen?

Frightened by their rigid, set, routine, by what I see as a righteous air
I have been distant always, wary and put off,
by the decent people, the old reliables, the ones who show up on time.
Am I, now, to be converted, to give up my life, to be an early-bird?
A dawn-breaker? Me? Today, tomorrow, forever, to be always more than
early?
Lord bless my soul and let me forge just one more chance.